Palgrave Studies in International Relations

General Editors:
Knud Erik Jørgensen, Department of Political Science, University of Aarhus, Denmark
Audie Klotz, Department of Political Science, Maxwell School of Citizenship and Public Affairs, Syracuse University, USA

Palgrave Studies in International Relations, produced in association with the ECPR Standing Group for International Relations, will provide students and scholars with the best theoretically informed scholarship on the global issues of our time. Edited by Knud Erik Jørgensen and Audie Klotz, this new book series will comprise cutting-edge monographs and edited collections which bridge schools of thought and cross the boundaries of conventional fields of study.

Titles include:

Pami Aalto, Vilho Harle and Sami Moisio (*editors*)
INTERNATIONAL STUDIES
Interdisciplinary Approaches

Mathias Albert, Lars-Erik Cederman and Alexander Wendt (*editors*)
NEW SYSTEMS THEORIES OF WORLD POLITICS

Robert Ayson
HEDLEY BULL AND THE ACCOMODATION OF POWER

Gideon Baker (*editor*)
HOSPITALITY AND WORLD POLITICS

Barry Buzan and Ana Gonzalez-Pelaez (*editors*)
INTERNATIONAL SOCIETY AND THE MIDDLE EAST
English School Theory at the Regional Level

Toni Erskine and Richard Ned Lebow (*editors*)
TRAGEDY AND INTERNATIONAL RELATIONS

Rebekka Friedman, Kevork Oskanian and Ramon Pachedo Pardo (*editors*)
AFTER LIBERALISM?
Liberalism in a Changing World

Geir Hønneland
BORDERLAND RUSSIANS
Identity, Narrative and International Relations

Beate Jahn
LIBERAL INTERNATIONALISM
Theory, History, Practice

Oliver Kessler, Rodney Bruce Hall, Cecelia Lynch and Nicholas G. Onuf (*editors*)
ON RULES, POLITICS AND KNOWLEDGE
Friedrich Kratochwil, International Relations, and Domestic Affairs

Also by Beate Jahn

THE CULTURAL CONSTRUCTION OF INTERNATIONAL RELATIONS

CLASSICAL THEORY IN INTERNATIONAL RELATIONS

Palgrave Studies in International Relations Series
Series Standing Order ISBN 978–0230–20063–0
(*outside North America only*)

You can receive future titles in this series as they are published by placing a standing order. Please contact your bookseller or, in case of difficulty, write to us at the address below with your name and address, the title of the series and the ISBN quoted above.

Customer Services Department, Macmillan Distribution Ltd, Houndmills, Basingstoke, Hampshire RG21 6XS, England

Liberal Internationalism

Theory, History, Practice

Beate Jahn

School of Global Studies, University of Sussex, UK

First published 2013 by
PALGRAVE MACMILLAN

Palgrave Macmillan in the UK is an imprint of Macmillan Publishers Limited, registered in England, company number 785998, of Houndmills, Basingstoke, Hampshire RG21 6XS.

Palgrave Macmillan in the US is a division of St Martin's Press LLC, 175 Fifth Avenue, New York, NY 10010.

Palgrave Macmillan is the global academic imprint of the above companies and has companies and representatives throughout the world.

Palgrave® and Macmillan® are registered trademarks in the United States, the United Kingdom, Europe and other countries.

ISBN 978–1–137–34841–8 hardback
ISBN 978–1–137–34842–5 paperback

This book is printed on paper suitable for recycling and made from fully managed and sustained forest sources. Logging, pulping and manufacturing processes are expected to conform to the environmental regulations of the country of origin.

A catalogue record for this book is available from the British Library.

A catalog record for this book is available from the Library of Congress.

For Justin

Contents

Acknowledgments

This book is the result of a long-standing, but not always conscious, interest in the role of liberalism in international politics. My reflections on this topic have, over the years, developed in response to, and in cooperation with, a great number of people who have in a myriad of ways contributed to this project. If I am not able to mention all of them here, this is due to lack of space and the unfortunate deterioration of my memory, for which I apologize.

Amongst the people who have made a major contribution to this project is Rose Shinko whose intellectual motivation, initiative, as well as organizational support were crucial in helping to organize a workshop on liberalism at the ISA conference in San Francisco in 2008. The workshop brought together a group of scholars whose work has been a great inspiration for this project, including Anna Agathangelou, Andreas Behnke, Linda Bishai, David Blaney, Tim Di Muzio, Barry Hindess, Naeem Inayatullah, Vivienne Jabri, Louiza Odysseos, Mustapha Kamal Pasha, Anna Stavrianakis, and Rose Shinko herself. Some of the papers that have arisen out of this workshop were subsequently presented at the ISA and the Millennium conferences in 2009 and I want to thank Rob Walker, Yale Ferguson, Cindy Weber, and Kirsten Ainley who, in their role as discussants, provided excellent comments that helped develop our thoughts further. I am also grateful to Patrick Jackson and his team at the *Journal of International Relations and Development* for the opportunity to publish some of the papers from this project as a special issue on 'Critiquing Liberalism' and for patiently and constructively guiding that project to completion.

George Lawson and John MacMillan invited me to participate in the ESRC-funded project on the Historical Sociology of Intervention. The workshops provided an excellent opportunity for intellectual exchange and greatly enriched my knowledge of, and reflections on, intervention. The last two sessions at the House of Lords, moreover, were unforgettable in showcasing the disjuncture between 'theory' and 'practice' and have inspired my thinking on this subject ever since. Thanks to George, John, and all the members of the project. Similarly, I am grateful to Christopher Hobson and Milja Kurki for the invitation to participate in the EU-funded project on the Political Economies of Democracy

Promotion. Thanks are due to the participants of the workshops for their excellent work which helped clarify my thoughts on liberalism and democracy promotion.

Over the past few years, I have been given the opportunity to present different aspects of my work on liberalism to audiences at the University of Wales in Cardiff, Oxford Brookes University, the University of Brno (Czech Republic), the University of Oxford, the University of Cambridge, the University of Bristol, the University of Warwick, LSE, Queen Mary University, the University of Aberdeen, Manchester Metropolitan University, Brunel University, the University of Reading, and Sheffield University. I would like to thank the hosts as well as the audiences in all these places for their valuable engagement.

In addition, my colleagues at the Department of International Relations at the University of Sussex have, for the past 15 years, provided a research environment without par: always challenging, always motivating – and never boring! Amongst them, Ben Selwyn has provided me with an annotated course outline on the political economy of development which gave me a heads-up for this project and a conversation with Cindy Weber regarding the REF inadvertently clarified the structure of this book in my mind. I also want to thank Motomichi Igarashi whose PhD on the relationship between trusteeship and humanitarianism was not only inspiring in general, but also provided great sources on liberal practices in the colonies.

At Sussex, I also owe a great debt of gratitude to Joanna Wood. Her commitment, intelligence, self-reliance, and organizational skills as administrator of CAIT and EJIR over the past year have enabled me to devote considerable time to work on this manuscript while running CAIT and taking over as editor of EJIR. In the end, Jo also helped with some literature research and the bibliography without which this book could not have been finished in time. Thank you!

Our visiting scholars at CAIT during the autumn of 2012, Feride Asli Ergul, David Blaney, and Knud Erik Jørgensen, have contributed to the completion of this book in their own way – by being unfailingly understanding of my rather brief appearances and limited hospitality. I also want to thank Knud Erik Jørgensen for suggesting the *Palgrave Studies in International Relations Series* for the manuscript. At Palgrave, Julia Willan and Harriet Barker have been incredibly helpful and efficient in getting this book into print. Thanks are also due to the reviewers of the manuscript whose comments, in addition to their enthusiasm, provided excellent feedback and suggestions for improving the manuscript. Their advice has been crucial for the revision of the manuscript.

Many of the ideas that come together in this study have had their beginnings laid in previous publications, though none of these publications are reproduced here. I began to explore the relationship between liberalism and colonialism in *The Cultural Construction of International Relations. The Invention of the State of Nature* (2000). This has also provided the motivation to think more systematically about the use of classical authors for the analysis of international politics, past and present, which has given rise to the edited volume on *Classical Theory in International Relations* (2006). A more systematic engagement with the Democratic Peace thesis has led, in 2005, to the publication of 'Barbarian Thoughts: Imperialism in the Philosophy of John Stuart Mill', in *Review of International Studies*, Vol. 31, pp. 599–618 and 'Kant, Mill, and Illiberal Legacies in International Affairs', in *International Organization*, Vol. 59, No. 1, pp. 95–125. I have explored the strengths and weaknesses of liberalism's methodological approaches in 'One Step Forward, Two Steps Back: Critical Theory as the Latest Edition of Liberal Idealism', in *Millennium: Journal of International Studies*, Vol. 27, No. 3, pp. 613–41 (1998) and in 'Liberal Internationalism: From Ideology to Empirical Theory – and Back Again', in *International Theory*, Vol. 1, No. 3, 409–38 (2009), as well as in my contributions to debates on these issues in 'Universal Languages?', in *International Theory*, Vol. 2, No. 1, 140–56 (2009) and 'A Liberal Vanishing Act: Response to Oisin Tansey', in *Journal of Intervention and Statebuilding*, Vol. 2, No. 1, 94–8 (2008). Methodological reflections on the study of liberalism also play a role in the introduction to the special issue 'Critique in a Time of Liberal World Order', in *Journal of International Relations and Development*, Vol. 15, 145–57 (2012). I began to develop my thoughts on the dynamics of liberal foreign policies in 'The Tragedy of Liberal Diplomacy' Part I, in *Journal of Intervention and Statebuilding*, Vol. 1, No. 1, pp. 87–106 and Part II, in *Journal of Intervention and Statebuilding*, Vol. 1, No. 2, pp. 211–29 (2007). Initial thoughts on democracy promotion led to the publication of 'Rethinking Democracy Promotion', in *Review of International Studies*, Vol. 38, No. 4, 685–705 (2012) and on humanitarian intervention to the publication of 'Humanitarian Intervention – What's in a Name?', in *International Politics*, Vol. 49, No. 1, 36–58 (2012).

Since their arrival, Benjamin and Joschka have given me more joy (and exasperation) than words can describe. They have enforced much needed breaks. But they have also been extremely tolerant of my recent preoccupation and unavailability. And it has been great fun to explain to them why it is that the completion of this book will definitely not lead to the kind of financial windfall that J. K. Rowling has enjoyed.

The greatest debt of gratitude, however, I owe to Justin to whom I promised an immanent critique of liberalism in a pub in London in 1995. The origins of this book thus go back to the – often quite heated – debates we used to have then about what was needed in International Relations: Political Theory or Sociology, a critique of Realism or of Liberalism. In a bid to help me finish the book in time, he gave me some (child)free time during the summer of 2012, taking over my Thursday afternoons with the boys in the autumn, and since January the weekends as well. Without his intellectual engagement, love, and generosity over the years, this book would not exist.

1
Introduction

During the 1990s, liberal internationalism experienced a remarkable 'comeback' (Gardner 1990). The end of the Cold War was widely interpreted – by academics, politicians, and the media alike – as ushering in a new, and liberal, world order. The 'triumph' of liberalism over its main competitor(s) seemed to support its core assumptions of a progressive historical development toward the realization of individual freedom, prosperity, and domestic as well as international peace and cooperation (Fukuyama 1989). Liberalism, in short, seemed to be exceptionally in tune with the 'global developmental processes' which had finally swept it to the top and led to a liberal hegemony in the international system (Ikenberry 2006: 146).

This liberal hegemony in turn 'opened up a vast potential for movement toward realizing the liberal vision worldwide' (Richardson 2001: 2). Hence, George Bush Senior announced the arrival of a 'new world order' in which the 'United Nations, freed from Cold War stalemate, is poised to fulfill the historic vision of its founders' (Bush 1991). This political vision involved the spread of democracy and respect for human rights to all states and peoples as well as an influential role for international organizations in the pursuit of these aims. Meanwhile, in the realm of economics, the neoliberal agenda entailed an expansion of capitalism into the closed economies of the past as well as deregulation, liberalization, and privatization of the world market more generally. In short, the largely unchallenged dominance of liberal actors, policies, and ideologies promised 'freedom and a better life for all' (Richardson 2001: 2). The historical validation of liberal theory in combination with the dominant position of liberal states (as well as NGOs and IGOs profoundly influenced by liberal ideas and actors) thus gave rise to a 'period of massive and profound optimism' (Sørensen 2000: 287). In the spirit of this optimism, liberal actors embarked on proactive foreign and international policies designed to realize these liberal promises.

Amongst these policies, democracy promotion played a prominent role. It was based on the liberal assumption that democratic rule is most conducive to the realization of the natural freedom of the individual (Mill 1998b) and that democracy is conducive to domestic and international peace (Doyle 1996). The spread of democracy thus promised respect for individual rights as well as peace. In practice, democracy promotion was pursued by a wide range of actors – states, NGOs, international organizations – and took a variety of forms. Democracy assistance usually entailed economic and political incentives for democratization as well as financial and technical aid for the consolidation of electoral processes. Yet, democracy promotion was also pursued through economic and diplomatic pressure such as conditional aid, widely used in relations with the developing world by states and international organizations alike (Carothers 2000: 185–9). Finally, and prominently, democracy promotion played a crucial role in a variety of military operations. The assumption that democracy provides a nonviolent way of managing and resolving domestic conflict and competition turned the establishment of democracy into a core aspect of UN peacekeeping operations during the 1990s (Paris 2004). And the pacific implications of democracy for foreign policy established democratization as a major goal of the interventions in Afghanistan and Iraq, triggered at least in part by (real or assumed) security threats emanating from those states.

In the economic realm, liberal theories hold that the protection of private property, free markets, and free trade provide the basis for economic productivity and efficiency. Hence, liberal foreign policies aimed to spread free-market and free-trade practices throughout the international system. To this end, liberal states supported privatization, financial deregulation, and trade liberalization – often, but not only, through the development of international organizations like the World Trade Organization (WTO). More specific targets of these policies were states of the former Soviet Bloc in which a market economy needed to be established from scratch and Third World states in which the state engaged in market intervention or played an important role as economic actor. In all these cases, proactive liberal policies aimed to widen and deepen the realm of the market and the freedom of trade – through multilateral and bilateral policies.

Finally, liberal theories hold that the institutionalization of liberal norms provides a basis for cooperation and reform of the international system at large. With the end of the Cold War, the possibility of integrating liberal norms more prominently into the legal and institutional structure of the international system seemed to have arrived. This included a more vigorous protection of human rights through a reform of the UN Human Rights Council as well as calls for the practice and legalization of the principle of humanitarian intervention which ultimately led to the adoption of the Responsibility to Protect. As a major barrier to these efforts, the principle of sovereignty and its concomitant rights was to be linked to liberal credentials: this included suggestions for gradations of sovereignty (Keohane 2003), an elevated position for liberal actors under international law (Rawls 2001; Slaughter 1995) and in international organizations like the UN (Clark 2009).

All these political plans were inspired by, and in accordance with, the one or other liberal theory. And yet, in practice, liberal actors often failed to live up to these theoretical expectations, while liberal policies failed to achieve their aims or led to highly paradoxical outcomes. Though liberal states occasionally used humanitarian arguments to justify particular interventions – in the case of Kosovo in 1999, for instance – they did not actively pursue the legalization of humanitarian intervention. Though peacekeeping operations aimed to appease local conflicts through the introduction of market democracy, the latter often – for example in Angola, Cambodia, and Liberia – failed in its pacifying mission and sometimes even exacerbated conflicts (Paris 2004). Though democracy promotion successfully helped establish electoral systems in many states, like Russia, these often serve decidedly illiberal policies (Zakaria 1997). Though the military interventions in Iraq and Afghanistan successfully replaced authoritarian with democratic regimes, these did not enhance the level of domestic and international security (Nash 2006; Rubin 2006a, 2006b). Though the spread of free trade and market economies certainly increased prosperity amongst some groups, it was accompanied by increasing poverty for others. And though liberal economic policies do engender economic growth, they also generate serious economic and financial crises. Though liberal actors aim to promote peaceful international relations, the post-Cold War era has seen them continuously embroiled in wars. Though liberal actors promote respect for human rights, they also prominently violate those rights, for example in Guantanamo or Abu Ghraib. Though liberal actors are committed to the rule of (international) law, they are widely judged to break that law and undertake illegal wars, in Kosovo and Iraq, for example.

In short, even a cursory glance at the post-Cold War era shows that liberal foreign policies frequently failed to achieve their goals and that liberal actors often failed to act in accordance with liberal principles. And it is partly this disjuncture between liberal theory and practice and the patchy or contradictory achievements of the latter that led observers to conclude that the rise of liberalism at the beginning of the 1990s had, by the end of the decade, already turned into a demise. Certainly, the optimism of the early 1990s that the international system could now be remade in accordance with liberal principles and would thus fulfill the liberal promises of respect for individual rights, prosperity, and peace world wide gave way to much more cautious assessments and policies. The establishment of market democracies in other countries was now recognized as a difficult, complex, and slow process which required long-term commitments (Jahn 2007b) and led Donald Rumsfeld to announce 'we don't do nationbuilding!' Similarly, the promotion of democracy now seemed to require a transformation of the political culture, civil society, judicial system, media, and so on in target societies as well as a considerable period of 'consolidation' (Diamond 1996). By 1999, WTO policies were widely seen to exacerbate poverty, inequality, and – through the TRIPS agreement – even to endanger the health of large sections of humanity and thus generated a period of systematic protests on the streets, ushered in by the 'battle of Seattle', as well as diplomatic resistance on the part of affected states. In sum, the optimism of the early 1990s was gone, and with it the readiness of liberal actors to engage in widespread 'missionary' foreign policies.

Hence, by the end of the 1990s the heyday of liberalism was gradually coming to an end – a process that was subsequently accelerated by the terrorist attacks in September 2001. Liberal states turned from the expansive goal of 'enlargement' and began to concentrate again on the 'defense' of domestic or intraliberal achievements. This gradual demise of liberal optimism stands in stark contrast to the at-times triumphalist assumption of the early 1990s that history had finally caught up with and validated liberal theory and practice. Indeed, by the end of the 1990s and even more so after 2001, the historical developments did not appear to unequivocally validate liberal theory any longer. Moreover, this ultimately very short heyday of liberal internationalism seemed to fit right into the general fate of liberalism in international affairs – which is by most accounts characterized by repeated ups and downs, by periods of exalted expectations and embarrassing failures.

And yet, liberalism, even at a low ebb, undoubtedly continues to play a tremendously important role in world politics. Liberalism is a defining feature of many of the most powerful actors in world affairs – from liberal states through international organizations set up by these states and largely operating within a liberal ideological framework to private companies and NGOs. The world economy is largely structured in accordance with liberal principles. And liberal norms – from human rights through to free trade – provide a general reference point for international politics. This crucial role of liberalism in world politics thus calls for analysis: for an explanation of the mixed results of liberal policies, of its contradictory role in world politics, and hence also of the nature of liberalism itself.

Such analyses have variously been undertaken, most recently by G. John Ikenberry (2009, 2011) and Georg Sørensen (2012). Both authors argue that 'the current dilemmas and tensions' have their roots, at least partly, 'in the unresolved intellectual and political tensions within liberalism itself' (Ikenberry 2011: 282). Tensions between commitment to the rule of law and the use of power politics, between liberal political and economic principles and interests, between its domestic and international conduct have informed, and led to inconsistent, liberal policies during the 1990s and are partly responsible for their mixed outcomes. What is more, it is the very 'success of the liberal project', its hegemony after the Cold War, that is at least partially responsible for this crisis (Ikenberry 2011: 225). And yet, the identification of these internal contradictions of liberalism does not lead to their resolution. With regard to practice, 'neither liberal Restraint nor liberal Imposition contains durable solutions to the world order challenges faced by liberal states' (Sørensen 2012: 3). With regard to its historical role, we are still left with two contradictory conceptions of the current world order: one that conceives this order as liberal on account of the overwhelming power (political, economic, normative) of liberal actors, institutions, and practices; and another that holds that a liberal world order will only come into being once liberal principles are generally, or universally, realized – that is, it remains 'a project to be realised' (Young 1995; Sørensen 2012: 3). And hence we are still confronted with two competing conceptions of liberalism – one based on power and the other on the realization of liberal principles – that call for a 'rethinking of the liberal project' itself (Sørensen 2012: 6).

Hence, while it is frequently recognized that 'an examination of the plight of liberal internationalism must shift to the flaws and limitations of liberalism itself' (Hoffmann 1995: 160), and while these are widely described, they have, so far, not been integrated into a conception of liberalism. This book thus aims to provide a conception of liberalism that accounts for its internal contradictions and core dynamics and thus provides the basis for a clearer assessment of liberalism's role in history as well as for the challenges facing liberal policies today. Though this sounds like a tall order, there is in fact an analytical approach specifically designed to explore the structure of concepts such as liberalism. This approach, an immanent critique, begins with the internal contradictions of contemporary conceptions of liberalism and then reconstructs the dynamics that have led, historically, to their production. It requires three core moves which inform the structure of this study. It is, first, necessary to establish the internal contradictions of liberalism in its contemporary manifestations. These, secondly, have to be traced back to their historical origins in order to recover the dynamics by which they came to constitute liberalism. On this basis, it is possible to formulate a comprehensive but preliminary conception of liberalism. Thirdly, it needs to be established in how far this 'historical' conception of liberalism is able to account for liberal theory and practice in the contemporary world.

The various incarnations of liberalism, as we have seen above, appear as so many disjointed pieces of a puzzle. In order to produce a general and broadly consistent picture of liberalism in world affairs, these pieces have to be assembled. For such an assembly to be successful, however, it makes sense first to take stock of the separate pieces and to investigate the rationale of their fragmentation. I will therefore begin in Chapter 2 by providing an overview over the range of liberal international theories and their relationship to (domestic) liberal theory as well as to other, especially realist, theories in International Relations. The chapter shows that liberal theory is divided into a variety of different strands: distinguishing between political, economic, and normative issue areas as well as its historical and contemporary, domestic or intraliberal and international, and theoretical or normative and practical or empirical dimensions. These distinctions, I will show, serve to provide fairly coherent conceptions of liberalism by avoiding some of its parts and making sense of others. On closer inspection it turns out, however, that the contradictory aspects of liberal thought and practice do not fall neatly onto either side of these divides. Traditional approaches thus generally tend to grasp only part of liberalism and fail to provide a satisfactory account of its systematic tensions and contradictions.

In order to put the pieces of the liberal puzzle back together again, I will return in Chapter 3 to the historical origins of liberalism and the work of John Locke. Locke provides an exposition of liberal principles that explicitly theorizes the constitutive and dynamic relations between them, and I will use his work to formulate a preliminary conception of liberalism that integrates its main dimensions. Locke's work is particularly suited to this exercise because it is located at a critical historical juncture: at a time when 'liberal' ideas and interests had begun to emerge but had not yet consolidated into a coherent world view or become embodied in political institutions. Locke's work addresses both these problems: he provides a systematic account of these ideas and interests and he works out how they might be realized in a contemporaneous 'nonliberal' environment. While the former gives rise to an explicit theorization of the relations between, and the co-constitutive nature of, the different dimensions of 'liberalism', the latter introduces a dynamic of fragmentation into liberal thought and practice. Liberalism, the Lockean work suggests, is both an ideology and a practice (indeed, the former arises from the latter and reconstitutes it). In order to test the validity of this conception of liberalism, the chapter ends by providing a brief sketch of the historical emergence and subsequent development of liberalism which, I will show, indeed broadly follows the trajectory outlined by Locke.

The remainder of the book picks up different pieces of the liberal puzzle in contemporary world politics and investigates whether, and the extent to which, these pieces can be assembled following the Lockean conception of liberalism. Chapter 4 provides an exposition of two core liberal theories focusing on political institutions: the democratic peace thesis and the democracy transition paradigm. These approaches provided the theoretical framework for a variety of democracy promotion policies that played a prominent role in the post-Cold War era. Yet, instead of leading as expected to democratization and pacification, these policies often contributed to the rise of 'illiberal democracy'[1] and even, on occasion, to violent conflict. These failures can be traced back to a narrow focus on political institutions inspired by theories largely reducing liberalism to political institutions. In contrast, I will show, the Lockean framework accounts for both the successes and the failures of these policies – and it does so by highlighting in particular the foundational role of economic organization for the development of liberal political cultures and institutions.

---

[1] The term has become widely used as a result of Zakaria's influential article on 'The Rise of Illiberal Democracy' (1997) where it connotes a contradiction between democratic institutions and the realization of liberal values. This juxtaposition has since been challenged with reference to the fact that in 'illiberal' states the quality of democratic institutions also tends to suffer (Møller 2008). I will nevertheless use the term as a simple shorthand connoting the existence of democratic institutions – particularly elections – in illiberal states.

Hence, Chapter 5 provides a brief account of the general assumptions of liberal economic theory and of their role in development theory and the economic strand of the democracy transition paradigm. These theories inspired, I will show, liberal economic policies during the 1990s, in general, as well as development policies and some democracy promotion policies, in particular. Again, however, the results of these policies provide a rather mixed picture – with prosperity rising in some quarters and poverty in others, with economic and financial booms followed by serious crises, and with successful transitions to capitalism accompanied or followed by a decline in political liberalism and, on occasion, a rise in violent conflict. While liberal 'political economy' does, as the term suggests, recognize an intimate link between the economic and political dimensions of liberalism, it tends to overlook the equally intimate link between the domestic and international sphere and its constitutive role for liberalism. International or global liberal economic policies thus often undermined the prospects of domestic liberalization and contributed to mixed results. Again, however, the Lockean conception of liberalism makes the constitutive role of the international/domestic divide for the development of liberalism explicit and thus provides an explanation for the contradictory outcomes of liberal economic policies.

Chapter 6 introduces normative liberal theories. These theories hold that the spread and institutionalization of liberal norms provide the basis for a realization of liberal principles like tolerance, individual freedom, distributive justice, and prosperity, as well as cooperation and peace. Inspired by these assumptions, policies designed to protect and spread respect for human rights – prominently in the form of humanitarian intervention and the responsibility to protect – and to reform international institutions and international law were widely advocated. Often, however, this advocacy was not particularly vigorously followed by action – and where it was, the outcome frequently fell far short of the aims. More often than not, political and economic interests seemed to trump or shape (with detrimental consequences) the commitment to realize liberal norms. While normative liberal theories may view these interests as compatible with, or even an integral part of, liberalism, they fail to recognize what the Lockean theory makes explicit: namely that these particular political and economic interests play a constitutive role for liberal norms themselves, which explains their pervasive role in frustrating normative projects (actively or passively).

On the basis of this analysis, in conclusion, the pieces of the liberal puzzle can finally be assembled to provide a conception of liberalism that integrates its major dimensions and accounts for its diversity both across space and time. This conception has profound implications for liberal theories, liberalism's role in history, and liberal policies. It shows that contemporary liberal approaches tend to provide only a partial conception of liberalism and thus, while offering excellent analyses of particular aspects, fail to grasp the core dynamics of the whole. The diversity of liberal thought thus tends to offer choices within liberalism rather than between liberalisms. In contrast, the conception of liberalism developed here provides the basis for a comprehensive analysis of the role of liberalism in history and practice.

In light of this concept, an assessment of liberalism's role in history has to be widened to take into account not only the diversity of liberal but also nonliberal actors, liberal practices not only within domestic or intraliberal environments but also in the international context, not just the historical achievements of liberalism but also the periods of their constitution. This framework shows that liberalism's role in world history was at once greater and smaller than generally acknowledged: the successful constitution of liberal actors was accompanied, as we shall see, by that of nonliberal actors; the constitution of domestic liberal states entailed the constitution of the international system in its modern form; the establishment of the rule of law was accompanied by power politics; and the production of development entailed the operation of 'underdevelopment'. The historical power of liberalism thus led to the establishment of a liberal world order already by the end of the 19th century. Yet, it was smaller than generally recognized inasmuch as these achievements do not add up to a progressive realization of liberal principles. Instead, they are driven by the fragmentary dynamics of liberalism whose internal contradictions, indeed, caused this liberal world order to fall apart again. And it is this very dynamic that plays itself out again in the liberal world order following the end of the Cold War.

Finally, these fragmentary dynamics explain the impulse, diversity, inconsistency as well as the paradoxical outcomes of liberal policies during the post-Cold War era. These policies produced exactly the results that a comprehensive conception of liberalism would suggest and imply that it was not liberal practice that failed liberal theory but rather liberal theory that failed to grasp the dynamics of, and therefore also misled, liberal practice. Since the fragmentary dynamics of liberalism entail the constitution of nonliberal forces, the attempt of a universal realization of liberal principles is bound to fail. The recognition of this dynamic, however, frees liberal policies from pursuing the kind of hubristic goals that led to its 'crisis of authority' (Ikenberry 2011) in the post-Cold War era. And it implies that the major challenge for liberal policies does not lie in confronting external challenges but in avoiding the production of internal fragmentation.

In sum, the strengths of an immanent critique lie in drawing together the different dimensions of liberalism and making explicit the dynamics that link as well as separate them. Yet, like any other approach, this one, too, has its weaknesses and limitations. These arise from its focus on the core dynamics of liberalism itself with consequences for both its internal constitution and its external relations. With regard to the former, the focus on the internal dynamics of liberalism runs the risk of overstating its coherence and/or historical consistency and continuity. While there are indeed good reasons for using the work of Locke for an initial reconstruction of liberalism, it may be argued that other liberal thinkers like Immanuel Kant, John Stuart Mill, or John Rawls would have provided a very different conception of liberalism. Indeed, the contemporary variety of liberal approaches – often traced back to, or supported by, different classical liberal writers – attests to this claim. Though this study does not compare these and other liberal authors, I will return to this question in the conclusion and show that the differences between liberal authors have their roots in, and are the result of, the dynamic of fragmentation that accompanies the historical development of liberalism and are thus accounted for in its conception.

Similarly, the focus on the core theoretical dynamics of liberalism entails the risk of marginalizing some of its historically and politically important yet contingent features – such as its intimate linkage to patriarchal, paternalist, or racist policies. Not only Locke but many later liberal writers are variously implicated here (for example, Glausser 1990). What unites these policies from a theoretical point of view is the fact that they all entail the establishment of hierarchical relations, domestically and internationally, and justify them with reference to supposedly natural or cultural differences between individuals or societies. This establishment of hierarchical relations does indeed play an important role in this study – particularly in the context of the liberal philosophy of history which is designed to provide precisely such justificatory accounts. The substantive content of these justifications – gender, race, culture, religion, development – however, changes over time. The constitution of liberalism, in other words, requires the establishment of hierarchical relations, but it is not inherently patriarchal – hence John Stuart Mill's essay against the subjection of women (1998c) – or racist – hence the crucial role of liberals in the anti-slavery movements (Porter 1999) – or even secular (Pasha 2012). The existence of such traits in liberalism must therefore be acknowledged here, even if their analysis is not systematically pursued in the remainder of this study.

Conversely, the focus on liberalism's internal dynamics marginalizes, at least in terms of space, attention paid to its external relations. And yet, this external context plays a crucial role for the development of liberalism and is accounted for, if briefly, in the discussion of the historical and biographical background to Locke's writings. Moreover, both the constitution of liberal and nonliberal actors occurs in the form of a transformation of preexisting (nonliberal) actors, institutions, and practices and results, accordingly, in a rich diversity of liberal and nonliberal actors. This diversity, in other words, embodies the active engagement between liberal and nonliberal actors, between external and internal forces. Finally, the fragmentary dynamics of liberalism also, as I show in conclusion, have the power to rupture a liberal world order. In short, while the focus of this study on the internal dynamics of liberalism excludes, for reasons of space, the explicit discussion of its external relations, the latter are nevertheless presupposed in, and constitute a part of, the former.

By the same token, a thorough comparison with other theories goes beyond the scope of this book and may give rise to the impression that liberalism is singularly bedeviled by internal tensions and contradictions. And yet, all theories undoubtedly contain tensions and contradictions and many, if not all of them, also play a substantive ideological role. My focus on liberalism does therefore not imply a comparative judgment on the logic and consistency of liberal theory but rather a comparative judgment on its historical importance and political power. The focus on liberalism, in other words, is motivated by its importance in and for world politics. Moreover, if this analysis pays particular attention to liberalism's constitution of nonliberal forces, this does not imply a neglect of its emancipatory potential. Particular attention is only paid to the former because the latter is widely acknowledged in, and propagated by, a wide range of liberal theories. Indeed, I argue throughout that the constitution of such nonliberal forces goes hand in hand with the constitution of liberal forces themselves, and is hence by itself no more definitive of liberalism than its emancipatory potential is.

In sum, while this study provides a comprehensive conception of liberalism which accounts for its diversity as well as for its core dynamics across space, time, and in theory and practice, it also provides the basis for a future research program that systematically explores the conditions and consequences of its internal fragmentation or diversification in concrete instances as well as its dynamic relations with concrete nonliberal historical forces and theories.

Finally, the comprehensive nature of the concept of liberalism arising from this study calls for its differentiation from concepts like capitalism or modernity.[2] Capitalism, modernity, and liberalism are, indeed, closely related. Capitalism is an essential component of liberalism and liberalism has no doubt played a major role in the development of what is usually described as modernity. And yet, capitalism describes a particular social system and modernity a historical period defined by certain social, technological, cultural, and intellectual characteristics. Both, thus, are largely explanatory concepts. Liberalism, in contrast, is a political concept: it offers a political vision, and it is this vision, born of the disjuncture between theory and reality, that turns liberalism into a political project and constitutes agency which may include, but is not reducible to, the logics of capitalism or modernity. It is this vision which establishes the power of liberalism.

---

[2] A question specifically posed by Rob Walker at the ISA conference in 2009 as well as by one of the reviewers of this manuscript.

2
Contemporary Liberal Theories

Introduction

Understanding liberalism's prominent, yet fickle, role in world politics requires, first of all, a definition of liberal internationalism. Yet, such a definition is not readily available. The term 'liberal internationalism' is sometimes used to narrowly denote 'missionary' liberal foreign policies, sometimes to indicate more broadly the application of liberal principles and practices to international politics, and sometimes simply the foreign policies of liberal states. Conversely, all these practices have also simply been called 'liberal' or even, as the foreign policies of liberal states during the Cold War period, 'realist'.

This chapter aims to show that the absence of a widely shared conception of liberal internationalism is not simply due to failing attempts to get a grip on the phenomenon. On the contrary, the subject matter of liberal internationalism seems to slip through a wide range of systematic attempts to pin it down. Why and how this is possible, I will explore in the following pages. In contrast to the common practice of providing a definition of the subject at the beginning of the study, therefore, this chapter will analyze the reasons for the absence of satisfactory definitions of liberal internationalism and identify the weaknesses of existing conceptions – and thus provide the theoretical framework for an alternative approach to defining liberal internationalism in the next chapter.

The process of definition is an eminently theoretical exercise and hence this chapter will focus on the theorization of liberal internationalism in a variety of contexts. In the first section, I will establish the role of liberalism within the discipline of International Relations in general and its relations to realism in particular. Liberal theories,

I will argue, have played a much more fundamental role in and for the discipline of International Relations than is often recognized. Within the discipline, moreover, liberalism is generally defined in contrast to realism – with unsatisfactory results that do not account for the complex and often complementary relationship between these two approaches.

The second part of this chapter provides an overview over a wide range of liberal theories and shows that these theories, in response to the diversity of liberal thought and practice, tend to introduce systematic distinctions between liberalism's substantive issue areas and between its temporal and spatial manifestations; a practice supported by methodological divisions similarly based on a systematic distinction between theory and practice. Prioritizing one of these binaries over the other, liberal theories tend to produce decidedly partial conceptions of liberalism.

The strengths as well as weaknesses of these conceptions, however, enable some crucial insights. It is, I will show, liberalism's composite and dynamic nature that constantly undermines and overruns the limitations of traditional – static – forms of definition. This analysis suggests, then, that a more fruitful definition of liberalism requires an explicit focus on the sources of liberalism's dynamism, and these sources lie in the relationship between its constitutive parts and dimensions.

In pursuit of this argument, I will adopt three – more or less – unconventional forms of representation in the following pages. First, since the main aim of this chapter lies in highlighting the fragmentation of liberal theory, the four core areas of fragmentation – substantive content, temporal trajectory, spatial manifestation, and methodology – will provide the framework for the discussion of liberal theories. The chapter thus does not provide a coherent account of individual liberal theories in their own right and it does not engage with their substantive claims – instead its aim is to demonstrate the pervasive practice of fragmentation and its consequences for our conceptions of liberalism. A thorough presentation of, and engagement with, the substance of individual liberal theories will, however, follow in Chapters 3 to 5.

Secondly, though this book is entitled 'Liberal Internationalism' and thus advertises its particular interest in, and focus on, the international dimension of liberalism, it will ultimately show that liberalism is by definition international. Consequently, I will not follow the conventional practice of first providing a separate account of liberalism which is subsequently extended into international relations. Instead, the international context provides the overall framework for this study and the relationship between domestic and international liberalism will be discussed as one of the dimensions of liberal internationalism in the second part of this chapter. The term 'liberal' will be used in both contexts. Where the distinction between its domestic and international meaning plays an important role for the argument, I will make it explicit. Otherwise, the term refers to the meaning established by the given context.

Thirdly, since conceptualization of liberalism itself is at issue in this book, and since the current chapter does not yet provide an independent definition, I will use the terms 'liberal', 'liberalism', 'liberal internationalism' in a largely common-sensical way – that is, for principles, actors, approaches, practices that either identify themselves and/or are widely identified by observers as liberal.

Liberalism and the discipline of International Relations

The dominant theoretical and practical paradigm within International Relations is generally taken to be realism – certainly from the time of World War II until, at least, the early 1980s.[1] Indeed, so strong is this association that the discipline itself and the essence of its subject matter is sometimes presented as perfectly aligned with realism (Hoffmann 1987: 396). Traditionally almost every alternative approach in the discipline is developed on the basis of a critique of realism. Marxists (Cox 1981; Rosenberg 1994; Teschke 2003), feminists (Tickner 1988; Runyan and Peterson 1991; Peterson 1992), postmodernists (Ashley 1988; Walker 1987, 1993; Campbell 1992), and, of course, liberals of all shades and colors (Beitz 1979; Linklater 1990; Keohane 1986; Baldwin 1993; Moravcsik 1997) define themselves in opposition to realism.

And yet, liberalism frequently claims at least equal status with realism as one of the two core mainstream approaches in the field and is as such presented in textbooks and recognized by its main competitor. Further, liberalism inspires a great number of theoretical and practical approaches in the discipline: From the democratic peace thesis to the cosmopolitan democracy project, from neoliberal institutionalism to structural and empirical liberalism, from globalization theories to normative liberal approaches liberalism pervades the discipline of International Relations. In addition, there are countless studies devoted to particular areas of liberal concern: on democracy and democratization

---

[1] The general claim for the dominance of realism is made, for instance, by Doyle 1997: 41; Brown and Ainley 2005: 28; Shimko 2005: 46; Dunne 1997: 109. Dougherty and Pfaltzgraff Jr., meanwhile, see the end of its dominance in the 1980s (1997: 58).

(Sørensen 1993), international law (Nardin 1983; Onuf 1989; Reus-Smit 2004), global governance (Rosenau and Czempiel 1992), human rights (Dunne and Wheeler 1999) to name but a few. Equally, there are analyses of liberal approaches to war and peace (Howard 1978; Macmillan 1998), development and modernization (Packenham 1973; Latham 2000; Shafer 1988), international organization (Keohane 1989). And recently some attention has been paid to the role and influence of liberalism in the early and pre-history of the discipline (Long and Wilson 1995; Long and Schmidt 2005). There is no doubt, then, that the discipline would be unrecognizable without this body of work.

And yet, while the central status of realism within the discipline is reflected in the large number of books and articles devoted to this approach as such,[2] general accounts of liberalism, with very rare exceptions (Richardson 2001; Ikenberry 2006, 2011; Sørensen 2012), are almost entirely restricted to textbook chapters (Zacher and Matthew 1995; Dunne 1997; Jackson and Sørensen 2003; Brown and Ainley 2005; Burchill 2001). In light of the veritable deluge of systematic studies of realism it is no exaggeration to say that the search for a comparative treatment of liberalism comes up virtually empty-handed.

The close association of realism with International Relations as a discipline as well as with its subject matter may be partly responsible for this difference. And yet, a closer look at the history of the discipline suggests that liberalism was neither so much less important nor so clearly distinguishable from realism. There is probably no work which has done more to substantiate the claim that realism is the dominant paradigm in the discipline than John A. Vasquez's 'The Power of Power Politics' (1998: 183). Vasquez starts his investigation with a kind of 'potted history' of the discipline. The starting date for this history is the establishment of a Chair in International Politics at Aberystwyth in 1919, followed by an idealist phase between the two World Wars, the realist take-over in the course of World War II, followed by the 'behavioral' revolt in the late 1950s and early 1960s (Vasquez 1998: 32–44). This is probably the most common version of the discipline's history, countless times imparted to students of International Relations (Dougherty and Pfaltzgraff 1997: Chapters 1 and 2; Brown and Ainley 2005: Chapter 2; Jackson and Sørensen 2003: Chapter 2).

---

[2] Williams 2005; Guzzini 1998; Haslam 2002; Sheehan 1995; Smith 1986; Spegele 1996 – to mention but a few.

And yet, this history is potentially misleading. In dating the beginning of the discipline in 1919 its core purpose is clearly associated with the pursuit of peace; and, indeed, the downfall of liberalism (or idealism) and the simultaneous rise of realism is directly linked to the failure of liberal policies to establish and maintain peace – especially through the League of Nations – and the realist claim that balance of power politics would be more successful. The idealist phase, argues Vasquez, has helped institutionalize the discipline and 'established its emphasis on questions of peace and war' (1998: 43).

Recent studies suggest, however, that a fuller picture emerges if systematic analysis of international politics in the second half of the 19th and the beginning of the 20th centuries is taken into account (Sylvest 2005, 2009). In this period before World War I a number of influential liberal studies of international politics were written, and their authors actively engaged in the institutionalization of the discipline (see Long and Schmidt 2005). These authors were interested in the growing economic and technological interdependence of the world, in the governance of this interdependence through free trade, international communication, cooperation, law and organization, and in the role of democracy, nationalism, imperialism, civilization, and race relations in international affairs. This substantive liberalism was accompanied by an equally familiar belief in science and rationality (Fritz 2005). While questions of peace and war were by no means absent, they were integrated into, and determined by, the economic, political, cultural and organizational developments analyzed by these authors. In fact, the common themes emerging from, and driving, this 'early' international theory were a 'dynamic interaction between imperialism and internationalism and not', as Long and Schmidt argue, 'the much discussed realist-idealist debate' (2005: 1).

Recognizing this early or pre-history of International Relations does not mean that conventional accounts of the interwar period focusing on the connection between liberalism, peace, and the League of Nations are wrong. However, this picture overlooks, firstly, the varied nature of liberal work on international affairs, secondly, the continuity of liberal approaches to international relations from before World War I through the interwar period up until today, and thirdly, a considerable overlap with realist work.

Leonard Woolf's *Empire and Commerce in Africa*, and *Imperialism and Civilization*, Hobson's *Imperialism*, Toynbee's *A Study of History, Civilization on Trial*, and *The World and the West*, Paul Rich's *Race and Empire in British Politics* all attest to the importance of imperialism in liberal thought of the interwar period demonstrating a continuity to earlier liberal writings on international relations and laying the foundations for the systematic study of imperialism thereafter (Long 1995: 322). Similarly, the foundations for the modern study of political economy were laid in the interwar period by authors like Hayek, Hobson, Keynes, Pigou, Robbins, and Staley (Long 1995: 322). In the study of international organization there is an unbroken line from the late 19th century to today. The early liberal works closely resemble contemporary work under the heading of regime theory, institutionalism, global governance, and complex interdependence (a term coined by Buell in 1925; see Vitalis 2005: 171; Gorman 2005), and can be seen as a precursor to David Mitrany's functionalism (Schmidt 2005: 67; Fritz 2005: 156; Long 1995: 322). Finally, liberal work in the interwar period tended to be state centric and, thus, to overlap in this respect with contemporaneous as well as later realist writings (Long 1995: 305).

Paying attention to this early history of systematic academic engagement with international affairs thus brings to light the broader concerns of liberal work in and on international relations. These included prominently questions of imperialism and political economy in addition to the widely recognized work on international organization. Such a wider definition of liberal work in International Relations, hence, relativizes some of the assumptions entailed in the familiar 'potted history' of the discipline. Firstly, liberal concerns with questions of war and peace cannot simply be reduced to studies of international organization in general or the League of Nations in particular. Before World War I questions of war and peace were part and parcel of studies of international interdependence and colonial or race relations. The issue of peace and war undoubtedly moved to the core in the interwar period (Pugh 2012), but not in such a way as to displace the broader framework of liberal thought on political economy and imperialism. The failures of the League of Nations and the outbreak of World War II, then, while they must be seen as a challenge for liberal thought – more so for some strands of it than others – do not necessarily indicate the failures of liberal international theory as such.

Secondly, recognizing the broader range of liberal work helps to identify continuities not just between the pre- and post-World War I periods but also between the latter and the post-World War II period. While liberal work clearly lost influence, authors like Mitrany, Deutsch, Haas, and Hoffmann were prolific and widely read. These were followed in the 1970s by Keohane and Nye's 'Power and Interdependence' which triggered the development of regime theory and liberal institutionalism.

Also in the 1970s, the publication of John Rawls' *Theory of Justice* gave a new boost to normative liberal theories. Broadly influenced by liberalism was also the area of peace research which became particularly influential in continental Europe. Moreover, the issues of imperialism and political economy led to the development of subfields like development studies and political economy within the discipline. Most importantly, however, they merged into the highly influential modernization theory after World War II. Hence, it is important not to exaggerate the rupture between these two periods with regard to liberal work.

Finally, state centrism – one of Vasquez's core assumptions defining the realist paradigm – appears not to be exclusive to that approach. There have been state-centric strands of liberal international thought in all three periods, just as there are now (see Deudney and Ikenberry 1999, for example). On the basis of these reflections it seems that the familiar 'potted history' of the discipline defines liberalism too narrowly and exaggerates the decline of liberal international thought.

And yet, these reflections do not necessarily invalidate Vasquez's general claim that realism provides the dominant theoretical paradigm in International Relations. Rather, having established that this dominance may not be quite as absolute as it appears, it is now necessary to investigate in how far this dominance is restricted to guiding research in the discipline of International Relations and in how far it extends to guiding political practice.

The Cold War is, indeed, widely seen as the quintessential realist balancing of power in operation, thus, in turn supporting the primacy of the realist paradigm in the study of international affairs. 'From 1939 to the present, leading theorists and policy-makers have continued to view the world through realist lenses' and it is this usefulness as a 'manual' for policy-makers which is often cited as a major reason for the dominance of the realist paradigm in International Relations (Dunne 1997: 110; Vasquez 1998: 318f). George F. Kennan and Henry Kissinger are prime examples for this claim – the former as the main architect of containment and the latter in his skillful use of balancing policies. And yet, neither Kissinger nor Kennan fit into Vasquez's definition of the realist paradigm as easily as one might assume for in both cases the separation of domestic and international politics is blurred. Kissinger distinguished between stable and revolutionary systems and, thus, made domestic political structure a 'key element' of international politics (Dougherty and Pfaltzgraff 1997: 79). And Kennan pursued stability in Western Europe through the establishment of domestic liberal capitalism while envisaging that the pressure this put on the Soviet Union would lead to internal contradictions (Moravcsik 1997: 546; Dougherty and Pfaltzgraff 1997: 75). In this view, the erstwhile architect of the Cold War based his recommendations on liberal arguments just as Schlesinger and Podhoretz and Krauthammer, the latter now widely seen as neo-conservatives, justified the intervention in Vietnam on liberal grounds (Moravcsik 1997: 546; Smith 1992: 214f). Indeed, politicians from Jean Monnet to Jimmy Carter and Ronald Reagan through Bush the elder, Clinton, and Bush the younger have all been identified as justifying their foreign policies along liberal lines (Smith 1992: 220; Doyle 1986: 1151; Hoffmann 1995: 159, 166f, 176). In light of these continuities, the unequivocal characterization of the Cold War as dominated by realpolitik has to be relativized.

Moreover, if one does not focus solely on the competition between the United States, the Soviet Union, and their respective alliances, the picture shifts even further in favor of a continued importance of liberalism. Western policies toward newly independent states in the Third World were characterized until the end of the Vietnam War by the so-called nationbuilding or modernization policies (and they have been and are again since the Reagan years). And these policies in turn were inspired by modernization theories. The latter were developed on the basis of an unequivocally liberal world view aiming at the transformation of the economic, political, and cultural system of Third World states along the lines of Western liberal capitalist states with the expectation of thus turning them into stable and productive allies (Packenham 1973; Shafer 1988; Latham 2000). And this approach had its own Kennans and Kissingers, most famously W. W. Rostow.

This admittedly cursory glance at the Cold War era shows, firstly, that liberalism was decisive in policies toward the Third World and, secondly, that the clear separation or even counterposition of realism and liberalism in terms of their practical influence cannot be upheld. In fact, while practitioners of realpolitik such as Kennan and Kissinger clearly integrated liberal attention to domestic affairs and regime type into their considerations, for the practitioners of modernization policies 'realist' security concerns constituted an integral part of the drive to spread market democracies in the Third World.

It becomes increasingly clear, then, that the relationship between liberalism and realism is rather complicated (Guzzini 1998; Williams 2005; Gismondi 2008). And this also finds expression in the debates between the proponents of these approaches. Liberalism is generally presented as in 'natural opposition' to, and in 'sharp' contrast with, realism (Dunne 1997: 148; Jackson and Sørensen 2003: 106). It is the 'paradigmatic alternative' to realism and institutionalism (Moravcsik 1997: 513, 522) and, thus, claims equal or even superior status as a theory at the core of the discipline (Moravcsik 1997: 542, 513; Deudney and Ikenberry 1999: 196). As such it is also recognized by realists who – from Carr through Morgenthau to Waltz – develop their position in explicit opposition to liberalism. And yet, the same authors also see liberalism and realism as 'complementary' (Moravcsik 1997: 542, 513; Deudney and Ikenberry 1999: 196; Doyle 1996: 50).

The foregoing discussion should suffice to underline the importance of liberal internationalism. It has played a constitutional, continuous, and important role as a theoretical approach at the core of the discipline of International Relations; it has inspired the foreign policies of major Western states; and it has considerably influenced the organizational and legal structure of the international system from at least 1918 onwards. After all, 'the "settled norms" of the contemporary international order are still essentially those of 1919 – national self-determination, nonaggression and respect for international law combined with support for the principles of sovereignty. The United Nations is, in effect, a revision of the League of Nations, even if it was convenient to gloss over this in 1945' (Brown and Ainley 2005: 28). Moreover, the sheer quantitative weight of liberal approaches in International Relations is staggering. Liberalism has thus proven to be 'remarkably resilient' (Brown and Ainley 2005: 28). Moreover, while liberalism is very frequently presented as the alternative to realism, in practice there appears considerable complementarity between these approaches.

Liberal theories

In light of this rather crucial role of liberalism in the constitution and development of the discipline as well as in international politics, the fact that there does not exist a coherent account of this approach appears rather curious. While the assumption of realism's dominance may play some role in explaining this lack of a systematic account of liberalism and its role in international relations, this does not account for the fact that liberals themselves – despite their explicit aspirations – have failed to provide such an account of their own approach. In short, as Moravcsik argues, a proper liberal theory of International Relations has simply never been formulated (1997: 514). Instead, the discipline boasts a wide array of approaches focusing on different areas of liberalism but failing to account for 'shared assumptions' and aggregate implications (Moravcsik 1997: 514, 534).

This diversity, I will show now, has its roots in the rich, diverse, complex and even contradictory range of policies associated with liberalism which present a challenge for theorization. After all, liberal theories, like all theories, need to specify their subject matter, identify its historical and spatial boundaries, and adopt an appropriate methodological approach for its analysis. And it is in pursuit of pinning down each one of these four dimensions of theory that liberal authors introduce systematic distinctions and prioritize some dimensions of liberalism over others.

The first of these distinctions concerns the subject matter of liberal theory. Liberalism, as we have seen, is associated with a wide range of policies from the promotion of democracy, through state- and nationbuilding, the development of international organizations and international law, the pursuit of prosperity and economic development to the protection of human rights that makes identifying the subject matter of liberal theory difficult. Moreover, the issues on this list are traditionally addressed by different disciplines – Political Science, Economics, Philosophy – highlighting the qualitative nature of the problem. Hence, liberal theories in International Relations reflect this disciplinary distinction and tend to focus either on the political or the economic or the normative issue areas. Hence, Moravcsik identifies ideational, commercial, and republican liberalism (1997: 515); Jackson and Sørensen sociological, interdependence, institutional, and republican liberalism (2003: 108); Dunne speaks of internationalism, idealism, institutionalism as well as their respective 'neo'-variations (1997: 150–4); Doyle of liberal imperialism, pacifism, and internationalism (1997: 206); Zacher and Matthew distinguish between republican, commercial, cognitive, sociological, and institutional liberalism (1995: 122–37); and Keohane between republican, commercial, regulatory liberalism (2002; see also Griffiths 2011) to mention but a few of these distinctions. Republican liberalism focuses on political institutions and regimes; commercial, interdependence and pacifist liberalism on the economic sphere; while ideational and cognitive liberalism focus on ideas, norms, and culture.

These distinctions provide the most fundamental source of fragmentation for liberal international theory – despite the fact that most sophisticated liberal theories explicitly recognize a connection between these dimensions. Although one occasionally finds a one-dimensional definition of liberalism – Russett, for example, defines a liberal state solely in terms of political institutions like voting rights, contested elections, and an executive responsible to an elected body (1996a) – most liberal theories explicitly provide definitions that include at least two and often all three of these dimensions. Hence, Owen's definition makes reference to liberal norms as well as political institutions (1996) and Doyle combines normative, political, and economic elements in his definition of a liberal state by the legal equality of citizens, representative government, private property, and a market economy (1996: 5–6). Similarly, Moravcsik explicitly states that 'economic development has a strong influence on the viability of democratic governance, with its pacific implications; liberal democratic governments tend in turn to support commerce' which can 'lead to transnational communication and...promote secularizing cognitive and ideological change' (1997: 534). Hence, in the abstract liberals widely recognize a connection between the political, economic, and normative aspects of liberalism, but in practice they rarely theorize this connection.

Explanations of the pacific nature or implications of liberalism provide a good example. Unlike realism, liberalism holds that international peace is actually achievable and much of liberal theory is concerned with showing why this is so and how this goal may be realized. Yet, focusing on different issue areas, liberals tend to develop different and potentially contradictory theories of this dynamic.

Liberal political theories like the democratic peace thesis focus – as the name suggests – on democratic political institutions for an explanation of the democratic (or liberal) peace. Democracy has pacific implications, it is argued, either because it allows for the representation of peaceful interests of the population in politics or because these institutions slow down the decision-making process and thus create space for alternative forms of conflict resolution. Though the 'spirit of commerce' adds 'material incentive' to these pacific dynamics, it only plays a supportive role (Doyle 1996: 26).

Normative theories, in contrast, hold that norms of nonviolent conflict resolution characterize the domestic political culture of liberal states; these norms over time also influence the foreign policies of these states – at least vis-a-vis other liberal states – and thus generate peaceful international policies (Russett 1996b). Liberal political and economic institutions are hardly even touched upon in the normative explanation of the liberal peace.

Finally, the possibility of international peace is also theorized by economic liberal approaches – yet for lack of reference to political institutions like democracy usually not included in the 'democratic peace' literature. According to economic theories, liberalism is conducive to peace because it fosters economic development and interaction – through the protection of private property, free markets, and free trade. The resultant economic interdependence militates against war which would be costly for all parties (Angell 1910) and it also provides the basis for enhanced transnational cooperation and mutual understanding (Barbieri 2002). For this explanation of peace, liberal political institutions or normative principles are strictly unnecessary – though they may well play a supportive role in practice.

On the one hand, this fragmentation of liberal theory according to substantive norms or issue areas reflects the genuine spread of liberal norms and policies. Yet, on the other hand, by focusing either on political, or normative, or economic dynamics as sources of peace, these approaches fail to establish whether, and if so how, these different norms and issue areas are related. While these alternative explanations may not be 'inconsistent with one another', they are nevertheless 'logically distinct from one another' (Keohane 2002: 17). These logical alternatives become problematic in practice when competing theories suggest different and competing policies in pursuit of the same end. Does the pursuit of peace require capitalist economic development or democratization? And if both contribute to peace, what is their relationship and how do they need to be combined? Does, for instance, the simultaneous introduction of market economics and democracy undermine peace but a sequential introduction contribute to peace (Paris 2004)? The fragmentation of liberal theory according to substantive policy areas thus has a direct impact on liberal policies.

More importantly for the purpose of this chapter, however, it also generates competing and partial conceptions of liberalism. By focusing on different substantive issue areas, these analyses generate (more or less) partial conceptions of liberalism which fail to grasp the meaning of the term 'liberal' as it is generally – if not precisely – applied in academic and political life. Though liberalism is undoubtedly intimately linked to democracy today, democratic institutions are not sufficient for a state to be recognized as liberal – Russia being a case in point (Zakaria 1997). Similarly, neither liberal norms and principles as endorsed by British rule in Hongkong, for instance, nor an economic system based on private property and free markets alone – such as in China – constitute a liberal state. The diversity of liberal political practices thus gives rise to a variety of liberal theories generally distinguished by the policy areas on which they focus.

A second and further layer of fragmentation is triggered by the varied and contradictory principles and practices of liberalism historically. Liberal political theories, as we have seen, widely present democracy as a core characteristic of liberalism. And yet, liberals were historically passionately opposed to democracy and actively resisted an extension of the franchise (Plattner 2008: 64–5; Przeworski 1992: 53; Di Muzio 2012). Much of liberal history is therefore not just un- but positively anti-democratic. More generally, history does not unequivocally support the contemporary assumption of a 'natural' link between liberalism and democracy: it is instead littered with examples of undemocratic liberal states (in European history) and democratic illiberal states (in ancient Greece as well as globally today).

In the economic realm, liberalism is today often associated with a (more or less extensive) welfare state in the domestic sphere and the regulation of free trade through international economic and financial institutions in the international sphere (Moravcsik 1997: 527, 529). And yet, neoliberal policies of liberalization, privatization, and deregulation as well as classical laissez-faire policies are equally associated with liberalism (Plattner 2008: 68). Moreover, while liberals certainly pursue free trade policies, they also have a history of protectionism, rent-seeking, slavery, colonialism (Moravcsik 1997: 530). And even liberal norms do not escape such contradictions. While liberalism is today largely associated with the protection of human rights and the realization of liberal norms like individual freedom or self-determination, historically liberalism was also intimately associated with slavery and colonialism.

Most commonly, liberal theories respond to this problem of contradictory historical evidence with the argument that early conceptions of liberalism were immature and often still mistaken in the interpretation and application of liberal principles. With regard to the tension between liberalism and democracy, for instance, it is argued that early liberals did not yet realize – but subsequently learned – that extending equal political rights to all citizens was logically required by liberal principles and 'need not lead to the outright plunder of the rich and the destruction of a productive economy and a civilized society' (Plattner 2008: 60, 68).

Similarly, 'as production becomes more specialized and effective trading networks more diverse and complex' political extraction of economic benefits become more disruptive and slowly recede (Moravcsik 1997: 530). In the normative realm as well, liberal principles were historically still poorly understood and applied in a limited manner. Human rights violations – in the form of violent conflicts, acts of genocide, and crimes against humanity – were in the past 'considered normal' (Müllerson 2009: 136) as well as protected by the historical principle of noninterventionism (Tesón 2003: 128). Moral principles have, however, undergone a process of universalization so that such atrocities can now be stopped 'in the name of cosmopolitan conventions whose time may have come' (Linklater 2000: 493). Processes of globalization, moreover, have undermined the standing of the state and provide an opportunity to introduce democratic forms of decision-making at the transnational and supranational level (Held 1996; Archibugi 1998).

Contradictory historical evidence is thus interpreted as a (potentially even necessary) step on the road to contemporary mature liberalism: that is, liberalism 'contains within itself the seeds of its own democratization' (Plattner 2008: 60) or, one might add, the universalization of its moral principles. Alternatively, historical developments of the world economy provide the basis for better and more mature forms of liberal economic policies as well as for the realization of liberal moral principles. The distinction between historical and contemporary liberalism thus allows observers to define liberalism on the basis of its contemporary manifestations and to exclude its (less savory) historical practices from the definition. Instead of undermining the identification of liberalism with democracy, free trade or universal moral principles, historical counterevidence here simply demonstrates its progressive development and learning capacity.

Interestingly, though, some authors use the same division between historical and contemporary liberalism to support a definition of liberalism based on its historical rather than contemporary performance. Here it is argued, for example, that liberalism does not require democracy in the widely shared contemporary sense of majority rule (Vanberg 2008: 146–7; Sartori 1995); that classical liberals were correct in their arguments for laissez-faire economic policies (Shearmur 1992); or that the emancipatory norms and dynamics of classical liberalism have, over time, been betrayed by the privileged classes that applied them (Richardson 1997).

In substantive terms, these two responses to contradictory historical evidence are polar opposites of each other. The first prioritizes contemporary evidence as definitive of liberalism and regards counterevidence as historically contingent. It thus identifies liberalism with democracy, embedded economic liberalism, and human rights. The second prioritizes historical evidence as definitive of liberalism and presents alternative contemporary practices as a deviation from true liberal principles – which are associated with the protection of individual rights instead of democracy, with the deregulation of markets, and with good (liberal) government (whether foreign or domestic). Both, however, use the division between past and present as a means to distinguish between the essential elements of liberalism and its historically contingent features (see also, van de Haar 2009).

Unfortunately, this solution to the problem of contradictory evidence is not satisfactory because the distinction between historical and contemporary liberalism simply overlooks that contradictory evidence cannot neatly be divided along temporal lines. The 'rise of illiberal democracies' today (Zakaria 1997) undermines the neat distinction between past and present as much as the undeniable interest of classical liberals in the principle of 'government by consent' (Locke 1994). Similarly, recent neoliberal policies of deregulation, privatization, and liberalization suggest some continuity with the classical laissez-faire policies (Plattner 2008: 68) and coexist in the present with social democratic and welfare type policies. Moreover, protectionism (by the US and the EU in agriculture, for example), the exploitation of power differentials in pressing for favorable economic policies, or even the use of force to secure liberal ends (interventions to protect or expand opportunities for foreign investment, for example) are by no means just a thing of the past. In addition, just as historically states also engaged in the protection of citizens in other countries (Chesterman 2001: 13–16; Jahn 2012a), liberals today explicitly contemplate (neo)imperialist policies (Cooper 2002; Ignatieff 2003: 309, 320; Bacevich 2003). Such evidence suggests that historical change alone does not account for, and explain, the contradictory performance of liberalism.

A third layer of fragmentation is engendered by the differential spatial performance of liberalism. Thus, Stanley Hoffmann argues that the performance of liberalism in the international sphere is characterized by ambition, insolence, rapine, brutality, racism, and intolerance; no liberal state has ever behaved as liberal abroad as at home (1987: 397). Hence, the United States guarantees individual or human rights in its domestic constitution but is averse to signing international human rights conventions (Alvarez 2001: 194). Moreover, while it largely respects these rights for its own citizens in the domestic sphere, it systematically violates those of foreigners (in Guantanamo) on foreign soil (through extraordinary rendition). Similarly, while liberal states tend to operate a – more or less extensive – system of domestic redistribution through the welfare state, they resist a redistributive system in the international sphere and actively discourage developing countries from establishing similar redistributive institutions, through Structural Adjustment Policies (SAPs), for example. And while liberal states tend to keep the peace with each other, they quite liberally go to war with nonliberal states (Doyle 1996).

This disjuncture between the domestic and international performance of liberalism finds its most prominent expression, of course, in the distinction between political, that is, domestic, liberal theories and international liberal theories. Traditionally, the former do not concern themselves at all with liberal foreign policies. Arblaster's *Rise and Decline of Western Liberalism*, for example, proceeds on the assumption that Western liberalism can be grasped without any attention to its external relations (1984). Just as in International Relations, in Political Theory, too, liberalism is recognized as a wide and varied tradition that is not easily defined (Freeden 2005). Three core concerns of the liberal tradition can nevertheless be identified. First, 'liberalism posits the individual as the fundamental unit of moral and political concern'; secondly, it is interested in government – with particular attention to the kind of political regime that best serves these individuals while safeguarding their freedom (usually some form of representative government); thirdly, it investigates civil society, the realm between the individual and government, with particular attention to the 'form of culture, or social order' (issues such as tolerance, nonviolent conflict resolution, secularism, interest-based forms of association, economic cooperation) necessary for the functioning of a liberal society (Evans 2001: 6–8). These traditional concerns of liberalism are clearly based on the assumption of a single society or state and thus, indeed, fail to address the problems of international relations directly. International concerns, however, have recently made some inroads into liberal theory. Liberalism's core concern with individuals is now frequently expressed through the notion of human rights (Rorty 1989) as well as challenged by communitarians who insist on the social nature of individuals and thus call for more attention to community (Sandel 1984). This challenge is logically based on the recognition of more than one community and historically linked to the – internationally generated – problem of minorities and their rights (Kymlicka 1989, 1995). Hence, Political Theory now engages directly with some international concerns and John Rawls' *Law of Peoples* (2001) explicitly addresses the question of extending liberal principles into the international sphere. For the most part, however, liberal theory frames its international concerns still as a problem of society in the singular rather than societies in the plural (Evans 2001: 11). That is, within the logic of the human rights agenda, the international system is simply seen as one cosmopolitan society populated by individuals and their rights – differing from the domestic context only in the absence of a central government and its means of enforcement. Conversely, the problem of multiculturalism, generated by refugees or migrants and hence a multitude of communities rather than individuals, is nevertheless generally treated as an issue of domestic government and civil society culture rather than as one of international politics.

Yet, these recent developments within domestic liberal theory provide some indication for the grounds of distinction between these two realms: the international system is traditionally seen to lack all three of the core assumptions of domestic liberal theory. That is, the international system is not populated by individuals but states, it does not have a government but is characterized by anarchy, and there is no realm of civil society. The international sphere thus provides an environment 'inhospitable to liberalism' (Hoffmann 1987: 405). The differences between the domestic and international context are thus made responsible for the contradictory performance of liberalism and provide the basis for a distinction between its definitive and contingent features. That is, liberal performance within the domestic sphere is definitive of liberalism. In concrete terms this means that liberalism is widely associated with the protection of individual or human rights, with an economically efficient and culturally tolerant (and hence also nonviolent) social order, and with some form of representative government. Meanwhile, liberalism's less savory record of slavery, colonialism, human rights violations, economic exploitation, and aggressive behavior are seen as the consequence of the 'illiberal' international environment and hence contingent.

Starting from the assumption that liberalism ultimately offers solutions to domestic conditions – individuals, civil society, government – liberal international theories generally aim to 'domestify' the international context. Broadly three versions of this move can be identified. The first simply interprets international politics in analogy to domestic politics, or conversely shows (explicitly or implicitly) that the achievements of liberalism in the domestic context can also be identified in international politics. Deudney and Ikenberry, for instance, argue that the liberal subsystem post-World War II managed to mitigate the dynamics of anarchy, enhance legitimacy, incorporate problem states, create interdependence, and facilitate integration. The means by which these feats were achieved include co-binding security practices, the reciprocal nature of American hegemony, mechanisms to incorporate semi-sovereign and partial great powers, the role of capitalism and a civic political identity (Deudney and Ikenberry 1999: 180–1). The reciprocal nature of American hegemony thus constitutes the international version of a liberal government – serving the states while recognizing their sovereignty. Co-binding security practices replace the state's monopoly of violence which guarantees the survival of the individuals, and capitalism constitutes the material basis of states in the international sphere just as it constitutes free individuals in the domestic sphere. International law and international organizations play the same role for the integration of problem or powerful states as the rule of law and social institutions and organizations play for the integration of asocial as well as powerful individuals. Finally, these (civil society) networks of reciprocal interaction, association, integration produce a civic political culture within the liberal subsystem of world politics just as they do for the domestic sphere of liberal states. While Deudney and Ikenberry's version of 'structural liberalism' identifies American hegemony as the analogous institution to domestic government, most liberal theories focus on transnational or international interaction in (implicit) parallel to domestic civil society and show how and to what extent this kind of horizontal cooperation integrates and socializes individual states or private actors, produces a self-perpetuating political culture of nonviolent competition and cooperation, and may even amount to 'governance without government' (Rosenau and Czempiel 1992; Keohane and Nye 1989; Hasenclever et al. 1997).

A second strategy for bridging the gap between the domestic and international spheres in order to make the latter more conducive to liberal theory and practice pursues this aim by 'liberalizing' its core actors – that is, by turning nonliberal into liberal states. This strategy is based on analyses that show that liberal states manage to realize liberal principles in their interactions even in the international sphere. Liberal states have more legitimacy because their democratic governments are based on individual consent (Buchanan 2003: 171); they meet standards for 'comparative moral reliability' (Buchanan and Keohane 2004: 19); they water down the principles of sovereignty (in the EU for instance) and thus develop more universalistic forms of community (Linklater 2000: 484); they are more peaceful, at least in relations with other liberal states (Doyle 1996); they contribute to the progressive development of international law (Slaughter 1995). Both these strategies translate the original distinction between the domestic and the international sphere at the international level into a sharp distinction between the liberal and nonliberal parts of the international system. In this vein, liberal authors have divided the international system into a zone of peace and a zone of war (Doyle 1996), a historical and a post-historical zone (Fukuyama 1989), a moral and a less moral zone (Buchanan and Keohane 2004) as well as, by adding intermediate spaces, into a pluralist, solidarist, and post-Westphalian zone (Linklater 1998), a graduated zone of law and an outlaw zone (Rawls 2001). The extension of the liberal zones, in both cases, therefore promise the realization of liberal principles in the international sphere.

In contrast, the third strategy of 'domestification' suggests that the days of systematic differences between the domestic and international spheres are numbered. Cosmopolitan liberal theories argue that transnational legal interaction between companies and domestic judiciaries provides the basis for the development of a liberal international law (Slaughter 1995); communications technology provides the basis for a global public opinion (Held 1996; Archibugi 1998); economic interdependence undermines the ability of states to deliver public goods and establishes a global market; and transnational interaction between individuals, companies, and NGOs establishes a global civil society. Taken together, these developments gradually constitute one cosmopolitan society populated by individuals and private actors and thus remove the traditional barriers to the introduction of liberal principles such as the global enforcement of human rights through humanitarian intervention (Wheeler 2000; Linklater 2000), the development of international criminal law (Megret 2001), the establishment of redistributive justice (Beitz 1979) as well as the introduction of democratic forms of decision-making (Held 1996; Archibugi 1998). Moreover, these three strategies of domestifying the international sphere are not mutually exclusive. Cosmopolitan authors regularly recognize the legitimacy and sovereignty of liberal states who are generally accorded with the right to nonintervention (Beitz 1979; Linklater 1998: 167) while liberal institutionalists equally stress the transformations of the international sphere through economic interdependence and organizational networks which also play a role in the cooperation of liberal states in structural liberalism. Since the limited or 'disaggregated' state (Slaughter 1995) is a core feature of liberal political theory, even statist theories like structural liberalism provide individual or private actors a role in world politics.

For both domestic and international liberal theories, the domestic context is definitive of liberalism. Hence, there is substantial overlap between domestic and international liberal theories. Long before Rawls expanded his theory to the international sphere in the *Law of Peoples* (2001), his political *Theory of Justice* inspired liberal international theories (Beitz 1979; Pogge 1989). This overlap and cooperation nevertheless relies on the prior distinction between the domestic and international spheres and the definition of liberalism in terms of its domestic achievements. And yet, just as in the case of temporal distinctions, the spatial distinction between domestic and international or liberal and nonliberal contexts do not satisfactorily resolve the problem of contradictory liberal practices for it obscures the fact that 'illiberal' practices occur within liberal contexts and it exaggerates the 'illiberal' nature of policies in international or nonliberal contexts. Hence, liberal states violate human rights even within the domestic sphere, for example in the context of the war on terror (Roberts 2004) and, as the Iraq war has made plain, they do not necessarily agree in their interpretation of international law. Companies and civil society associations like NGOs are neither democratic institutions nor necessarily an alternative to the state who often provides funding and explicitly uses these organizations to do their bidding (Stavrianakis 2012). Likewise, liberal states – and even more so private actors like companies – often engage in constructive, peaceful, and law-governed relations with nonliberal actors in the political as well as the economic field (Alvarez 2001). Hence, alliances between liberal and nonliberal states were as much a feature of the Cold War period as they are now (Westad 2005). The contradictions attending liberal policies can thus not be resolved by distinguishing between liberal and nonliberal spaces. Hence, definitions of liberalism based on their domestic or intraliberal performance grasp only part of the phenomenon.

Finally, the distinctions between different substantive issue areas, between historical and contemporary, and between domestic and international liberalism are supported by methodological choices that either approach liberalism through its principles or through its practices. Liberalism is associated with norms such as individual freedom and equality, justice, tolerance, nonviolent conflict resolution, and in the international sphere with human rights, justice, cooperation, and peace. Yet, as we have seen already, these norms are frequently violated even in liberal practice. Hence, liberals have had no problem of combining the norm of individual freedom with the practice of slavery. Many liberal states produce high levels of inequality between citizens (currently widely under attack). Justice is often reduced to the rule of law – which may well produce unjust outcomes. Liberal states also engage in systematic human rights violations, support a highly unequal international economic order, and widely use military means to settle conflicts. In light of this disjuncture between liberal principles and practice, normative liberal theories elaborate liberal norms and principles and hold them up against the imperfect reality. This counterposition serves, on the one hand, to criticize the failure to live up to liberal principles and, on the other, to propagate practice better in line with these liberal norms.

Hence, the lack of democratic accountability in the current international system is exposed and new forms of democratic decision-making advocated (Held 1996). Similarly, material inequality in the world is criticized and new principles of redistribution are elaborated and advocated (Beitz 1979; Pogge 2002). And in order to strengthen the protection of human rights, even new international institutions are advocated (Buchanan and Keohane 2004). Normative theories thus define liberalism with reference to its normative principles; and these principles (or the methods for establishing and elaborating them) are usually taken from or inspired by the work of classical liberal authors – with Immanuel Kant by far the most influential today. Indeed, Kant plays a crucial role in Rawls' work; he is present in the statist democratic peace thesis (Doyle 1996) as well as in a wide array of cosmopolitan literature (Held 1996; Archibugi 1998; Linklater 1998; Franceschet 2002; Macmillan 1995). In light of the complexity of liberal thought and practice, normative theory draws a line between liberal principles and ideals on the one hand and liberal practice on the other – and it defines liberalism through its principles and ideals while excluding contrary practice from the definition. When applied to historical development, this distinction leads to the identification of two different strands of liberalism: grassroots or 'radical liberalism' as the bearer of emancipatory liberal principles and 'offical liberalism', or that of the privileged in positions of power who practice a version of liberalism shorn of its emancipatory elements (Richardson 1997).

And yet, the same distinction between theory and practice is used by empirical theorists to define liberalism in terms of its practices. Accusing normative approaches of collecting disparate views held by classical liberal authors and defining liberalism in a teleological manner, Moravcsik aims to formulate a liberal theory based on testable assumptions (1997: 514); that is, a theory that can account for the varied practices of liberalism instead of ignoring them in favor of liberal principles. The same approach is also employed in neoliberal institutionalism (Keohane and Nye 1989), regime theory (Hasenclever et al. 1997), and structural liberalism (Deudney and Ikenberry 1999). Such theories analyze and explain varied liberal practices and define liberalism on the basis of this evidence. These definitions succeed in integrating rather 'illiberal' practices into the definition; yet by doing so they tend to lose major aspects of the distinctive character of liberalism (Jahn 2009) and produce significant overlaps with realism, such as states as the main actors in an anarchical international system that act in accordance with their interests. This common ground arises from the fact that both approaches apply the same method to, largely, the same material, namely the foreign policies of liberal states, if for different reasons. Liberals focus on these states because they are liberal, while realists focus on them because they happen to be particularly powerful in the current world order. In light of these commonalities it is not surprising that empirical liberal theorists characterize their relationship to realism as simultaneously complementary and competitive (Moravcsik 1997: 513, 522, 542; Deudney and Ikenberry 1999: 196). From a normative standpoint, these positivist approaches are, accordingly, accused of sacrificing the norms definitive of the liberal tradition and with them its moral and emancipatory character or potential (Long 1995; Reus-Smit 2001).

In both cases, however, the distinction between norms and practices underpins a partial definition of liberalism – based on either one or the other. This solution is not only unsatisfactory because of its competing outcomes. There is also evidence in support of both positions. Normative theories, as we have seen, largely take their inspiration from Kant while other classical liberal thinkers like Locke, Smith, or Mill are comparatively rarely mentioned. Though it may be argued that classical liberal authors generally share certain core values like freedom, equality, and justice, they nevertheless tend to provide rather different accounts of these norms, of the relationship between these norms, and of their implications for political practice. The Kantian monopoly thus suggests, indeed, a rather 'disparate' and unsystematic basis for the definition of liberalism. Further, the cosmopolitan and statist interpretations of Kant highlight that there is no agreement even between normative liberals on the interpretation of these classical liberal principles. Most importantly, however, the distinction between theory and practice itself does not fit the evidence. Classical liberal authors themselves, far from just elaborating pure liberal ideals, have also systematically propagated a variety of rather 'illiberal' principles. While Locke developed the principle of government by consent, he also argued for the restriction of political rights to property holders; Mill distinguished between civilized and barbarian peoples and justified – as well as practiced – colonialism (Jahn 2005a and 2005b); Kant wrote the Perpetual Peace, yet accorded war with a variety of progressive characteristics (Behnke 2012).

Conversely, the empirical approach to liberalism does not help to overcome the contradictions entailed within liberal practices. Hence, as we have seen, liberal actors actively engage in peaceful as well as aggressive policies; the United States, for example, supports international organization in the case of the WTO but fails to do so in the case of the International Criminal Court (ICC). In addition, however, liberal practices in one area may contravene those in others. Hence, 'liberalism

tends to be peacefully oriented' but its 'extension of economic interests worldwide... may entail the use of force' in the protection of these
interests – hence interventions like the ones in Guatemala, Cuba, and
Chile (Keohane 2002: 27). Yet, by taking these contradictory practices
into account, and by excluding liberal norms from playing a definitive
role, it becomes more and more difficult to identify what exactly is 'liberal' about these policies; and hence positivist approaches do not insist
on the label 'liberal' but are ready to consider other names like 'societal',
'state-society', 'social purpose', or 'preference-based' theories (Moravcsik
1997: 548–9; Keohane 2002). Ultimately, however, the liberal label sticks
because it helps define these approaches in relation to realism. Most
importantly, however, the varied practices of liberal actors are regularly
justified with reference to liberal norms (such as the dangers of Weapons
of Mass Destruction (WMDs), the lack of democracy and human rights
in Iraq) while the latter are clearly advocated with a view to reform practice. A conception of liberalism based on either the one or the other
thus fails to account for the intimate relationship between them. Neither normative nor empirical approaches, hence, provide a satisfactory
solution to the diversity and tensions within liberalism – but they do
add a further layer of fragmentation to the already fragmented field of
liberal theory.

In sum, this exercise of taking stock of liberal theory through the
four major theoretical dimensions confirms, first, Moravcsik's injunction that a liberal theory of international relations (as such) has
simply never been formulated (1997: 514). Though liberal authors
frequently provide a wide and encompassing list of liberal characteristics, these abstract definitions remain sterile and do no work in the
theories themselves. The explanatory or interpretative parts of liberal
theories prioritize a particular issue area over others; they define this
issue area in either its contemporary or its historical manifestation;
they prioritize its domestic over its international performance; and
methodologically approach liberalism through either its principles or
its practices.

Each of these exercises in trying to pin down liberalism in terms of its
contents in time and space, thus, leads to a partial conception of liberalism that does not live up to the rich – if imprecise – meaning of the
term 'liberal' as it is generally applied in academic as well as political discourses. For none of these theories accounts satisfactorily for the
fact that the term 'liberal' is applied to political, economic, and normative theories as well as policies and, conversely, for the fact that
political actors are only recognized as 'liberal' if and when they live up
to liberal standards in all three areas. The same problem arises in the case

of the temporal and spatial distinctions. The definition of liberalism in terms of its contemporary or historical incarnations respectively fails to account for the fact that we call both classical and contemporary principles and practices 'liberal', and thus recognize that many of these principles and practices are found in both periods. Liberalism's definition in terms of its domestic or intraliberal performance, too, ignores the widespread use of the term 'liberal' for the foreign policies of liberal actors – liberal peacebuilding, liberal nationbuilding, neoliberal economic policies, liberal human rights policies – or even the depiction of the entire world order as liberal; and it obscures the fact that 'nonliberal' practices can be found in the liberal as well as in the international sphere.

Moreover, while these distinctions to some extent account for tensions within liberalism, they do so by externalizing what is perceived to be its less savory, or in the case of methodology its less coherent aspects. In other words, liberalism is defined in political terms versus a reductionist economic or normative conception and vice versa; liberalism's immature past is pitched against its degenerate present, its domestic achievements are held up against its international machinations, its utopian principles vie with its imperfect practice. In other words, these distinctions lead to competing accounts of liberalism and can hence not simply be combined with each other. And it is this 'diversity' of liberalism that gives rise to the notion that a general definition of liberalism is impossible since it would 'paper over significant differences' (Tansey 2008: 89–9).

Conclusion

At the end of this investigation, we are therefore confronted with a genuine problem. On the one hand, the partial conceptions of liberalism embedded within the wide range of liberal theories simply do not begin to grasp the richness and diversity of liberal principles, practices, and actors implied in the general use of the term. On the other hand, the genuine differences and tensions within liberal thought and practice appear to militate against the possibility of such a general definition. And yet, this investigation provides some insights into the nature of liberalism.

First, there is no doubt that each of the liberal theories discussed above correctly highlights a crucial aspect of liberalism. That is, liberalism indeed seems to entail a political, economic, and normative dimension. What is missing from the existing theories, therefore, is simply an account of how these substantive issue areas are related to each other. Moreover, existing theories of liberalism correctly identify systematic differences between historical and contemporary liberalism. Yet, the fact that there clearly also exist significant historical continuities suggests that it is a dynamic historical phenomenon whose different temporal incarnations are nevertheless intimately connected. In short, what is missing is an account of the relationship between historical and contemporary liberalism. Liberal theories are similarly correct in identifying systematic differences between liberalism's performance in the domestic and international spheres. Yet, the significant extent of liberalism's activities in the international sphere as well as its contradictory performance even within the domestic sphere suggests a close connection between the two. What is missing from existing liberal theories, then, is an account of the nature and dynamics of this relationship. And finally liberal theories are, of course, right to point to systematic differences between liberal principles and practices. And yet, liberal practices are routinely justified with reference to liberal principles; and these principles are in turn routinely advocated as a guide to practice. Existing methodological approaches thus simply fail to provide satisfactory access to the dynamic relationship between liberal principles and practices. Hence, taken together the insights from existing liberal theories suggest that liberalism is a composite phenomenon which changes over time and from place to place. What these theories do not capture is the fact that there appear to exist dynamic relations between liberalism's constitutive parts – between its substantive issue areas, its historical incarnations, its spatial performance, and its principles and practice.

Liberalism, then, appears to be a composite and dynamic phenomenon or, in Max Weber's terms, a complex cultural phenomenon, that is, 'a complex of elements associated in historical reality which we unite into a conceptual whole from the standpoint of their cultural significance' (Weber 1984: 47). In other words, we attach the conceptual term 'liberalism' to the historical coming together of different elements – particular political, economic, and normative arrangements – that in combination play a significant role in shaping our cultural framework. Defining such phenomena is difficult, first, because their significance arises from the relations of their constitutive elements to each other, which are obscured in theories distinguishing between them; secondly, because as historical phenomena they are changing over time and thus defy static forms of definition prioritizing one historical period over others; thirdly, because the cultural significance (meanings and outcomes) of such phenomena varies within different social and political contexts; and finally because the changing forms liberalism takes on the ground feed back into its theoretical conception and vice versa. Consequently, Weber argues that for complex cultural phenomena of this kind, the 'definitive concept cannot stand at the beginning of the investigation, but must come at the end' (1984: 47). At the end, that is, of a thorough historical investigation that traces the changing relations of the different dimensions of liberalism. In other words, trying to grasp a complex cultural phenomenon is by no means impossible, but it does require extensive historical research. In the case of liberalism, with a history that arguably goes back several hundred years and whose impact can be traced in every part of the globe, following Weber's lead amounts to the task of a lifetime and is thus impossible within the confines of this study.

Instead of giving up, however, I suggest that the analysis of the strengths and weaknesses of existing liberal theories provides the necessary insights to develop an alternative route (or shortcut) to a better understanding of liberalism. Given that complex cultural phenomena draw their meaning from the interaction between their constitutive elements, an alternative conception of liberalism needs to focus on the relationship between these dimensions. In order to recover the relationship between these different dimensions of liberalism, therefore, I will return in the next chapter to the historical origins of liberalism's fragmentation.

3
Classical Liberal Theory

Introduction

Liberal internationalism is a composite and dynamic phenomenon: it is made up of a number of different political, economic, and ideational principles and practices which, moreover, change over time and take on different forms in different social and political contexts. The form and meaning of liberal internationalism is thus constantly in flux and it is this multifaceted nature and historical fluidity that presents a challenge to conventional forms of definition that aim to fix meaning in time and space.

And yet, the terms 'liberal', 'liberalism', 'liberal internationalism' are widely used in academic and political discourse. Though this usage clearly entails a variety of meanings – with different associations in Europe and America, for instance – it arguably also attests to the fact that the common connotations of these terms outweigh their differences. Within a political context such terms need to effectively provide common ground for (or against) a cause, otherwise they fail to fulfill their most important function. Of course, a variety of associations with a particular term can be very useful, in that it mobilizes and brings together different constituencies. Yet, even in that case some minimal common ground or assumed linkage between the different meanings is necessary – otherwise political fragmentation is bound to result. Hence, if we are to analyze liberal (international) policies or even a liberal world order, it is necessary to attempt a clarification of these terms.

The aim of this chapter is, therefore, to provide a preliminary conception of liberal internationalism that integrates its different dimensions and that can subsequently be tested in the context of contemporary liberal foreign or international policies.

Since the existing fragmentation of liberal internationalism tends to follow roughly the disciplinary distinctions in the modern academy – Political Science, Economics, Philosophy, History, Sociology, International Relations, Political Theory, the Humanities and Social Sciences – an interdisciplinary approach designed to overcome these distinctions seems promising. And yet, on closer inspection interdisciplinary approaches generally do not manage to provide a theorization of the relations between different subject areas. The constitution of separate academic disciplines rests on the claim that their respective subject areas differ qualitatively from each other and thus require particular tools for their analysis. These tools of analysis are hence designed to highlight the specificity of their respective subject area. Once this distinction is historically established, therefore, interdisciplinary approaches can take two forms: either they apply the methodology of one discipline to the subject matter of another or they apply a range of different methodological approaches to the same subject matter. An example for the former is Kenneth Waltz's application of economic modeling to the material of international politics – which results in an economic model of international relations with states acting like firms in the market (Waltz 1979). Though this approach may well provide interesting insights, a theorization of the relationship between politics and economics is not among them; instead it subsumes the former under the latter.

The alternative of applying different methodological approaches to the same subject matter simply results in producing and juxtaposing alternative narratives – as is most obvious in the theoretical fragmentation of the discipline of International Relations itself which has its roots in the application of different approaches to the subject matter of international politics. Irrespective of the rich insights these stories entail, they do not provide an account of their relationship to each other. In sum, the distinction between different dimensions of social and political life is constitutive of individual disciplines and henceforth reproduced by them. Combining such centrifugal forces thus does not overcome the problem.

Instead, I will trace the fragmentation of liberalism back to its historical origins in order to recover their common roots and co-constitutive dynamics. That is, I will return to a historical juncture at which liberal ideas had begun to develop but did not yet constitute a coherent world view, on the one hand, and had not yet become embodied in particular political or economic institutions (and thus fragmented), on the other. Though it is impossible to put a precise date on the origins of liberalism and many authors have contributed to the emergence and development of liberal thought (Manent 1994), it is perfectly possible to identify the historical period during which these developments occurred. What is more, though liberalism does not have an unequivocal founder who played the role Marx, for example, played for Marxism (Rapaczynski 1987: 6), it is in Locke's work that 'the central elements of the liberal outlook crystallized for the first time into a coherent intellectual tradition expressed in a powerful, if often divided and conflictual, political movement' (Gray 1986: 11). For this reason, among the early contributors to this tradition, Locke is widely seen as 'the only unqualified liberal' (Rapaczynski 1987: 14; MacPherson 1962: 262). Locke, in other words, stands out because he drew disparate liberal ideas together and explicitly theorized the relations between them. Moreover, this synthesis of liberal thought was developed before 'liberalism' came to be recognized and named as an established political project in the early 19th century and prior to the disciplinary fragmentation of the modern sciences, and hence allows us to circumvent the problem of disciplinary fragmentation.

In the first part of this chapter, I will set out the Lockean theory and show that, how, and why all the different dimensions play an integral and constitutive role for liberalism. Despite this integrated account of liberal principles, the second part of this chapter shows, the Lockean theory already contains the seeds for its own fragmentation. The disjuncture between liberal ideas and the realities on the ground introduced tensions and contradictions into liberal theory and practice which led to processes of fragmentation. The third section provides a brief overview over the historical development of liberalism and confirms the conception of liberalism derived from Locke's work. It shows that each of the familiar dimensions of liberalism plays an indispensable role for its establishment and dynamic development. On the basis of this theoretical and historical material, the chapter concludes with the formulation of an integral and dynamic, if preliminary, conception of liberalism.

Liberalism in Lockean theory

The emergence of liberal ideas in general and Locke's contribution to this development in particular is historically located at a time of intersecting intellectual, social, and political change, and Locke ended up making an important contribution to all three areas.[1] Within Europe, the fragmentation of religious unity in the 16th century led to religious wars and a crisis of political authority. Locke (1632–1704) lived through the Civil Wars in England, Cromwell's Protectorate, the execution of the King, the Glorious Revolution; he was expelled from Oxford for political reasons, had to go into exile, and became an influential political figure within the Whig movement.

John Locke was born into a family of minor gentry and went to Oxford at the age of 20 where he eventually specialized in medicine. Though he was interested in politics, Locke was originally a traditionalist and authoritarian. This changed radically when he met Anthony Ashley Cooper, later the first Earl of Shaftesbury, in 1666. Shaftesbury was rich from investments in England and overseas. He also occupied high political positions (Chancellor of the Exchequer, Lord Chancellor) and though he first hired Locke as his physician, Shaftesbury soon set Locke to educate his grandchildren as well as to contribute to his political interests and activities. Locke wrote for (and sometimes with) Shaftesbury on education, knowledge, the rate of interest, religious freedom, colonial administration, and ultimately also the *Two Treatises of Government*. Under Shaftesbury's influence Locke turned from an authoritarian to a 'radical' with considerable influence in the Whig movement. Shaftesbury, moreover, provided Locke with a number of political positions and Locke continued to hold political offices after Shaftesbury's death under the patronage of Lord Somers. Locke was secretary to the Lord Proprietors of Carolina (1668–71), secretary to the Council of Trade and Plantations (1673–4), a member of the Board of Trade (1696–1700); he invested in the slave-trading Royal Africa Company (1671), the Company of Merchant Adventurers to trade with the Bahamas, and the East India Company; he was a Landgrave of the proprietary government of Carolina, wrote parts of the Fundamental Constitutions of Carolina, handled the day-to-day correspondence with the colonists in Carolina, and Edisto Island was originally called Locke island (Tully 1993: 140–1; Tuck 1999: 167; Laslett 1994). In short, 'without Shaftesbury Locke would not have been Locke at all' (Laslett 1994: 27). Though a scholar by inclination, under Shaftesbury's influence Locke began to write about the big political questions of his time and developed what

---

[1] This chapter focuses on Locke's (international) political thought. For a more general overview over Locke's work, see Chappell (1994).

can only be described as new foundations for intellectual, social, and political life.[2]

Core principles

The starting point of Locke's theory, perfectly in line with contemporary conceptions of liberalism, is the claim that the state of nature of all men is 'a *State of perfect Freedom* to order their Actions, and dispose of their Possessions, and Persons as they think fit' (Locke 1994: 269). Yet, upholding this freedom requires self-preservation (Locke 1994: 271). And it is this requirement, Locke argues, that can only be fulfilled if 'every Man has a *Property* in his own *Person*' and 'the *Labour* of his Body and the *Work* of his Hands' (Locke 1994: 287f). Self-possession, property in one's person and the fruit of one's labor, thus allows individuals 'the taking any part of what is common, and removing it out of the state Nature leaves it in, which *begins the Property*' (Locke 1994: 289). According to Locke, this natural right to private property underpins and upholds not just the life of the individual who would otherwise perish (Locke 1994: 289, 294); it also makes the individual independent of others for its survival and thus establishes its freedom. This natural freedom of the individual then militates against absolute government. 'Men are naturally free, and the Examples of History shewing, that the Governments of the World ... had their beginning laid on that foundation, and were made by the Consent of the people' (Locke 1994: 336). And since this freedom is based on property, the 'great and *chief end* therefore (of government) *is the Preservation of their Property*' (Locke 1994: 351).

This argument lies at the core of Locke's theory and it entails the three substantive areas of liberal thought: private property or economics, the norm of individual freedom, and the political institution of government by consent. In Locke's work, however, these three dimensions are intimately linked to each other. Private property constitutes individual freedom and individual freedom requires government by consent whose main task in turn is the protection of private property and thus that of individual freedom.

This core Lockean theory, however, encountered a fundamental problem: namely that it did not reflect the social and political conditions at the time of Locke's writing. In fact, it was precisely because most governments in Locke's time and throughout history had not been governments by consent, and because private property was not protected,

---

[2] For biographies of Locke, see Woolhouse (2007) and Cranston (1985).

that Locke developed this theory and propagated it against the prevailing political positions, such as Filmer's defense of paternal government which he attacks in the first treatise (1994). Locke thus had to solve two problems. The first was to provide a satisfactory explanation for this disjuncture between his theory and the historical evidence. The second was to demonstrate how this disjuncture could be overcome in practice. For, after all, he thought it is 'evident that there is a difference in degrees in men's understandings, apprehensions, and reasonings to so great a latitude, that one may, without doing injury to mankind, affirm, that there is a greater difference between some men and others in this respect, than between some men and some beasts' (Locke 1959, II: 446). A liberal polity could therefore not be established by simply providing all people with the right to consent to government or, in contemporary terms, by introducing elections. Locke thus had to show how society could be based on the principles of private property and government by consent in the absence of a majority of individuals supporting such developments or, conversely, how the majority of the population could be convinced to establish and maintain such a polity. In other words, Locke saw himself confronted with the task of promoting 'liberalism' in a nonliberal environment. And it was in the course of solving these two problems that the historical and spatial dimensions became an integral part of liberalism.

Time

Locke solved the first problem by introducing a philosophy of history that accounted for the predominant existence of authoritarian governments and radical material inequality. Like many writers at the time, Locke supports his theoretical argument with reference to indigenous societies in America. Information (if often partial or inaccurate) about these societies had become widely available in Europe since the Spanish discoveries and provided a fundamental challenge for the heretofore authoritative religious scriptures with wide-ranging implications for the European world view. Amerindian societies were widely taken to represent humanity in the state of nature and this concept of the state of nature provided the starting point for virtually all modern European social and political theory.[3]

---

[3] See, for example, Meek (1976) on its role in the social sciences, Bitterli (1982) and Pagden (1993) on its influence on European world views, Pagden (1995) on ideologies of empire, Todorov (1999) on intercultural relations, Jahn (2000) on its role in International Relations, and Inayatullah and Blaney for its role in International Relations and International Political Economy (2004, 2012).

In order to substantiate his claim about the natural right to private property and its consequence, the natural freedom of the individual, Locke cites indigenous communities in America as empirical evidence. While god gave the earth and its bounty to man in common, the latter, if he is to make use of it and to keep himself alive, must be allowed to remove his necessities from this common state – to appropriate them for his private use. 'Thus this Law of reason makes the Deer that *Indian's* who hath killed it' (Locke 1994: 289). In the state of nature, therefore, the right to turn common into private property establishes the 'Indian' as a free man and hence government in indigenous American societies is based on the consent of these free men. In the olden days, the indigenous people in Peru and contemporaneously in Brazil and Florida, Locke argues, 'were actually *free*' and 'by consent were all *equal*' and hence 'their *Politick Societies* all *began* from a voluntary Union, and the mutual agreement of Men freely acting in the choice of their Governours, and forms of Government' (Locke 1994: 335).

This was originally a peaceful state because 'Man had a Right to all he could employ his Labour upon, so he had no temptation to labour for more than he could make use of. This left no room for Controversie about the Title, nor for Incroachment on the Right of others' (Locke 1994: 302). And yet, there is a definite limit to this state of affairs because everyone can only take us much as he or she needs and no more in order not to encroach upon the share of others. Since 'nothing was made by God for Man to spoil or destroy' cultivation of the soil or intensive production could not be undertaken without violating that law (Locke 1994: 290).

The solution to this problem, Locke argues, was the invention of money, for money made it possible to exchange surplus production of goods that would spoil for metal which would not spoil (1994: 301). 'Find out something that hath the *Use and Value of Money* amongst his Neighbours, you shall see the same Man will begin presently to *enlarge* his *Possessions*' (Locke 1994: 301). The invention of money thus triggered the enclosure of large tracts of land which could now be 'improved', that is, more intensively cultivated. Since the surplus product would be exchanged for money, humanity as a whole benefited from the increased production. 'This partage of things, in an inequality of private possessions, men have made practicable out of the bounds of Societie, and without compact, only by putting a value on gold and silver and tacitly agreeing in the use of Money. For in Governments the Laws regulate the right of property, and the possession of land is determined by positive constitutions' (Locke 1994: 302). Private property and the invention of money thus lay the foundations for the constitution of states, and Locke clearly justifies states based on private property. For through their protection and regulation of private property, such states guarantee individual freedom, economic cooperation, and prosperity for their populations. Yet, this internal settlement only exported the problem into the international sphere. The introduction of private property in land and 'the Increase of People and Stock, with the *Use of Money* had made Land scarce' and generated a state of war. In order to solve this problem, 'several *Communities* settled the Bounds of their distinct Territories' (Locke 1994: 299). Thus, Locke also justifies sovereignty in the external sense as the mutual recognition of the property in land held by different communities, and thus as an important means to avoid war.

Nevertheless, war between these communities generated by struggles over scarce land brought military leaders to the fore. And while these leaders first occupied a position of preeminence based on their virtue and recognized by their countrymen, over time 'Successors of another Stamp' were swept into power under whose rule the people did not find their properties 'secure' and who would justify their rule with reference to the authority and 'Sacredness of Customs'; and under such government the people 'could never be safe nor at rest, *nor think themselves in Civil Society*, till the Legislature was placed in collective Bodies of Men, call them Senate, Parliament, or what you please' (Locke 1994: 329). In other words, Locke explained the existence of despotic government in his time and throughout much of (known) history as the result of a two-sided historical development: on the one hand, the combination of the natural right to private property and the invention of money has the positive effect of generating increased productivity and hence prosperity. On the other hand, it gives rise to competition over land between individuals and communities and thus leads to the constitution of states that regulate and thus pacify this competition. In the absence of safeguards against abuse (which had not been necessary in the state of nature), these state institutions were vulnerable to usurpation by men who would violate the property rights of individuals for self-serving purposes and justify their despotic rule with reference to custom and tradition.

The core elements of this narrative sound familiar today because it is widely deployed to explain the lack of, and justify strategies for, development. The World Bank, for example (as well as other international institutions, politicians and the media in liberal states), has identified corruption (self-serving politicians in government who do not protect the property of the population) and its justification with reference to traditional culture as a major barrier to development (particularly in

Africa) – an explanation which provides the justification for the 'good governance' agenda of the Bank (Williams and Young 1994).

In sum, Locke argues that material inequality in society – the fact that most people did not hold any property – is a natural rather than political fact. He is emphatic that already in the state of nature, 'Men have agreed to disproportionate and unequal Possessions of the Earth', because 'a man may fairly possess more land than he himself can use the product of, by receiving in exchange for the overplus, Gold and Silver, which may be hoarded up without injury to any one' (Locke 1994: 302). This material inequality is morally justified because private property generates increased production which benefits all people. In other words, Locke formulates the still so influential 'trickle-down' argument as justification for material inequality. Hence, the right to private property entails the right of all human beings to appropriate property by removing it from the commons through labor as well as the protection of already existing (unequal) private property. But it does not entail the right of all people to own property. This argument, in other words, lays the foundation for the liberal principle of equality as opportunity rather than outcome. Since the 'initial partage' of things occurred in the state of nature, real existing material inequality was 'natural' and did not undermine the principle of equality.

Despite the fact that Locke thus justified material inequality, it is important to note that his work does not preclude all forms of redistribution. In fact, he does formulate limits to the power of private property when he argues that the transformation of common into private property was justified only for as long as 'there is enough, and as good left in common for others' (1994: 288). All people had to be given the chance to fulfill their rights and obligations to god, that is to work for their upkeep. This limitation on private property can in principle be used to justify a relatively generous measure of redistribution within a liberal state, or the liberal 'welfare state' (for example, Tully 1982). Both the 'conservative' and the more 'socialist' interpretation of Locke have come to play an important role historically, as we shall see later.

Locke thus accounts for the disjuncture between his theoretical claims – of the natural freedom of all individuals and the concomitant need for government by consent – and the real existing unfreedom of individuals and the predominance of authoritarian government in his time by developing a speculative history. Fundamental for this philosophy of history is the conception of the state of nature as its starting point. As empirical evidence for this state of nature, Locke systematically refers to indigenous societies in America (and elsewhere). His library contained large numbers of books on all aspects of European exploration, colonization, and on aboriginal peoples. And it was this concrete historical and anthropological material on which Locke drew in developing the concept of the state of nature (Arneil 1996: 21–3; Tully 1993: 140). The natural laws governing this state of nature, in particular the natural right to private property and the invention of money, Locke speculates, trigger a historical development that leads to the deviation from these laws accounting for the contemporary counterevidence. The implications of this philosophy of history, however, extend into the future. Having rediscovered the state of nature and its laws, Locke argues, humanity now has the obligation to reform society in accordance with its principles. The philosophy of history thus plays a crucial role in liberalism by bridging the gap between theory and practice: it moves the theory (liberal principles) into the past (the state of nature) and projects practice according to these principles into the future, and hence accounts for their lack of congruence in the present.

Space

Having identified the natural law principles for social and political organization in the state of nature, Locke turned to working out how individual freedom and government by consent could once again be established in practice. His solution to this problem accorded the international sphere a crucial role in the constitution of domestic liberalism. The starting point for Locke's solution was faithful to the fundamental premises of his theory, and in particular to the linkage between freedom and private property. If private property was the basis of individual freedom, Locke argued, property owners would demand that government protect private property and hence their freedom. He thus advocated the extension of full political rights to property owners only, and the concomitant denial of these rights to those who did not own property. '*Paternal Power* is...where Minority makes the Child incapable to manage his property; *Political* where Men have Property in their own disposal; and *Despotical* over such as have no property at all' (1994: 384).[4]

---

[4] This does not mean that the emancipatory potential of Locke's thought is strictly limited to property owners. Locke simply aims to exclude those deemed unable or unwilling to uphold this principle as foundational for society from political rights. Once based on this principle, society could curtail individual property rights for purposes of international competition and defense and in order to allow every individual to fulfill its rights and obligations to God – that

This solution, however, directly contradicted his claim that, in principle, all people were born free and equal and thus had a right to consent to government. Moreover, Locke saw the tiny minority of property owners, 'the rich', who would have been accorded full political rights, as 'mostly corrupt' (Dunn 1969: 217). Hence, Locke was interested in extending the franchise and, perfectly in line with his theory that private property provides the basis for individual freedom and the rights that follow from this, he argued that an extension of the franchise could be achieved by turning more, and ideally all, sections of society into property owners. This was a neat theoretical solution, but in practice it threw up the problem where all this additional property was to come from. Once private property had been naturalized and Locke had committed himself to its protection, large-scale redistribution was not an option. So, Locke argued that private property was more productive than common property and thus of greater benefit to all of humankind (1994: 296–8). It was therefore justified to turn common into private property: God gave the land 'to the use of the Industrious and Rational' (Locke 1994: 291). People could simply attain property by mixing their individual labor with the original common property. The privatization of common property was thus the solution to the problem, and it was this solution that provided a crucial role for the international sphere.

Assuming that land – at the time the most important additional source of wealth and of particular importance to Locke, as we shall see – in England was too scarce to provide the vast and rising number of poor with property, Locke looked abroad: 'Yet there are still *great Tracts of Ground* to be found, which (...), *lie waste*, and are more than the People who dwell on it, do, or can make use of, and so still lie in common' (Locke 1994: 299). It was this common land in America which could be used, at least in principle, to furnish all individuals with property and thus make them eligible to full political rights. In short, 'Locke...was offering the New World, specifically the colonial settlements of America, as validation of his sociopolitical philosophy' (Lebovics 1986: 577). Hence, Locke (and Shaftesbury) were deeply invested (both financially and politically) in the advocacy of colonialism as well as in its administration. Locke's writings, political and theoretical, cover all aspects

---

is, to work for its upkeep (Arneil 1996: 159; Tully 1982: 63; Dunn 1969: 246; Laslett 1994: 105). Similarly, political rights could be extended to nonproperty owners well socialized into the principles and practices of such a society.

of colonialism and consistently defend it (Tully 1993: 140–1; Tuck 1999: 167).[5]

The parameters of Locke's advocacy of colonialism were given. On the one hand, Locke and Shaftesbury had to establish English rights to land in America in competition with the Dutch, the Spaniards, and of course the indigenous population. On the other, they had to convince domestic public opinion which was strongly opposed to colonial 'adventures' that were seen to enfeeble the nation and drain it of its resources; hence Locke and Shaftesbury had to wage a concerted public effort in favor of colonialism (Arneil 1996: 91f). Finally, in light of the fact that the cruelty of Spanish colonialism had been sharply criticized all over Europe, and especially in protestant England, Locke had to develop a basis for English colonial policies which distinguished it from the Spanish and which could be ethically defended.

Much of Locke's theory provides a counterargument to the domestic association of colonialism with a drain on productive people and resources and with potential competition against England (Arneil 1996: 93). Like other advocates of colonialism – Josiah Child, Charles Davenant, and Thomas Mun – Locke was at pains to establish two points: first, that 'tis *Labour* indeed that *puts the difference of value* on every thing' (Locke 1994: 296). Land, he insists, is worthless without the labor that improves it. According to Locke, 'there cannot be a clearer demonstration' of this than the example of the Amerindians who 'are rich in Land, and poor in all the Comforts of Life', who though nature has provided them with plenty of fruitful soil, 'for want of improving it by labour, have not one hundreth part of the Conveniences we enjoy: And a King of a large and fruitful Territory there feeds, lodges, and is clad worse than a day Labourer in *England*' (Locke 1994: 296–7). And if labor really raised the value of land 10 times, 100 times, even 1000 times (Locke 1994: 298) the employment of agrarian labor in the colonies would make England independent of its competitors in Europe. Moreover, the products would have to be shipped entirely in English ships, thus producing jobs. And the colonists would need products manufactured in England, producing work in the manufacturing industry (Arneil 1996: 94–107). Agrarian labor was to be preferred to mining or grazing, too, because the latter tended to enrich the private colonists more than the mother country and they led to the enclosure of such large tracts

---

[5] On Locke's support for colonialism, see also Arneil (1996), Armitage (2004), Boucher (2006).

of land that they were indefensible (Arneil 1996: 99, 101). In short, Locke's theory of property provided the basis for a model of agrarian colonialism that would generate rather than drain resources and benefit not just the individual colonialist but the home industry and mother country as well.

The same argument was used to deny the indigenous population property rights. While all land in the state of nature was held in common, individuals had the right to appropriate 'as much as any one can make use of to any advantage of life before it spoils... Whatever is beyond this, is more than his share, and belongs to others' (Locke 1994: 290). Since Locke held that the indigenous population either did not engage in agricultural labor or worked land that was commonly held, and since they had not introduced money to allow for the exchange of perishable goods for nonperishable money, the Amerindians did not improve the land and had the right only to as much as they could individually make use of. In contrast, private land holdings under English law and their use of money to exchange overproduction of perishable for nonperishable goods entitled the English to all the land they could intensively cultivate and that was not needed to satisfy the individual subsistence needs of the indigenous population. The surplus, after all, would flow back into the (world) economy and benefit all people. In addition, the indigenous population would benefit from English knowledge, skills, and technologies (Arneil 1996: 114–16).

Dutch land claims in the Americas and those of colonists who had taken to buying land from the indigenous population, like William Penn, were also undermined by this argument. Since the indigenous population, according to Locke, had no communal rights to the land (only individual subsistence rights), it was not their property to sell. Land appropriation in America therefore could and should proceed without their consent. In addition, the purchase of land did not establish property rights unless this land was cultivated and hence the English were entitled to take over all uncultivated Dutch land.

And finally, by basing the freedom of the human being on his right to property, Locke rejected the Spanish land claims based on conquest, for conquest interfered with the individual rights to property and it did not necessarily lead to intensive cultivation. The English could therefore also take over land claimed by the Spaniards.

The realization of 'liberal' principles in England (or any other society) required first that property owners (or their political representatives) gain political power and deny similar political rights to nonproperty owners. This power could then be used to codify laws to systematically protect existing private property and to support the transformation of common into private property, that is, expropriation. The resulting spread of private property in society would then provide the basis for an extension of the franchise. The core contradiction of liberalism thus lies in the pursuit of political emancipation and economic appropriation through political oppression and expropriation, which at least in the short run do not lead to a wider distribution of property in society. And it was this contradiction that the constitution of the international sphere was designed to mediate. Colonialism, the expropriation of indigenous communities based on common property, was advocated by Locke as the most important policy in pursuit of this aim. These policies in turn were justified with reference to differential stages of development. The international sphere in the form of opportunities in America and the realization of these opportunities through foreign policies of colonialism thus played a constitutive role for the establishment of domestic liberalism.

In sum, liberal principles were developed in response to the instability generated by the religious and civil wars of the early modern period in Europe that led to political and economic insecurity for a great number of people – including Locke and Shaftesbury. Hence, Locke developed the (for his time) radical argument in the *Two Treatises* as a call for, and justification of, political change (Laslett 1994: 47). Liberalism is thus, as Tom Young has aptly put it, a political 'project to be realized' (Young 1995). The aim of this project consisted in the political empowerment of wealthy citizens who would then be able to establish the protection of private property and with it their own individual freedom. In order to justify this radical political program, Locke argued that the principles of private property, individual freedom, and government by consent in fact had their basis in human nature – and hence also in god's law – as life in the state of nature exemplified by indigenous communities showed. This political program was thus not radically new but simply a return to original principles that had been forgotten and pushed aside by adverse historical developments. Moreover, once these principles were realized and wealthy individuals established in government, the privatization of land in the domestic as well as the international sphere would lead to increased production and, consequently, a wider spread of property within society; this in turn would provide the basis for an extension of political rights to previously disenfranchised sections of society.

The key difference between this Lockean theorization of liberal principles and much of contemporary liberal theory lies in the necessary role that all its dimensions play for the constitution of liberalism.

Thus, without private property there can be no individual freedom (in the liberal sense); without individual freedom there can be no government by consent; and without the political participation of property-owning individuals, the protection of private property would not constitute the raison d'etre of government. Moreover, the realization of these principles required their historical justification and their internal contradictions – generated by appropriation through expropriation and political freedom through political oppression – could only be glossed over with reference to external opportunities.

The fragmentation of liberalism

Locke's work, I have shown above, provides an explicit account of the relations between the core liberal principles and their temporal and spatial dynamics. And yet, contemporary liberal theories are, as we have seen, characterized by the separation between all these dimensions. Why and how this fragmentation has come about, I will set out in this section. Despite Locke's theorization of the dynamics between liberal principles and practices, his work also provides insight into the roots of this fragmentation, which lie ultimately in the disjuncture between liberal theory and social and political reality. This disjuncture forces Locke – as well as subsequently his interpreters, as we shall see – to integrate the separation between theory and practice into liberalism where it generates fragmentation in all its key dimensions.

Locke's theory, as we have seen, advocated a solution to contemporaneous problems that was very favorable to the interests of a small group of rich men – and not at all in the interests of the vast majority of the population who had nothing to gain and potentially a lot to lose from a system based on private property. In other words, Locke had to convince his contemporaries that this system was in principle, at least, in everyone's interest. And he did so by presenting the historically specific interests of a small group of his contemporaries in private property, individual freedom, and government by consent as *natural* principles of human life. That is, he interprets features of contemporaneous indigenous communities as expressions of these principles; he then produces a composite picture of a society made up of these elements; and finally presents this society as 'a Pattern of the first Ages' of human social life (Locke 1994: 339) – that is, as a society in the state of nature. And it is this abstraction from the actual historical context that encourages the interpretation of the state of nature as a purely theoretical construct, and subsequently leads to the intellectual fragmentation of liberalism.

Indeed, 'the notion of a state of nature, and the claim that this condition is one of perfect freedom, were assumptions wholly foreign to the Roman and Renaissance texts' (Skinner 1998).

Hence, while commentators on Locke generally recognize that the state of nature lies at the heart of his theory, they also, until recently,[6] passionately insisted that the state of nature was a hypothetical rather than an empirical historical concept (Cox 1960: 111f) which cannot be criticized on historical or anthropological grounds because it 'has literally no transitive empirical content whatsoever' (Dunn 1969: 103, 106f). Though Locke's construction of the state of nature was, indeed, a theoretical act, such concepts are nevertheless generally interpreted with reference to their historical and intellectual context.[7] Moreover, Locke interpreters do engage in contextual analysis with reference to the domestic or European political and intellectual developments at the time even while they ignore, or explicitly deny, the international context to which the extensive and explicit use of the Amerindian 'material' in Locke's work points.

In substance, this abstraction of the concept of the state of nature from the actual empirical and historical material on which it obviously rests lays the foundations for the fundamental distinction between theory and practice which haunts liberal theories to this day. This distinction, as Dunn explicitly notes, serves the purpose of protecting liberal principles from empirical critique. And such protection is warranted for two reasons. First, empirical support for Locke's claims, as we have seen, is exceptionally thin and the supportive evidence he does present – the presentation of contemporary features of a variety of societies as representing the state of nature – is highly questionable (on empirical, logical, and methodological grounds). Secondly, liberal principles do require protection from a thorough investigation into their particular historical origins which seriously undermines their claim to universal validity based on the state of nature.

Yet, while this distinction between theory and practice manages to separate liberal principles from the empirical data on which they rest, it does so at the price of splitting liberal theory along methodological lines

---

[6] Locke scholarship has lately taken a dramatic turn in paying particular attention to the historical and anthropological material in Locke's theory and highlighting its political implications, especially for colonialism (Armitage 2004; Arneil 1996; Tully 1993; Tuck 1999; Boucher 2006; Mehta 1999).

[7] Quentin Skinner has made this case most famously and even his critics generally do not take issue with the argument for contextual analysis as such (Tully 1988).

into competing normative and positivist camps and competing conceptions of liberalism based on either its principles or its practices. As a
result of this split, liberal theory is henceforth incapable of providing a
satisfactory account of the dynamic and constitutive relations between
its principles and practices in all its dimensions.

Secondly, the distinction between theory and practice results in the
marginalization of the Amerindian material from Locke's theory, and
since this material happens to entail the most important international
dimension of Locke's theory, the distinction between theory and practice also leads to a split between the domestic and international context.
Hence, 'Lockeian liberalism' (Laslett 1994: 22) was traditionally seen
as an eminently domestic affair; it expressed the 'ambivalence of an
emerging bourgeois society' (Macpherson 1962: 247); it is rooted in
'Calvinist social values' (Dunn 1969: 259); and the individual lies at its
core (Rapaczynski 1987: 9). As much as these interpretations of Locke's
work differ, they concur that the origins and motivations of Locke's
work are domestic.[8] Moreover, though Locke's work is accorded great
political influence (Laslett 1994: 78, 92; Tully 1982: x; Dunn 1969: 267),
this influence, too, always plays itself out in the domestic sphere: Did
Locke's theory of property politically strengthen the rich or the poor,
the property owners or the laborers (Dunn 1969: 216; Laslett 1994: 105;
MacPherson 1962: 248; Tully 1982: 173)? This interpretation of Locke
constitutes a vision of the domestic sphere as open to progress, justice,
and the good life – all of which find their limits in the international
sphere which is characterized by conflicts for wealth and power (Dunn
1969: 159; Rapaczynski 1987: 188) and not open to the same level of
consent as domestic government is (Laslett 1994: 119).

Locke was, to be sure, motivated by the contemporaneous problems of
domestic politics, but domestic was not strictly separated from international politics at the time. The English civil wars were closely linked to
similar developments on the continent; one of the contributing factors
to the religious fragmentation underlying these wars was the Spanish

---

[8] An exception to this focus on the domestic sphere is presented by Cox, who
argues that Locke's conception of the state of nature was very close to that
of Hobbes and that, accordingly, his theory posits the primacy of foreign over
domestic policy (Cox 1960: xixf). In this reading, Locke propagates capitalist
forms of production and trade, including the liberation of labor, as the most
efficient way of strengthening England in mercantilist international competition
(1960: 179f). But even this position is based on the assumption of a hypothetical state of nature and thus completely disregards the role of colonialism in
Locke's work.

discovery of the Americas and its intellectual as well as political implications; Englishmen like the Earl of Shaftesbury had made their riches in domestic as well as foreign trade; European rulers were closely related to each other; and most importantly, Locke explicitly advocated colonial policies in support of his domestic political program; colonialism in turn began to play a crucial role for individual European states as well as for their relations with each other. The distinction between domestic and international politics, therefore, neither reflects accurately the nature of politics in Locke's time nor the dynamics of his own political theory.

Yet, Locke interpretations that ignore the empirical international context either at the time of Locke's writing or in his text miss this disjuncture between theory and practice, and hence also the fact that instead of reflecting an existing distinction between domestic and international politics, Locke's theory served to establish that distinction. For the core concept of liberalism, 'property' (Williams 1996: 91–2, 97) does not only constitute the free individual but also the state. Locke wrote chapter V, the chapter on property, at the same time as he revised the Fundamental Constitutions of Carolina (Armitage 2004) and in this context the concept of property referred to communities rather than individuals – that is, it served to negotiate land rights in the Americas between the English, Dutch, Spanish, and Amerindian communities (Arneil 1996: 133).[9] Communities based on private property were accorded with political rights – sovereignty over their land – while communities based on common property were denied political rights and had to make do with individual subsistence rights. In theory, therefore, this concept of property underpinned the modern international system consisting of sovereign states.

In practice, however, Locke recognized that 'tis true, in *Land* that is *common* in *England,* or any other Country, where there is Plenty of People under Government, who have Money and Commerce, no one can inclose or appropriate any part, without the Consent of all his Fellow-Commoners: Because this is left common by Compact, *i.e.* by the Law of the Land, which is not to be violated. And though it be Common, in respect of some Men, it is not so to all Mankind; but is the joint property of this Country, or this Parish' (Locke 1994: 292). In other

---

[9] Paying attention to this context may well explain why Locke used the term 'property' sometimes with reference to material property only and at other times included life and liberty (MacPherson 1962: 246; Rapaczynsk 1987: 117; Laslett 1994: 106; Tully 1982: 154). In chapter V, at any rate, the term is used consistently with reference to material property (especially in land) only.

words, common property existed not just amongst indigenous communities but also in England and other states – just as conversely, of course, laws and government also existed amongst indigenous communities, as Locke knew very well. Being common to all communities, the presence of these features thus did not provide grounds for according international political rights (sovereignty) to some and their denial to others. Indeed, the English law of the land protects its commons against outsiders while the Amerindian laws do not. In practice, the difference between these communities consisted simply in human and material power: England had 'plenty of people', 'commerce', and 'money', and thus the means to deny international political rights of sovereignty to peoples with a small and materially relatively poor population. In practice, therefore, the realization of liberal principles (according to Locke) required the expropriation of other peoples' land and this goal could only be realized through the systematic exploitation of power differentials. Power politics, however, clearly contradict liberal principles (that were, after all, developed with the aim to replace might with right). Locke thus provided a theoretical justification for the denial of political rights to some communities, and hence for the practice of power politics in the international sphere.

The theoretical distinction between the domestic and the international sphere thus, again, protects liberal principles from empirical critique. It suggests that liberal power politics has its roots in the nature of the international sphere rather than in the logic of liberal principles; and hence liberalism can only be judged with reference to its performance in the domestic sphere. Yet, this protection of liberal principles leads to a further round of fragmentation. First, the distinction between the domestic and international spheres overlooks that Locke's concept of property was constitutive not just of individual freedom (within the domestic sphere) but also of the modern sovereign state (and hence international relations). Within the liberal tradition, this distinction subsequently leads to competing cosmopolitan and statist conceptions of liberalism. Secondly, it provides the basis for the differentiation between Political Science and Theory on the one hand and International Relations on the other.[10] In short, the abstraction of liberal

---

[10] For a contemporary formulation of this distinction, see Martin Wight (1966). It also provides the basis for the argument that 'illiberal' behavior on the part of liberal actors has its roots in the different, or inhospitable, nature of international politics (Hoffmann 1987), as discussed in the previous chapter.

theory from its empirical basis constitutes – instead of confirming – the distinction between domestic and international politics.

Third, the distinction between theory and practice has serious implications for the interpretation of Locke's philosophy of history. This distinction allows commentators to argue that Locke made the discussion of politics independent of historical examples (Laslett 1994: 78) and that his philosophy of history therefore is to be understood as nothing but 'expository and polemical rather than logically essential' (Dunn 1969: 106f). And yet, if Locke's theory was indeed nothing but abstract philosophical reflections, then why did he spend so much time amassing empirical evidence to back up his conception of the state of nature? How did he manage to separate these philosophical reflections from his practical work for the political projects of Shaftesbury and others as well as in the administration of a variety of practical domestic and colonial policies? And how are these philosophical reflections to be separated from his (and his patron's) investments and hence material interests in practical political issues?

Yet, if we consider Locke's work as a theoretical contribution to practical politics, these contradictions are immediately resolved. As a contribution to political practice, providing a philosophy of history and backing it up empirically (as best as possible) was absolutely essential. The philosophy of history explained (away) the blatant contradictions between Locke's claims and the political knowledge and experience of his contemporaries; it provided his principles with historical (and, indeed, religious) pedigree and justification; and it demonstrated that and how these principles could be realized in practice. All three functions are indispensable for political mobilization of any kind. The philosophy of history thus provides a necessary, and necessarily concrete (if not necessarily accurate), link between theory and practice, and it has done so ever since.

The presentation of the philosophy of history – on Locke's part and that of his interpreters – as purely theoretical obscures the highly practical role it played in Locke's time and ever since. The philosophy of history introduced a stagist conception of historical development locating different societies at different levels of development – most importantly the Amerindians as occupying the bottom rung and the English further up the developmental ladder (Jahn 2000; Meek 1976). These differential locations were then used to justify differential rights and obligations – specifically, they justified a denial of political and hence also land rights to Amerindian communities and accorded political and land rights (including rights to Amerindian land) to the English. Yet, the practical importance of Locke's philosophy of history is not exhausted by these early cases of colonial appropriation. Rather, as an integral part of liberal theory, the philosophy of history has ever since been a dynamic tool protecting liberal theoretical claims from empirical counterevidence. Favorable historical conjunctures (such as the end of the Cold War) – in which liberal forces appear to dominate – are interpreted as supportive evidence for liberal claims, while adverse historical conjunctures, instead of undermining liberal claims and principles, are simply interpreted as the result of lower levels of historical development. And just as in Locke's time, the differential locations of different actors on a developmental scale are accompanied by unequal rights and obligations. Hence, the familiar division of the world in historical and post-historical, or pluralist, solidarist, and post-Westphalian zones (Fukuyama 1989; Linklater 1998) that provide the basis for according the higher developed actors more rights – especially rights of intervention and the right to use force. In short, the philosophy of history protects liberal principles from empirical counterevidence and provides the justification for the establishment of unequal law and political practices.

Yet, even while this interpretation of the philosophy of history as a purely theoretical (or polemical) construct excludes liberalism's unsavory historical practices from its definition, it also creates a distinct split between historical and contemporary liberalism with the former not any longer seen as an integral and constitutive part of the latter. More importantly, inasmuch as the liberal philosophy of history provides the justification for denying weaker communities political and economic rights, its purely theoretical conception obscures those practices as part of liberalism, and with it the role liberalism plays in constituting the targets of those policies as 'backward', 'illiberal' or simply 'poor' and an international system defined by unequal rights and obligations more generally. The theoretical interpretation of the philosophy of history thus contributes to the disciplinary distinction between History on the one hand and Political Science/International Relations on the other. By obscuring the constitutive role of liberalism for other states as well as for the states system itself, moreover, this reading of the philosophy of history provides the basis for the comparative method which applies common developmental criteria and standards to separate societies, without realizing that these criteria have played a constitutive role for their separation.

Finally, Locke locates the core liberal principles of private property, individual freedom, and government by consent in the state of nature and thus provides the basis for an ahistorical interpretation of these principles. Though this move protects the claim to a universal validity of these principles from being undermined with reference to their historically particular origins, it simultaneously severs their relations to each other. For these relations are themselves historical, private property *in time* constitutes individual freedom which only *subsequently* leads to government by consent that *in turn* protects private property. In other words, these principles are established through a historical process. Presenting the state of nature as a logical construction thus juxtaposes these principles as equal and ahistorical characteristics of human life that can be studied independently of each other – a move which contributes to the rise of independent disciplines like Economics, Philosophy, and Politics.

The Lockean theorization of liberal principles, as we have seen in the first section, clearly establishes constitutive relations between them and is triggered by and derived from particular historical circumstances (in space and time), which thus become an integral part of liberal theory and practice. And yet, as I have shown in this section, this theory also lays the groundwork for the subsequent fragmentation of liberalism (in theory and practice) and it contributes to the fragmentation of the human and social sciences, in substantive as well as methodological terms. The theoretical root to this fragmentation lies in the construction, presentation, and interpretation of the state of nature – by Locke and his interpreters – as a purely theoretical concept, despite the fact that it was clearly motivated by particular historical circumstances and interests and extensively supported with reference to real existing contemporaneous indigenous societies. This distinction between theory and practice – which manages to protect the theoretical claims from empirical critique – contributes to the separation between domestic and international politics, between history and theory, and between the substantive principles of liberalism (as the next section and the conclusion will show in more detail). In each case, what gets lost in this fragmentation is the productive dynamic between liberal theory and practice, domestic and international politics, past and present, and of course between politics, economics, and ideas. Yet, as the next section will show, the historical development of liberal theory and practice follows broadly the integrated and dynamic conception initially outlined by Locke.

Liberalism in history

Contemporary approaches tend to identify liberalism with the one or other of its core principles and thus to ignore the crucial relationship between them. Consequently, the historical development of liberalism itself is presented as following the (competing) logic of these principles leading to a variety of separate and distinct versions of liberalism in theory and practice. Based on the distinction between theory and practice, the historical development of liberalism, moreover, is presented as a measure of approximation to (or deviation from) purely theoretical and ahistorical liberal principles. In other words, the antidemocratic or colonial policies of early liberalism are interpreted as immature practices that did not live up to the liberal ideal of freedom – while today's democratic and anticolonial liberalism are taken to indicate the transcendence of these contradictions and thus evidence for the emancipatory potential of liberal principles. In contrast to these assumptions, I will now provide a (necessarily brief) sketch of the historical development of liberalism focusing on the dynamic relations between its different dimensions as initially outlined by Locke. This narrative confirms the widely noted diversity of liberal thought and practice. But it also shows that this diversity is not based on competing liberal principles but rather on the constitutive dynamic between these principles applied in different historical settings. In addition, this narrative confirms liberalism as a tremendously powerful driver of historical change. But it also shows that this change is driven by and reproduces contradictions internal to liberalism rather than resolving them. The development of liberalism, in sum, attests to the historical nature of its principles rather than to a natural history of humanity.

According to conventional accounts, the origins of liberalism lie either in a particular European political culture characterized by secularization, tolerance, and the 'taming of politics' (Sartori 1995: 104, 106; Fukuyama 1992b) giving rise to liberal political ideas and institutions, including in the long run democratization as well as economic development (Talavera 1992). Or the sources of liberalism are seen to lie in economic development (and capitalism) in early modern Europe which provides the material foundations for the development of individuals and groups independently of the state, and thus for a liberal political culture and ultimately democracy (Huntington 1991; Berger 1992). At a first glance, these narratives appear to recognize intimate constitutive relations between the political, economic, and ideational dimensions of liberalism. This intimate linkage is, however, interpreted as a matter of historical contingency and explicitly denied the status of a theoretically necessary element of liberalism. While one side argues that economic development or capitalism 'must be a necessary (though not sufficient) condition' for liberal democracy (Schmitter 1994: 66), the other holds that 'economic development is neither a stable nor a sufficient condition' for stable liberal democracy (Fukuyama 1992a: 108), though their historical conjuncture is seen as very helpful by both sides. The two accounts, despite their overlaps, thus clearly provide competing logics of the origins and development of liberalism, but they share the assumption that these logics are of a strictly European and endogenous character. That is, liberal thought and practice arose from within Europe and led to the transformation of individual domestic societies.

A brief look at the origins of liberalism through the lenses of Locke's integrated conception, however, suggests otherwise. The period prior to the development of Locke's ideas was characterized by extremely violent and wide spread civil and religious wars. It was thus the absence, rather than the presence, of a secular, tolerant, and relatively nonviolent political culture that provided the motivation for Locke's work. These conditions quite literally threatened the economic interests, liberties, and lives of the population in general and of men like the Earl of Shaftesbury under whose influence Locke began to develop his ideas in particular. It was these men, land owners and merchants who had become rich from trade with the colonies, who sought solutions to these problems based on property. And Locke's theory provided such a solution – based on the separation of the private and the public sphere – in the form of a 'privatization' of religion. The public sphere or 'political society', in Locke's terms, 'is instituted for no other end but only to secure every man's Possession of the things of this life' and thus has no right to adjudicate on matters of the afterlife (1983: 48). Conversely, while individuals may follow their particular faiths in the private sphere, they may not 'obtrude those things upon others, onto whom they do not seem to be the indubitable Doctrines of the Scripture' (Locke 1983: 57). Yet, the privatization of religion requires the protection of the private sphere which in turn rests on the protection of private property. Secularism, tolerance, and a tame political culture (inasmuch as they do materialize) are thus the result of protoliberal developments – rather than their roots.[11]

The protection of private property, however, also became the bedrock of the public sphere. In line with Locke's argument, men like

---

[11] Tolerance is one of the characteristics very widely associated with liberalism. Yet, it can be argued that the 'privatization' of religion as conceived by Locke does not constitute tolerance because it results in an individualization of religion and its removal from the public sphere, thus eliding the need for tolerance (Seligman 2009: 121, 123).

Shaftesbury increasingly demanded political rights with direct reference to their property, leading to a huge increase of members in the House of Commons (Perelman 2000: 175; Acemoglu and Robinson 2006: 350). Their political representation resulted in the establishment of a liberal state characterized by the transference of *de jure* political power into the hands of commercial and capitalistic interests and the stabilization of property rights in 17th-century Britain (Acemoglu and Robinson 2006: 349–50). Hence, just as Locke had argued, private property constituted individual freedom which in turn provided the basis for government by consent. Moreover, this property itself frequently had its roots in 'international' economic activities like overseas trade. And European technological and economic growth was dependent on property rights, including discoveries and intellectual goods, and a competitive market (Talavera 1992: 113). That is, large-scale technological and economic development were the result of, rather than the condition for, the establishment of protoliberal institutions.

These early incarnations of 'liberal' thought and practice were, as widely recognized, riddled with contradictions – asserting the universal right to government by consent while oppressing democratic movements at home and systematically pursuing colonialism abroad; hailing the economic benefits of privatization while impoverishing vast amounts of people through expropriation (Di Muzio 2012). And yet, today liberalism is associated with democracy and anti-colonialism as well as with economic prosperity and at least some measure of redistribution. This development of liberalism is variously explained with reference to the power and logic of liberal ideals or with reference to economic progress. Just as in the case of liberal origins, however, both are invariably seen as a matter of endogenous development in individual European (settler) societies – thus giving rise to a variety of liberalisms. In general, however, this historical development is interpreted as a gradual realization of abstract liberal principles. And yet, as we shall see, it was the internal contradictions of liberalism that drove this development every step of the way.

While the protection of private property accorded propertied classes with economic freedom, political rights, and a private sphere in which they could pursue their religious interests undisturbed, none of these gains were available to the vast majority of the nonpropertied population. On the contrary, once in power the ruling elite systematically pursued the privatization of common property and justified it with reference to its productivity. Thus, Locke's work was frequently cited in Parliament in support of private enclosure acts which, between 1710 and 1815, transferred 6.5 million acres or 20 percent of the total land from common into private property (McNally 1988: 62, 8–9; Perelman 2000: 175).[12] This large-scale privatization of common land led, within the domestic sphere, to the impoverishment of wide sections of society and thus contributed to upheavals, rebellions, and the threat of revolution (Tilly 2004; Kim 1992: 24). In other words, these protoliberal policies did not just constitute free liberal individuals – they simultaneously constituted anti-liberal forces. These groups, just as Locke had argued, could not be expected to uphold private property rights and therefore had to be denied political rights (Przeworski 1992: 53; Plattner 2008: 64–5). In short, the realization of liberal principles produced an economically and politically deeply divided society.

For early 'liberal' actors already involved in international commerce, the international sphere offered possibilities to relieve this domestic tension. Hence, Locke's systematic justification of colonialism and his theory of property were subsequently widely used by 'preachers, legal theorists, and politicians' to base first the land claims of the British colonists and then those of the American citizens on the enclosure and cultivation of land (Arneil 1996: 169). The same argument was also influential in Australia, New Zealand, and Canada throughout the 18th and well into the 19th centuries (Ivison 2003: 93).

These policies of colonialism allowed the European elites to appropriate 'foreign' land; that is, to pursue a considerable part of their economic interests abroad, thus easing the economic burden on the domestic poor. Moreover, colonialism provided an opportunity for the poor to emigrate and to 'improve' their prospects through the appropriation of other peoples' land; and it allowed the government to export its poor, its criminals, its orphans as well as to offer employment for the middle and higher classes in the administration of the colonies, and thus eased political pressure on domestic government. Most importantly, however, colonialism provided common political ground – namely the interest in expropriating foreign land and hence a commitment to the principle of private property which justified this expropriation – for rich and poor alike and thus bridged the gap between their otherwise mutually exclusive interests.

These dynamics resulted in the constitution of 'new' societies – in settler colonies – and the gradual transformation of 'old' societies in Europe

---

[12] McNally reports that in 1710 the first private enclosure act was presented in Parliament, followed by 100 between 1720–50, 139 between 1750–60, 900 between 1760–79, and 2000 between 1793–1815 (1988: 11).

as well as the constitution of the modern international system. Settler colonies like America offered huge amounts of 'common' land – yet the appropriation of this land in practice required large numbers of individuals willing and able to first wrest it from their indigenous owners and then to actually enclose and work it. The necessary manpower was provided through large-scale immigration and motivated by promises of land ownership. Consequently, settler societies were characterized by a relatively wide distribution of property as well as by the common political interest in the expropriation of the indigenous population and thus a commitment to the protection of private property underpinning these policies. There was no need to fear revolution and hence universal franchise was generally introduced earlier in settler societies.

In Europe, meanwhile, where land was scarce and already privately owned, a wider distribution of property was slower to develop. However, the enclosure of commonly owned land domestically, colonial appropriation of land internationally, and the industrial revolution contributed to economic growth (Marks 2007; Washbrook 1997) that eventually led to a wider distribution of property in society and hence to the development of a sizable middle class (Przeworski et al. 2000; Acemoglu and Robinson 2006: 58). These developments enabled the ruling elite to lower the property threshold for voting rights gradually, thus extending the franchise, but only to those sections of society that had actually achieved a measure of individual freedom based on private property and who therefore had a stake in upholding the liberal character of government.

Yet, as a result of the industrial revolution, other parts of the population experienced a new round of impoverishment and deprivation, coupled with horrific working conditions, which were also, however, conducive to political mobilization. Hence, the development of workers' movements and renewed threats of revolution in the 19th century. At this point, however, colonialism could no longer provide a relief for these domestic tensions, because there was hardly any territory left to colonize. The division of Africa between the European powers largely completed the colonial appropriation and division of the world, and unlike America, New Zealand, or Australia, Africa was already inhabited by large numbers of people and thus did not provide the same opportunities for emigration and appropriation. In order to prevent revolution, European elites thus began to make a range of economic compromises (factory regulation in England, for example, and welfare legislation in Germany). Internationally, the end of opportunities for colonial expansion led to competition between European powers and contributed ultimately to World War I, finally leading to revolution (in Russia and Germany) and the subsequent more or less immediate introduction of universal franchise also in European states.

This historical development of liberalism, first of all, challenges the claim that liberalism 'contains within itself the seeds of its own democratization' (Plattner 2008: 60) in the form of liberal ideas whose universal appeal ultimately undermines traditional privileges of all kinds, as evidenced by the fact that the ruling classes themselves eventually outbid each other in introducing universal franchise (Plattner 2008: 66). Though liberal ideas were of course used by the various emancipatory movements, 'most moves toward democracy happen in the face of significant social conflict and possible threat of revolution. Democracy is usually not given by the elite because its values have changed. It is demanded by the disenfranchised as a way to obtain political power and thus secure a larger share of the economic benefits of the system' (Acemoglu and Robinson 2006: 29; Kim 1992: 24).

Secondly, the diversity of liberal developments – such as the relatively early democratization of settler societies – was not due to a more radical political culture there in comparison with a backward and traditional political imagination in Europe (Plattner 2008: 62). It was, after all, in Europe that radical political movements frequently challenged the ruling elite and European political culture is to this day more radical than its American counterpart. Instead, it was the spread of property in America that constituted a liberal political culture and allowed for an early introduction of universal franchise. And it was the need to make economic compromises (factory regulation, welfare) that delayed democratization in Europe and provided the basis for a more 'social democratic' or 'welfare' type liberalism here. In short, variations in the politico-economic context give rise to different forms of liberal political culture, even within Europe, all of which nevertheless arise from the same core dynamics. None of these different incarnations of liberalism, moreover, is more 'liberal' – more in tune with abstract liberal principles – than the others. They simply represent the appropriate form of liberalism in different contexts.

Thirdly, although this historical development indeed provides support for the importance of economic dynamics, it nevertheless radically challenges the assumption that modernization was an essentially endogenous development 'linked to national, economic, and political independence' (Przeworski 1992: 55). Instead, it was the international practice of colonialism that provided the European ruling elites with the economic and political opportunities to delay the extension of political rights in the domestic sphere and thus ensured the liberal character of democracy when it was eventually introduced (Bova 1997: 116; Ake 1992: 33–4). Meanwhile, American liberalism has its roots in a population of colonists settling on land entirely appropriated from indigenous peoples. Most importantly, however, these developments are not independent of each other: it was, after all, European people populating American indigenous land and 'American' economic and political opportunities that contributed to the development of liberalism in Europe. European and American liberalism are thus constitutive of each other – an international dynamic that undermines a comparative approach treating individual polities as independent cases of endogenous historical developments.

Finally, by undermining the belief in the endogenous nature of liberalism that subsequently encounters the international as an alien sphere that awaits 'liberalization', this history shows that liberal thought and practice were actually constitutive of the modern international sphere. Colonialism, after all, required the denial of political rights to weaker communities, and thus it established the international as a sphere of power politics in contrast to the domestic which was at least in principle based on the rule of (liberal) law. Liberal thought and practice thus led to the legal construction of independent sovereign states based on property and an international sphere in which these entities could compete over spheres of influence and appropriation. And it was this constitution of the modern international sphere that played a crucial role in ameliorating the centrifugal implications of liberal policies in the domestic sphere: that contributed to the development of national unity and the pursuit of the good life based on international diversity as a realm of war.

In light of this history, there can be no doubt that liberalism is a powerful historical force. Liberal thought and practice successfully managed to transform traditional identities into free individuals in the liberal sense and thus liberal political cultures; it played a crucial role in reconstituting crisis-ridden political communities into bounded sovereign nation states based on the protection of private property and the rule of law, today largely associated with democracy; and the concept of sovereignty led to the establishment of the modern international system inhabited by 'like units' competing over influence and resources. Liberalism, moreover, has not just been influential in transforming the world of (international) politics, it has also transformed itself from a passionately anti-democratic and ruthlessly exploitative political program to one committed to democracy and at least some measure of economic regulation.

Yet, this development does not indicate a transcendence of the original contradictions of liberalism and thus a closer approximation to ahistorical liberal principles. After all, it was precisely the tension between liberal theory and practice that gave rise to contradictory policies – political emancipation and oppression, economic privatization and expropriation – and these contradictory policies constituted not just liberal individuals but also nonliberal ones, not just liberal political communities but also nonliberal ones, not just sovereign states but also dependent colonies. The original tension within liberalism thus is now embodied in the *relations* between these new actors, ideologies, and structures. Indeed, it is the very success of these liberal policies that demonstrates most clearly the continuing operation of its internal tensions. Hence, it was the very success of dividing virtually the entire globe into sovereign states (often colonial powers) on the one hand and dependent colonies on the other that, by the early 20th century, put an end to colonial expansion, and thus turned the tension inward in the form of enhanced competition (and ultimately war) between these sovereign states. The very same success in establishing colonial empires eventually also undermined the neat distinction between inside and outside and turned the contradiction between despotic government for the population in the colonies and government by consent for that in the mother country into a domestic issue. And it was the very success of establishing the vast majority of citizens as liberal individuals on the basis of private property, welfare, and other economic compromises that led to the democratization of liberalism and thus made its political survival dependent on maintaining these economic benefits. Hence the wide spread challenges to the liberal order from the right as well as the left in those societies during the 1920s and 1930s that were not able (or willing) to provide these benefits. In the absence of opportunities for further colonial expansion, the survival of liberalism in democratic societies, in short, depended on finding new ways to generate economic growth.

After World War II and in light of a real existing and relatively powerful alternative embodied in the Soviet system, Keynesianism provided a temporary solution that involved raising the buying power of the majority of the population, thus generating economic growth and providing political stability. Internationally, liberal principles were embedded in a range of economic and financial organizations – the Bretton Woods institutions – that provided a multilateral framework for the regulation of the international economic order. And it was this 'separation' of political sovereignty from economic integration at the international level which also played an important role in the decolonization process.

Colonial powers generally resisted the demand for independence. Either they had to be forced out by wars or they delayed the process of decolonization (in some cases, like India, for decades) by making it conditional on a range of reforms that would ultimately ensure the largely liberal character of the newly independent state, rather than a socialist or communist one. This prominently involved, of course, the political protection of private property in the domestic sphere and an incorporation of the economy into the liberal world economy, regulated through the Bretton Woods institutions.[13] As a result of this separation of politics and economics the eventual transfer of political power did not seriously undermine liberal economic interests and principles; rather, it established unequal economic relations between the First and Third Worlds and thus allowed the former the continuing import of economic benefits from the international sphere and the export of its political fall-out to newly independent states. The differences between the colonial and postcolonial periods thus simply pertain to the means by which inequality is established and maintained, not to the fact of it. While establishing control over other peoples' land required the use of force and direct political rule, in today's world economy, such control is largely (if not solely) established through economic (inter)dependence and their legal and political maintenance through international economic organizations (all of which embody unequal power relations between members explicitly or implicitly).

Throughout this entire history of liberalism, the transformation of common into private property remains at the core of liberal strategies to foster economic growth, and not just in the international sphere. The last two decades have seen a remarkable revival of liberalism in the form of market economics, the privatization of state-owned industries, and the trimming of welfare benefits by liberal democracies (Plattner 2008: 68). This latest round of 'privatization' and 'liberalization' targeted communal ownership of water and electricity supplies, education, health care, and the establishment of 'new enclosures' in the form of intellectual property rights over natural products and their uses (May 2000). Policies of privatization and marketization also lie at the core of the development policies of international organizations like the International Monetary Fund (IMF) and World Bank as well as those of individual liberal states. Hence, the end of colonialism does not indicate a radical departure from this Lockean dynamic even if its goal is not any longer the appropriation of other peoples' land (Wendt 1999: 284, 293)

---

[13] Grovogui (2000) describes this process beautifully for the case of Namibia.

and the democratization of liberalism has not put an end to practices of appropriation in the domestic or the international sphere that require the maintenance and pursuit of unequal power relations by economic, political and at times military means.

In sum, liberalism is today rightly associated with democracy and the principle of self-determination. But this democratic and anticolonial liberalism is neither more nor less 'liberal' than its previous antidemocratic and colonial incarnations. It attests instead to a historical dynamism driven by the internal contradictions of liberalism that even while they are successfully reconstituting actors and structures also reproduce the core tensions between them, and hence force liberalism to adjust its core practices to ever changing circumstances. With regard to these core practices, however, the historical development of liberalism demonstrates astonishing continuity: in separating politics, economics, ideas, domestic, and international spheres as well as past and present, it manages to obscure and displace in space and time the intimate and constitutive linkage between its emancipatory and oppressive, its liberalizing and exploitative practices, so far, however, without resolving these contradictions.

Conclusion

Locke's political philosophy, as we have seen, provides an explicit account of the relations between the core liberal principles of private property, individual freedom, and government by consent, an account which is sorely missing in contemporary conceptions of liberalism and liberal theories. And it was the very fact that this was a *political* philosophy, responding to and formulating answers for a particular political crisis that forced Locke to provide a justification for these principles that did not seem to find much support in contemporaneous or historical evidence. Hence, he provided a philosophy of history explaining this divergence between theory and practice and justifying these principles as in accordance with human nature (and by extension divine law). Yet, the realization of this political program in practice also required a bridging of the gap between theory and practice which Locke achieved by advocating colonial policies, thus providing both the philosophy of history and the international realm with a logical and necessary role in liberal thought and practice.

Despite this integration of the various dimensions of liberalism, however, Locke also laid the groundwork for its subsequent and today so familiar fragmentation. Though he systematically based his philosophy of history on empirical information about contemporaneous indigenous societies, he presented the latter as representatives of the state of nature of humanity, and thus the principles supported by this material as natural and universally valid. Subsequent interpretations of Locke, until recently, thus considered the state of nature as well as the philosophy of history based on it as purely hypothetical constructs that could not be criticized on empirical grounds. And with this distinction between theory and practice, liberal principles became established as ahistorical ideals obscuring their particular historical origins and dynamics. This abstraction of liberal principles from their historical origins also obscured the central and constitutive role of the international for liberal theory and practice. From now on, any disjuncture between liberal theory and practice required an adjustment of the latter without touching upon the validity of the former.

In its broad trajectory, I have shown, the historical development of liberalism is in line with Locke's *political* philosophy. It successfully reconstitutes individuals, communities, and the international system itself through processes of appropriation and governance. Despite its powerful transformative role, however, this development does not lead to the realization of liberal principles but to the reproduction of its internal tensions in the relations between these actors. Liberalism thus continually reinvents itself by applying its core practices to changing circumstances. Underneath its flexibility and diversity, however, its core dynamic is constant. And it is this continuity through change that makes a preliminary conceptualization of the relations between liberalism's core dimensions possible.

Liberalism is a political project that aims to establish individual freedom through private property and to protect and extend this freedom through government by consent. It pursues this goal through the privatization/expropriation of common property which requires the maintenance of unequal power relations (by economic, political, ideological or military means). And it justifies this inequality through a philosophy of history that attributes to different actors different levels of development corresponding to different rights and obligations.

4
Politics

Introduction

The concept of liberalism developed in the previous chapter now has to prove itself in the contemporary context. While the critical historical juncture at which John Locke was writing – after the emergence of liberal ideas and interests but before their systematic institutionalization – promised to provide insight into the coherence as well as political dynamics of the realization of liberalism in theory and practice (and seemed to be broadly supported by the subsequent historical development of liberalism), it nevertheless remains to be seen whether and in how far this concept is capable of grasping the dynamics of liberal thought and practice today. To this end, this and the next two chapters will describe a range of liberal theories that have played an important role in guiding liberal politics since the end of the Cold War and analyze the results of these policies. In each case, I will show, contemporary liberal theories fail to provide a satisfactory account of these political dynamics while the preliminary conception of liberalism based on Locke's work does.

The end of the Cold War was widely regarded as ushering in a new and liberal world order. This order, however, was not yet fully developed but to some extent a 'project to be realized' (Young 1995). Although the dominant and largely unchallenged position of liberal states after the Cold War contributed to this order's liberal character, the realization of liberal principles, practices, and institutions was by no means complete. In the absence of a powerful counterforce, however, this project could now be pursued more proactively. The 1990s were hence associated with the development or intensification of so-called liberal foreign policies, prominently amongst them democracy promotion, neoliberal economic policies, and humanitarian intervention.

These policies tend to focus, just like contemporary liberal theories, on either the political or the economic or the normative dimension of liberalism. Such distinctions are by no means watertight and there are considerable overlaps between these foreign policy areas, in theory as well as in practice. And yet, I will show, liberal foreign policies during that era were guided by liberal theories that were not themselves under the pressure to narrow their remit for purposes of operationalization and yet tended to focus on either one of these areas while neglecting the others, and this separation played a major role in the widespread failure of these policies.

This chapter thus focuses on foreign policies with the primary aim to establish and spread liberal political institutions – that is, democracy. I will briefly introduce two of the most prominent and influential liberal theories – the democratic peace thesis and the democracy transition paradigm – that provide the theoretical framework for these policies. I will then, secondly, provide an overview of the range and fate of the liberal foreign policies during the post-Cold War era inspired by these theories. The promotion of democracy has, in general, either led to paradoxical outcomes or to outright failure. Though the failure of these policies is widely analyzed, as I will show in a third step, they are mistakenly blamed on the 'illiberal' or inconsistent behavior of liberal actors. In fact, these practices are perfectly in line with the conception of liberalism derived from Locke's work in the previous chapter. What accounts for the disjuncture between theory and practice is a truncated theoretical understanding of liberalism rather than its practice. Liberal theories and policies focusing on political institutions, the chapter concludes, fail to integrate the economic and normative dimensions of liberalism and thus contribute to mistaken expectations.

Liberal political theories

Classical liberalism, as we have seen in the previous chapter, was passionately antidemocratic. Dynamic historical developments, however, led to its gradual democratization and liberalism is today rightly associated with democracy. Not only are the older and most powerful liberal states generally democratic, democracy is also theoretically identified as the regime type that best reflects and protects the core liberal norm of individual freedom. In addition, however, international liberal theories also link democratic political institutions to domestic and international peace. Amongst such theories, especially since the end of the Cold War, are the democratic peace thesis and the democracy transition paradigm. These two approaches advocate the spread of democracy as an important means toward a more cooperative and pacific domestic and international order and they have, indeed, inspired the foreign policies of liberal actors.

The Democratic Peace thesis was initially formulated in order to make sense of statistics indicating that democratic states 'have yet to engage in war with one another' (Doyle 1996: 10). Although some authors define these regimes narrowly by voting rights for a substantial number of citizens, contested elections and an executive either elected or responsible to an elected body (Russett 1996a), most include into their definition other characteristics like the legal equality of citizens, a representative government, private property, and a market economy (Doyle 1996: 5f), or a liberal ideology and the leverage of citizens over war decisions (Owen 1996). Democracy in the context of the democratic peace thesis thus widely refers to liberal democracy.

The most influential statement of the democratic peace thesis was provided by Michael Doyle.[1] Following Kant, Doyle argues that citizens are overwhelmingly interested in peace because they pay the price of war – in taxes, disruption of trade, material destruction, and lives. Hence, democracies in which the interests of the population are represented in government tend to be more peaceful than states in which rulers do not require the consent of their citizens to go to war (Doyle 1996: 21, 24f; Kant 1957: 12f). Alternatively it is argued that the norms of peaceful conflict resolution in the domestic affairs of democratic states are projected onto foreign affairs or that the constraints operating in democratic decision making provide time for alternative forms of conflict resolution (Russett 1996b). Either way, however, liberal democratic societies are associated with peace.

Over time, these liberal democratic states establish trust amongst each other, based on growing economic interdependence which provides

---

[1] The democratic peace thesis has generated an entire cottage industry of publications that deal at length with its every twist and turn. Hence, it is impossible to provide an encompassing overview over the relevant literature. However, for a discussion of the democratic peace thesis in the mainstream literature, the edited volume by Brown et al. (1996) provides a good starting point. For engagement with the democratic peace thesis from the perspective of more critical theories, see Barkawi and Laffey (2001). A brief but useful compilation of the core problems of this thesis can be found in Gates et al. (1996).

material incentives for peaceful behavior (Doyle 1996: 26; Kant 1957: 20–3), similar political institutions and values, and a history of non-violent conflict resolution. And it is this development which leads, according to the democratic peace thesis, to the establishment of a separate peace between democratic states which explains the statistical evidence (Kant 1957: 16–20; Doyle 1996: 26). Hence, the peaceful nature of domestic liberal society leads to peaceful international relations between such societies.

This argument entails, however, the converse implication that nonliberal states tend to be more aggressive. Since in those states the interests of the population are not represented in government, and since illiberal governments themselves can benefit from war – either materially as Kant argued and/or because wars can be used to distract from domestic problems – liberal states distrust illiberal states. In pursuit of peace, therefore, illiberal states easily become targets of liberal 'missionary' policies (Doyle 1996: 31f) which explains the empirical fact that they do quite 'liberally' go to war with nonliberal states (Doyle 1996: 10, 25; Russett 1996b: 92).

The logic of this theory suggests that a pacification of international politics is possible. It requires the spread of liberal democracy to as yet nonliberal states. Once a nonliberal state has become liberal, it can enter the pacific federation between liberal states, thus extending the realm of peace in the world (Kant 1957: 24–32). The aim of a liberal foreign policy thus lies in a systematic promotion of 'liberal principles abroad' (Doyle 1996: 49), that is, in changing the cultural, economic, and political constitution of nonliberal states. This systematic promotion of liberal principles requires a clear distinction between liberal and nonliberal states; 'we must have no liberal enemies and no unconditional alliances with nonliberal states' (Doyle 1996: 50). This distinction between liberal and nonliberal states thus serves to strengthen the liberal peace internally, to demonstrate the benefits of peaceful cooperation to nonliberal states, and to put pressure on nonliberal states by denying them those benefits prior to establishing liberal democracy.

While the democratic peace thesis provides the broad theoretical outlines of an association of liberalism with peace and nonliberal regimes with war and aggression, the democracy transition paradigm is located between this theory and practice. Within the framework of the core theoretical assumptions of the democratic peace thesis, the democracy transition paradigm aims to provide a model of successful democratization and to develop foreign policy prescriptions based on that model.

It has its historical origins in the period of decolonization following World War II in which powerful liberal states were concerned about the consequences of a large number of nonliberal states entering the international system. The break-up of the European colonial empires following the end of World War II raised the specter of an increase in nonliberal – communist – states (Westad 2005: 26f; Morse 1976: 2, xivf; Pye and Verba 1965: 5; Rostow 1971: 166). The West was thus confronted with the task – taken on by modernization theorists – of finding ways of 'controlling', 'stabilizing', and 'governing' this new international system; in other words, of providing a developmental model for Third World countries under the auspices of the democratic and capitalist world (Rostow 1971: 134, 104f). While modernization theories and policies were ultimately not particularly successful (Jahn 2007a: 99–100), their core ideas were taken up again in what is now known as the democracy transition paradigm (Cammack 1997) which assumes, in line with the democratic peace thesis, that nonliberal states present a danger to international peace and stability.[2] Third World states are internally unstable because they lack economic development, and economic failure leads to state failure (Sachs 2001: 187). While technologically and economically developed states have nothing to gain from war, war can still benefit Third World states. Territory and resources are more important in an underdeveloped economy; war can distract from domestic malaise; poverty produces mass migration, drug trafficking, disease, and even terrorism (David 1992/3: 135f; Sachs 2001: 187; Hamre and Sullivan 2002: 85; Marten 2002/3: 35f; Rotberg 2002: 85).

Moreover, Third World states, it is argued, are politically unstable. They are young and lack the cohesion and stability of Western states because colonial borders have produced ethnically mixed states and destroyed traditional institutions which have not been replaced with efficient new ones. Unlike in the early phases of the European development of the nation-state, the population in the Third World is educated and wants to participate in the political process. This domestic instability provides fertile ground for civil wars as well as for inter-state war (David 1992/3: 131–4). In addition, Third World states suffer political

---

[2] A good overview over 'the conceptual politics of democracy promotion' can be found in Hobson and Kurki (2012) and in-depth engagements with all aspects of the transition paradigm in Carothers (2004). Studies of the role of democracy promotion in American foreign policy are collected in Cox et al. (2000). Much of the ongoing debate on the transition paradigm and democracy promotion takes place in the *Journal of Democracy* and *Democratization*.

failure because of bad leadership and corruption (Rotberg 2002: 93; Froning 2001). The lack of democracy in Third World states makes them war prone. Elites do not need the support of the population to go to war and may do so in order to stay in power. They will not be punished if they lose a war because they can simply increase the oppression of the population (David 1992/3: 138–40). And, of course, lack of democracy creates hospitable conditions for terrorism (Windsor 2003).

These economic and political incentives for war are compounded by cultural factors. The Third World is characterized by militarism and hyper-nationalism. Third World ideologies are more supportive of war because of religious, ethnic, and political hatred which vilify and dehumanize enemies in the press and textbooks. Religious, particularly Muslim, fundamentalism is worrying because it generally pursues extreme policies. Muslim schools promote a personality not well suited to democracy. These cultural factors stand in the way of domestic political and economic development. Moreover, they narrow the range of foreign policy options for the West; deterrence policies cannot be pursued since it is unclear what these cultures would consider as unacceptable costs just as it is 'as dangerous as it is foolhardy' to assume that the cultural and religious beliefs of fundamentalist leaders would have no effect on their economic behavior (David 1992/3: 150, 136–8; Haass 2003: 145).

In short, 'there have been no fundamental changes in ideas and attitudes in much of the Third World' (David 1992/3: 138). And it is this economic, political, and cultural 'backwardness' – just as in modernization theories – which causes domestic and international instability and war. And just as in modernization theory, the characteristics of transitional states are defined in opposition to those of liberal capitalist states: 'war is more likely in the Third World ... because many of the reasons put forth for why war has become obsolete among the developed states simply do not apply to much of the Third World' (David 1992/3: 138, 131).

These assumptions regarding the dangers emanating from nonliberal Third World states (Duffield 2001) are perfectly in line with those implied by the democratic peace thesis. And like the latter, the democracy transition paradigm aims to counter these dangers by spreading liberal democracy. To this end the democracy transition paradigm generally models the historical development of liberal democracy in successful cases; these models then guide policies designed to spread democracy. This paradigm falls broadly into two strands: one focusing on the political, the other on the economic sphere. I shall discuss the former in the context of this chapter and return to the latter in the next chapter.

Liberal democracy is understood as a conglomerate of characteristics generally found in, or associated with, European (settler) states. These states and their transition to democracy provide the main model for both major periods of democracy promotion since World War II: modernization theories and policies in the 1950s and 1960s (Jahn 2007a) and transition theories and democracy promotion policies especially in the 1990s (Diamond 1996: 35; Paris 1997: 57; Jahn 2007b). In addition, the cases of Germany and Japan after World War II are frequently cited in support of the notion that democracy can successfully be promoted by foreign actors.[3] Since then, the case of South Africa seemed to prove that democratization was possible in deeply divided societies; Spain became a model for step-by-step democratization of authoritarian regimes; and Hungary and Poland played a similar role for the 'triple' transition from communism, including the transition of political institutions, economic organization, and military alliance (Whitehead 2009: 217–9). Modernization theories widely assumed that 'various national preconditions and deep structural factors' such as 'levels of socioeconomic development, degrees of socioeconomic equality and group polarization, patterns of land ownership or agricultural production, the prevalence of certain beliefs or cultural traits' were necessary for a successful transition to democracy (Rose 2000/1: 191; Jahn 2007a: 94–102). Yet, in 'The Third Wave' of democratization (Huntington 1991) political factors seemed to play an important role and provided grounds for a narrower focus on political institutions for democratization policies in the post-Cold War era (Rose 2000/1: 192–3).

According to the political approach, the emergence and democratization of liberalism in Europe and America has its roots in a particular political culture, characterized by secularization and the 'taming of politics' which led to the 'invention' of liberal ideas (Sartori 1995: 104). The subsequent expansion of liberalism is explained by 'the spread of liberal ideas of the natural freedom and equality of all human beings' which 'doomed any special and substantial privileges enjoyed on the basis of heredity' and 'eventually undermined any effort to exclude people from political participation on the basis of such factors as race, religion, or sex' (Plattner 2008: 67).

This development of liberal and democratic political institutions was historically frequently accompanied by technological and economic

---

[3] For a critical analysis of this assumption, see Jenkins and Plowden (2006).

development (Bova 1997: 116; Fukuyama 1992a: 108). Yet, while economic development is widely seen as 'very helpful' for the process of
democratization, it is 'neither a necessary nor a sufficient condition for
stable democracy' (Fukuyama 1992a: 108). Since liberalism was, a hundred years ago, not at all associated with providing economic benefits,
'a "poor democracy" is equally conceivable and possible' (Sartori 1995:
105). Indeed, economic development itself, according to this account,
has its roots in technological innovation which, in turn, was made possible by the culture of logic and rationality the West inherited from
ancient Greece (Sartori 1995: 106; Fukuyama 1992b). In short, both
economic and technological development as well as liberal political
institutions have their roots in a particular, Western, political culture.

Democracy promotion policies based on this narrative therefore identify a traditional political culture as the main barrier to the development
of liberal democracy and propagate policies focusing on the spread
of liberal ideas and institutions. These variously include support for
elections, citizenship, civil society, the rule of law, decentralization,
anticorruption, and others that are designed to address this political
backwardness (Plattner 2008: 53; Carothers 2004: 5).

Both, the democratic peace thesis and the democracy transition
paradigm hold that conflict and war have their roots in nonliberal
regimes. And both aim to spread liberal democracy in order to ensure
peaceful conflict resolution in the domestic and the international sphere
as in the interest of individuals and states in general. Historically, as
Doyle points out, a dominant tendency of liberal foreign policies was
thus 'interventionism' (Doyle 1996: 37). Since such 'missionary' foreign
policies may prove counterproductive, Doyle explicitly advocates the
extension of the right of military nonintervention to nonliberal governments (Doyle 1996: 48ff). Specifically, instead of force he advocates
economic means – sanctions or restricted interaction with nonliberal
states and extended aid and trade with liberal or transitional states – to
promote liberal principles abroad (Doyle 1996: 48, 50ff). Such 'carrots
and sticks' policies are also the preferred option for the democracy transition paradigm and characterize democracy promotion policies during
the post-Cold War era.

Democracy promotion policies

In practice, democracy promotion played a part in a wide variety of
contexts in the post-Cold War era and it was pursued not just by the
United States and other liberal states as well as their national development agencies, but also by international organizations ranging from the

UN through the Organization for Security and Co-operation in Europe (OSCE), the European Union (EU), North Atlantic Treaty Organization (NATO), the Organization of American States (OAS), the International Monetary Fund (IMF), and the World Bank as well as many NGOs (Paris 2004: 22–35). Since the end of the Cold War, all these institutions participate, in one form or another, in the promotion of (market) democracies in as yet nonliberal societies. Democracy promotion policies have played a role in roughly four different policy contexts ranging from general diplomacy through direct democracy assistance, peacebuilding operations and military interventions with the aim to replace nonliberal regimes. Yet, as I will show now, these policies have not been particularly successful.

Diplomacy

Liberal theories suggest that liberal states should build alliances and deepen cooperation with other liberal states and avoid closer ties with nonliberal states. These alliances are expected to enhance the security and cooperation between liberal states, to deter aggressive behavior by nonliberal states, and to provide an example of the benefits of liberalism and peaceful cooperation to nonliberal states.

And, indeed, cooperation between liberal states takes a multitude of forms in current world politics. Liberal states have played a crucial role in setting up and developing international economic organizations – from the Bretton Woods institutions after World War II to the WTO in the post-Cold War era. Originally also based on economic cooperation, the EU is by now one of the most advanced experiments of political cooperation between liberal states, even in the face of its manifold problems and limitations. Finally, NATO is a prime example for extensive military cooperation between liberal states.

But these examples of liberal cooperation do not quite live up to the predictions or prescriptions of liberal theories that insist on a qualitative distinction between intraliberal and liberal–nonliberal relations. After all, 'the most distinctive aspect of Liberal international relations theory is that it permits, indeed mandates, a distinction among different types of States based on their domestic political structure and ideology' (Slaughter 1995: 2). It is this 'distinctive quality of relations among liberal democracies' (Slaughter 1995: 2) *in contrast to and in combination with* the exclusion of, or pressure on, nonliberal actors that lies at the core of these theories and constitutes the main liberal tool of convincing the latter – with carrots and sticks – to emulate the former.

In light of this requirement, the examples of liberal cooperation mentioned above do not provide strong support for liberal theories. None of the international economic institutions excludes nonliberal states. On the contrary, these institutions aim to widen their membership and/or to spread and deepen liberal economic principles such as a 'substantial reduction of tariffs and other barriers to trade' (WTO Preamble 1994) in the international economic order. Moreover, liberal states like the United States permit vertical enforcement through domestic courts of bilateral investment treaties, 'mostly with non-liberal nations' (Alvarez 2001: 196). Politically, liberal states frequently cooperate with nonliberal states. While membership of the EU is indeed restricted to liberal states, membership of the UN is not. Liberal states not only played a major role in the establishment of the UN as an inclusive rather than exclusive organization, they cooperate with nonliberal states within its bounds as well as bilaterally. Thus, during the Cold War a wide range of nonliberal states were actively supported by and counted as allies of the Western or liberal camp (Westad 2005) even while democratic regimes, for example in Iran (1953), Guatemala (1954), or Chile (1973), were overtly or covertly undermined or attacked. Moreover, widespread cooperation between liberal and nonliberal states continued during the post-Cold War period. Liberal states have widely propped up undemocratic regimes in the Middle East – for example in Egypt and Saudi Arabia – and fail to recognize and provide support for democratically elected governments – for example in Algeria or Palestine. The democratization movements in the course of the Arab Spring (2011–12) provided a good example for the dilemmas of liberal foreign policies. While democratization in Egypt, for example, was in general welcomed, the fear that democracy might bring 'illiberal' parties like the Muslim Brotherhood to power provided a break on support for democratization. This political cooperation with nonliberal regimes extends into the military sphere. Hence, Turkey, accused (whether rightly or wrongly) of lacking liberal credentials by the EU, is nevertheless a member of NATO; there is extensive military cooperation between the West and Saudi Arabia; and nonliberal states frequently participate in peacekeeping operations. Liberal states, in short, do not appear to systematically distinguish between liberal and nonliberal states in their economic, political, or military relations.

Conversely, cooperation between liberal states does not necessarily support the claim of a 'distinctive' quality of intra-liberal relations. 'Trade wars' between Europe and the United States are a standard feature of international economic relations and make up most of the conflicts that come before the WTO dispute settlement mechanism. In contrast to the vertical enforcement of BITs (bilateral investment treaties) with nonliberal states, amongst themselves liberal states have failed to agree on measures that would provide their investors with directly enforceable treaty rights (Alvarez 2001: 199). Moreover, the EU, individual liberal states, and the United States also regularly disagree on the use of sanctions and trade restrictions with regard to Iran and China for example. There is strong disagreement between liberal states regarding environmental policies and agreements in general and issues of global warming. There is similarly strong disagreement regarding the development and institutionalization of the International Criminal Court (Wedgwood 1999; Hafner et al. 1999) and during the course of the 'war on terror' even regarding the interpretation and application of the Geneva Conventions and Human Rights Law. Most prominently, however, liberal states are on occasion deeply divided on fundamental issues of security and war. While the United States and Britain favored intervention in Iraq, France and Germany passionately opposed it; while Britain, France, and the United States favored intervention in Libya, Germany opposed it.

These disagreements in all areas of international politics do not undermine the fact of widespread cooperation between liberal states. But the range and depth of differences between liberal states in international affairs in combination with widespread cooperation between liberal and nonliberal states suggests, at the very least, that liberal states do not systematically act according to liberal theories regarding either their cooperation with each other or their noncooperation with nonliberal states. Overall, the behavior of liberal states results in a mixed picture of liberal diplomacy (broadly defined) and it is this very mixture that undermines the claim of a clearly identifiable model of intraliberal relations attracting emulation in light of an unattractive alternative. Prosperity, cooperation, and peace are clearly not a monopoly of liberal states and intraliberal relations; they are in fact also enjoyed by nonliberal states and in liberal–nonliberal relations, thus reducing the pressure to become liberal.

Democracy assistance

Democracy promotion, however, is not restricted to the general attractions of liberalism or the disadvantages of nonliberal regimes and relations. Instead, direct democracy assistance constitutes a core aspect of the foreign policy of liberal states which, though it has a long history, at least in the foreign policy of the United States (Cox et al. 2000: 10), has gained particular prominence after the end of the Cold War with roughly 2 billion USD per year spent on democracy-related aid projects (Carothers 2004: 2). And this amount is, since the end of the Cold War, even outweighed by other international actors like the EU (McFaul 2005: 156). The positive side of democracy assistance entails the extension of diplomatic and economic support and privileges as well as the funding of concrete democracy programs. Most often, the latter consist of election aid, but it can also entail aid to reform the police and military, judicial aid and aid to rewrite constitutions, as well as support for NGOs, human rights institutions, and independent media (Carothers 2000: 186–9). The negative side of such policies consists in exerting diplomatic and economic pressure and in extreme and very rare cases of military intervention to restore democracy. With the exception of military intervention, the term 'conditional aid' covers much of these policies and indicates that they have not just been pursued by the United States but prominently also by other liberal states and international organizations (Carothers 2000: 185f).

Democracy is generally taken to entail free and fair elections, separation of powers, a fair and independent judicial system, a free and inquisitive press, the widespread sharing of democratic values, respect for human rights and ethnic minorities, and the presence of civil society (Rutland 2000: 246). These are the criteria, then, by which democracy assistance programs must be assessed.

One of the largest shares of democracy assistance at the end of the Cold War went to Russia which can therefore serve as a good example for this form of democracy promotion (Carothers 2000: 185). Russia has had fairly free elections; and yet, its political spectrum is fragmented, the only party with a national presence and coherent organizational structure is the successor of the former communist party. The new constitution gave tremendous influence to the president and deprived government and parliament of real power. Hence, Yeltsin ruled by issuing thousands of decrees not subject to legislative review; 'his style of rule was that of a monarch, unchallenged and absolute' but legitimated by periodic elections (Rutland 2000: 255). Instead of an independent judiciary, corruption mushroomed; most of the national newspapers do not circulate outside Moscow and the local press remains under the control of provincial political bosses. The strong performance of authoritarian parties in elections throws some doubts on the development of widely shared democratic values. While far from being perfect, in the area of human rights Russia initially made progress since communist times. Civil society associations have also sprung up, yet they remain largely dependent on outside funding and do not generate the political power necessary to act as incubators of democratic values and experience. The latter have been actively suppressed under President Putin who follows in Yeltsin's footsteps regarding the authoritarian leadership style. Putin's return to government after Medvedev led to a 'renewed crackdown on opposition figures and government critics' (Kramer 2012: 3). Despite large amounts of democracy assistance, 'Freedom House has been documenting Russia's steep and steady decline in democracy and human rights' and comes to the conclusion that 'neither the parliamentary nor the presidential election was free and fair' (Kramer 2012: 2, 5). In sum, Russia is a prime example for what is variously called an 'electoral democracy', 'authoritarian democracy', or 'low-intensity democracy' (Sørensen 2000: 290; Gills 2000).

Electoral or authoritarian democracies are defined through the electoral establishment or legitimation of an essentially authoritarian government. Apart from Russia such authoritarian democracies can be found in Brazil, Burkina Faso, Congo, El Salvador, Indonesia, Kenya, Malaysia, Tanzania, Turkey, Ukraine, Uganda, Ethiopia, and Zambia (Sørensen 2000: 290). 'Many of the putative "democratic transitions" of the late 1980s and early 1990s, especially in Africa, Central Asia, the Caucasus, and South-eastern Europe are not following the path of initial opening, elections, and progressive consolidation' (Carothers 2000: 195). Indeed, the most common and natural regime type in the world today is located somewhere between dictatorship and democracy (Carothers 2002: 18). While electoral assistance has often been successful in helping to conduct relatively free and fair elections, it has certainly not instigated a self-perpetuating process of democratization.

Peacebuilding

Peacebuilding can be defined as 'action undertaken at the end of a civil conflict to consolidate peace and prevent a recurrence of fighting' (Paris 2004: 38).[4] For this purpose, peacebuilding operations in the 1990s generally included the deployment of military and civilian personnel from several international agencies. In accordance with the belief that market democracies provide for internal and external peace and security,

---

[4] Roland Paris' study of peacebuilding operations during the 1990s provides a theoretical analysis as well as excellent case studies (2004) of what has now become known as the 'liberal peace'. He also provides a good overview over the subsequent debates (2010). For more critical literature on the 'liberal peace', see MacGinty and Richmond (2007), Chandler (2006), Heathershaw (2008). Ongoing contributions to the debate can be found in *Journal of Intervention and Statebuilding*.

these operations included the organization of elections, retraining of judges, lawyers, and police officers, support for indigenous political parties and nongovernmental organizations, design and implementation of economic reforms, reorganization of governmental institutions, promotion of free media, and emergency humanitarian and financial assistance (Paris 2004: 39). There is considerable overlap, then, between the nonmilitary component of peacebuilding operations and democracy assistance.

Democracy promotion in the context of peacebuilding operations needs to be judged by slightly different criteria since in this case the promotion of political and economic liberalization, first and foremost, is meant to produce internal and external peace and stability (Paris 2004: 19–35). In how far this goal has been achieved by peacebuilding operations in the 1990s is the subject of Roland Paris's analysis (2004). While results differ from case to case, broadly three different outcomes can be identified.

In the first group of states, the rapid introduction of elections led to renewed fighting and/or a continuation of the previous conflictual policies. This was the case in Angola where elections triggered two years of renewed fighting killing more people than the previous 18 years of civil war. International donors forced the Rwandan government into democratization and the acceptance of structural adjustment policies. The resulting economic downturn as well as the political liberalization of civil society and especially the media served as a catalyst for the genocide (Paris 2004: 63–78). In Cambodia, too, every election campaign led to a flaring up of violence and it appears as if only Hun Sen's reintroduction of democratically legitimated authoritarian rule has provided some stability for the country. Similarly, in Liberia Charles Taylor reverted back to authoritarian rule immediately after the elections and fighting resumed (Paris 2004: 79–96). And the 1996 elections in Bosnia brought the very ethnic leaders into power who were responsible for the civil war in the first place and were unwilling to cooperate and overcome the ethnic divisions. When, as a result of this experience, peacebuilders openly favored moderate Serb leaders in the 1997 elections, they were accused of rigging the elections – and the moderate forces proved unsuccessful nonetheless (Paris 2004: 97–107). In these cases, democratization policies neither produced security nor did they initiate a self-perpetuating process of democratization. Instead, in some cases political and economic liberalization played into the hands of parties to the conflict (de Zeeuw and van de Goor 2006: 276).

More successful were peacebuilding operations in Croatia, Namibia, and Mozambique. And yet, in all these cases one partner to the violent conflict was actually an outside power – South Africa in the cases of Namibia and Mozambique, and Serbia in the case of Croatia. Strictly speaking, therefore, these cases cannot be defined as 'civil conflicts' – and their resolution was made possible by the withdrawal of this external power from the conflict. The Serb minority in Croatia was not supported by Serbia any longer and became largely politically inactive. In this situation, elections brought in more moderate politicians (Paris 2004: 107–10). The withdrawal of South Africa from the conflicts in Namibia and Mozambique put an end to violence in both cases (Paris 2004: 135–47). It seems, then, that reconciliation in these cases was less a product of democracy promotion and more that of the removal of an outside party to the conflict.

Mozambique, however, simultaneously falls into the third group of states in which the imposition of economic liberalization has led to increased poverty and, as a result, to an upsurge of criminal violence. The same is true for Nicaragua, El Salvador, and Guatemala. In all these cases, political violence was successfully ended but economic liberalization resulted in greater inequalities between the rich and the poor, and thus reproduced the causes of the original conflict whose violent consequences were now simply 'privatized' in the form of crime (Paris 2004: 114–33). Hence, economic and political liberalization in these countries have not addressed but rather exacerbated the original causes of the conflict and, thus, cannot be said to have led to greater stability and peace.

Most peacebuilding operations have, thus, not achieved the goal of establishing domestic peace and stability through the introduction of political and economic liberalization nor do they have a successful record in instigating a democratization process. The results of these operations are judged as 'fragile at best' and many cases show 'clear signs of backsliding' (de Zeeuw and van de Goor 2006: 281). Paris comes to the conclusion that, generally, peacebuilding operations either rekindled conflicts or recreated the conditions which led to conflict in the first place (2004: 155).

Military interventions

Finally, military interventions with the aim to replace an authoritarian by a democratic government are justified with reference to the actual or perceived aggression emanating from authoritarian governments and the belief that internal as well as international security can be enhanced by installing market democracies. In this case, a major military operation removing the authoritarian government is followed by the same list of civilian functions undertaken in peacebuilding operations with the military securing the state during the transitional period.

The obvious cases here are Afghanistan and Iraq. In both cases it was argued that the authoritarian governments produced domestic insecurity for their citizens, by violating their human and civil rights, and international insecurity, in the case of Afghanistan by providing shelter to terrorists, and in the case of Iraq by potentially aggressive foreign policies (based on weapons of mass destruction and support for terrorism). Overthrowing these governments and establishing market democracies in their place, it was argued, would remove the security threat and produce internal and external peace and stability. These, then, are the criteria by which the military interventions in these countries have to be assessed.

In both cases, the military intervention and subsequent removal of the governments of the Taliban and Saddam Hussein respectively was successful. And yet, the expected outcome of internal and external peace and stability is sorely missing. In March 2006 the situation in Afghanistan was characterized by:

> an ever-more deadly insurgency with sanctuaries in neighboring Pakistan . . . ; massive arms stocks despite the demobilization of many militias; a potential denial of the Islamic legitimacy of the Afghan government by a clergy that feels marginalized; ethnic tensions exacerbated by competition for resources and power; interference by neighboring states, all of which oppose a long-term US presence in the region . . . ; constitutional requirements to hold more national elections . . . than the government may be able to afford or conduct.
>
> Rubin (2006a: 2–3)

Above all, the antigovernment insurgency in Afghanistan was growing and judged to present 'a greater threat than at any point since late 2001' (Rubin 2006a: 2).

In September 2006 an update of this report concluded that the Taliban-led insurgency had 'increased its effectiveness and both broadened and deepened its presence' and the increased tempo of suicide bombings (before Iraq unknown in Afghanistan) 'has spread insecurity into Kabul itself' (Rubin 2006b: 3). Violent riots in May demonstrated opposition to the government and the United States from groups that had previously led the resistance to the Taliban and 'people are increasingly patronizing Taliban courts, seen as more effective and fair than the corrupt official system' (Rubin 2006b: 3).

Ten years after the beginning of the Afghanistan war 'a deadly and resilient insurgency persists'; the government is highly corrupt and does not enjoy the trust of the population; the military gains made in the South as a result of the 'surge' in troop numbers are judged 'fragile and reversible'; neighboring Pakistan with its nuclear arsenal and relatively safe havens for 'terrorists' has become destabilized (Bajoria 2011). It seems fair to say, then, that the establishment of a democratic regime and holding elections in Afghanistan has neither led to an improved security situation domestically or internationally nor has it generated a self-perpetuating development toward democracy.

In the case of Iraq, the general trend with regard to the development of democracy and internal and external security is much the same as in Afghanistan. Here, too, the removal of the despotic regime of Saddam Hussein was successful and democratic elections were held. And yet, in 2006 Nash reported that despite the establishment of a democratic government and the holding of relatively successful elections, 'the bottom line is that today there is an insurgency, there is a civil war, there is rampant crime, and the Iraqi people have far less security than before the US invasion' (Nash 2006: 2–3). In response to a 'rising tide of violence, largely caused by their own policy mistakes', the United States began a program of rapid remilitarization within Iraq and these security forces now provide the basis for developments away from democracy. 'As things stand' in 2012, 'the trajectory of Iraqi politics is clearly heading towards a new authoritarianism with the concentration of power in the hands of one man, Nuri al-Maliki' (Dodge 2012). Hence, the invasion of Iraq does not appear to have led to a self-sustaining process of democratization and it failed to provide domestic security or regional stabilization.

Judged in terms of the aims of initiating a natural process of democratization and, thus, improving domestic and international security, these democracy promotion policies are widely seen to have failed. A deepening process of democratization is rarely in evidence while internal and external security have either not improved as a result of these policies or even deteriorated. In fact, the optimism of the *Third Wave* has empirically ended in stagnation and even decline – especially of the liberal variant of democracy – giving rise to the question, 'Is the Third Wave Over?' (Diamond 1996: 28). Overall, observers agree that democracy promotion policies had, at best, 'very modest success' and 'little to show for themselves' (Finkel et al 2006: 86; Rose 2000/1: 192–3; Carothers 2004: 5; Diamond 1999: 23).

Analysis

The failure or paradoxical outcomes of these policies have, of course, been widely analyzed. These analyses, I will now show, attest to the limitations of contemporary liberal theories and tend to reproduce their shortcomings in practice. Yet, both the successes and the weaknesses of democracy promotion policies are easily explained by the alternative Lockean conception of liberalism.

To begin with, democracy promotion policies were inspired by contemporary liberal theories (Smith 2007) and, in particular, the belief that 'the natural evolution of developing states is toward market democracy, and that this evolution, once initiated, is self-perpetuating' (Paris 1997: 57; Carothers 2002: 15). This assumption is based on the belief that democratic institutions are the natural expression of human freedom. Perfectly in line with Locke's philosophy of history, what stood in the way of their realization was the historically deviant development of dictatorships. Once these dictators were removed, human freedom would automatically assert itself. On the basis of this assumption democracy promotion policies in all their incarnations were originally designed as short-term approaches. Democracy assistance programs generally provided aid until the first 'successful' election had been held and were then quickly withdrawn (Carothers 2002). Similarly, peacebuilding operations were based on the 'quickly in and out' approach and promoted a rapid constitution of market democracy (Paris 2004: 19; Orr 2002: 142). And the lack of preparation for civil reconstruction following the military interventions in Afghanistan and Iraq beyond the plan to hold elections, too, were based on the assumption that a removal of the illiberal regimes would automatically be followed by liberal practices on the part of the population (Packer 2006: 113, 147; von Hippel 1999: 99; O'Donnell 1996a: 47; O'Donnell 1996b: 163–4).

When it turned out that these approaches did not achieve their aims, two core areas of weaknesses were identified. The first lay in a lack of attention to particular local conditions (Carothers 2002: 16, 18; O'Donnell 1996a: 38; de Zeeuw and van de Goor 2006: 276) leading to much too optimistic assumptions about the nature of indigenous society in target states. Instead of the initial optimistic assumption that nondemocratic states basically just needed elections, by the end of the 1990s the countries in the 'grey zone' were seen to be in need of 'strengthening state capacity, liberalizing and rationalizing economic structures, securing social and political order while maintaining basic freedoms, improving horizontal accountability and the rule of law, and controlling corruption...strengthening political parties and their linkages to social groups, reducing fragmentation in the party system, strengthening the autonomous capacity and public accountability of legislatures and local governments, and invigorating civil society' (Diamond 1996: 33).

Similarly, the failure of peacebuilding or post-conflict reconstruction has been blamed on the lack of an appropriate political culture in target states. 'Postconflict reconstruction' must be characterized by longer-term and nonmilitary activities in target states which have to be rebuilt from scratch. Apart from the provision of security, this includes the constitution of a legitimate government, the mobilization of civil society, building state capacity and administration, providing justice and reconciliation, fighting corruption, and crafting conditionality (von Hippel 1999: 99, 103f; Hamre and Sullivan 2002; Orr 2002; Marten 2002/3; Barton and Crocker 2003). In short, what was required was 'a shift in political culture' (Diamond 1996: 33; Orr 2002; Hamre and Sullivan 2002; Rotberg 2002; von Hippel 1999; Marten 2002/3; Barton and Crocker 2003; Williams and Young 1994: 96).

This analysis held that democratic political institutions needed to be based on a liberal political culture which was often missing in the target states. It was therefore necessary to constitute such a culture and to this end, as we have seen, observers suggested the establishment of a wide range of additional social and political institutions. What was missing to make democracy work was a functioning civil society, and hence support for civil society became fashionable. When funding civil society organizations did not provide the 'hoped-for dramatic results', democracy promotion policies turned to deficiencies in the rule of law and began to support judicial reform whose disappointing results in turn led to support for decentralization and this in turn to anticorruption policies (Carothers 2004: 5). In other words, a liberal political culture was to be generated through a range of political and societal institutions – NGOs, parties, and law – widely associated with, or found in, mature liberal democracies.

While this answer to the problem was perfectly in line with liberal theories focusing on political institutions as the source of liberal policies and polities, it failed to account for the paradoxical results of democracy promotion policies. After all, it was not the case that the introduction of elections and other institutions failed entirely. Instead, in many cases the introduction of democratic elections was successful, but contributed to the 'rise of illiberal democracy' (Zakaria 1997). Instead of advancing democratization, elections were in these cases used to validate author-itarian regimes – Russia being a case in point. Electoral competition has also frequently led to renewed civil conflict, for example in Angola and Cambodia. Similarly, civil society associations were successfully established but subsequently used to advance decidedly illiberal policies (de Zeeuw and van de Goor 2006: 276), a free press can and has served, in Rwanda for instance, as a catalyst for civil conflict and even geno-cide (Paris 2004: 63–78), and parties often become vehicles for ethnic or religious competition like in Bosnia or Iraq (Paris 2004: 97–107).

These paradoxical results of democracy promotion policies suggest that institutions – even of the kind usually found in mature liberal democracies – are for the most part vehicles for the organization and expression of existing social and political interests. They certainly do not appear to generate a liberal political culture where it does not exist. In contrast to contemporary liberal theories that treat liberal insti-tutions as a source of liberal culture, however, in Locke's theory the freedom of the individual and hence also a liberal political culture are not constituted by political institutions but rather by private prop-erty. The Lockean theory thus offers an alternative explanation for the paradoxical outcomes of these policies.

The logic of Locke's theory suggests that political institutions advance liberal norms and principles if they are based on a liberal political cul-ture which is in turn the result of individual freedom based on private property. The absence of a liberal political culture thus indicates a lack of individuals constituted through private property. In other words, in a society in which private property is not widely distributed and/or in which the lives and liberties of individuals are based on common prop-erty and a communal division of labor (ethnic, religious, gendered or otherwise), a liberal culture cannot be expected to develop. Instead, in such a situation it makes perfect sense for people to use social and polit-ical institutions like civil society organizations, parties, elections, laws to advance the interests of their respective communities rather than to pursue the protection of private property and individual freedom. In short, the Lockean theory suggests that the reason for the absence of a liberal political culture may be found in the economic organization of society rather than in its political institutions. More importantly, it has the potential to explain the paradoxical results of democracy promotion policies – their successes in establishing liberal political institutions and their failure to generate a viable democratization process.

Though liberal theories focusing on political institutions generally hold that 'economic development' is 'very helpful' for democratization, they nevertheless insist that it is 'neither a necessary nor a sufficient condition for stable democracy' (Fukuyama 1992a: 108). After all, they stress, a hundred years ago liberalism was not at all associated with providing economic benefits and thus 'a "poor democracy" is equally conceivable and possible' (Sartori 1995: 105).[5] Having thus explicitly reduced liberalism to its political institutions, contemporary liberal theory not only tries to establish a liberal culture through such institutions; it can only address the failure of such policies by returning to, and adding more, institutions. In response to the initial failures and in the absence of alternative sources of liberal culture, observers return to the institution of democracy or democratic elections, break these down into further constitutive elements – parties, civil society organizations, free press, legal institutions – and support, demand, or establish this further layer of institutions in an attempt to generate a liberal political culture. This dynamic leads to ever more intrusive policies that compound the second major weakness of liberal democracy promotion policies.

This weakness lies in a fundamental contradiction between the stated emancipatory ends of democracy promotion and the authoritarian means necessary to achieve this end. Once a missing liberal culture is identified as responsible for the failure of democratization, analysts conclude that these societies have to be rebuilt from scratch and thus call for a renewed commitment to state- or nationbuilding (Marten 2002/3; Barton and Crocker 2003; von Hippel 1999; Carothers 2002: 16; Paris 2004: 177). Having identified the need for 'statebuilding' in the Third World, Paris points out that classical liberal theorists all presupposed and recognized the importance of the state: effective government is necessary, and not illiberal, and needs to be put into place in Third World societies (Paris 2004: 46–51, 185f). In practice, this translates into the recommendation to delay elections, to limit political freedoms, to promote 'good' civil society institutions while suppressing its 'bad' manifestations, until the government is stable and the outcome of elections and other forms of liberalization is secure (Paris 2004: 185–204). Occasionally, such intervention is even advocated as a preventive measure in weak states (Rotberg 2002: 94f).

And yet, this solution carries with it its own contradictions. It is, as Paris puts it, 'paradoxical' and 'unfortunate that international officials

---

[5] The notion that a 'poor democracy' is possible does not necessarily contradict the logic of Locke's theory which does not focus on absolute levels of prosperity but rather on the relative distribution of property and other economic benefits in society as a basis for democratization.

must suppress certain forms of political expression in order to build the foundations for a stable and peaceful democracy'; in short, peacebuilders have to act 'illiberally' in the course of establishing a liberal market democracy (Paris 2004: 209). This contradiction between 'liberal' ends and 'illiberal' means, however, is not restricted to peacebuilding policies that entail the use of military force. On the contrary, as Diamond points out, the ideological hegemony of democracy itself is partly based on the 'increasing use of pressure and conditional assistance to promote democratic development' on the part of the Western countries (1996: 35). And the tension between ends and means can be observed in all variants of democracy promotion policies. In some cases, like Cambodia, peacebuilders took over the entire government of the country; in others like Rwanda (desperately necessary) aid was made conditional on political and economic liberalization; in yet others like Iraq and Afghanistan military force and a military occupation were used to effect regime change and to establish liberal institutions. More generally, the establishment and training of police forces has become a standard feature of democracy promotion policies. Even the positive version of direct democracy assistance in the form of funding for elections or civil society organizations cannot escape the basic tension between the goal of enabling the target population to make their own political choices through democratic institutions and the fact that these institutions are funded and established by outsiders.

Moreover, it is important to note that this tension does not just exist on the theoretical level. Rather, the application of these 'illiberal' means directly undermines the 'liberal' ends in practice. Hence, conditional aid makes governments more responsive to donors than to the electorate and thus does not contribute to the development of indigenous democratic practices (De Waal 1997: 628). Intensified policies of statebuilding – entailing long-term intervention and the reconstruction of every aspect of the economic, political, and cultural constitution of target societies – literally undermines the freedom of the population to make their own choices and can only confirm suspicions about foreign domination (Ollapally 1995: 434). And, finally, the use of force – whether in the form of outside military intervention or the establishment of 'democratic' military or police forces in the target state – threatens the freedom of the population. Thus, when the military intervention in Iraq led to criminal violence, civil war, and insurgency, the United States responded by reestablishing the military as a powerful domestic force, the same force on which Nuri al-Maliki's current bid for authoritarian power rests. Similarly, threats to domestic peace and security today emanate frequently from the reformed and retrained Afghan police force.

Hence, the failures of the 'light footprint' of quick and superficial interventions lead democracy promoters to adopt a 'heavy footprint' of sustained and comprehensive intrusion in target societies which only exacerbates the tensions between freedom and oppression, as Paris rightly notes (2010: 343). Yet, there does not appear to be a 'right footprint' since all democracy promotion policies display this tension. Hence, where the democracy transition paradigm fits well – 'in the small number of clearly successful transitions – the aid is not much needed. Where democracy aid is needed most, in many of the grey-zone countries, the paradigm fits poorly', leading Carothers to call for 'the end of the transition paradigm' (Carothers 2004: 180–1). The problem, in other words, appears not so much to lie with the practices of democracy promotion but rather with the theories that guide these practices and fail to account for these tensions.

Here again, Locke's theorization of liberalism provides an alternative that does account for these tensions – albeit without resolving them. Confronted with the challenge of having to establish liberal principles in a nonliberal environment, Locke too advocated the extension of political rights to properly constituted liberal individuals and the denial of those rights to others. The result was liberal despotism – that is, government capable of realizing liberal principles like the protection of private property, individual freedom, and a gradual expansion of political rights through the oppression of nonliberal sections of society – or the passionately antidemocratic liberalism of much of liberal history. This Lockean theory suggests that the reduction of liberalism to democracy or democratic political institutions in contemporary liberal theories is seriously misleading (Hobson 2009). It misses the fact that the realization of liberal principles was, for a long time, only possible by suppressing democracy, as Paris rightly notes. In other words, it is democracy that is a contingent element of liberalism rather than its defining feature while political oppression is an *integral* part of the emergence of liberalism rather than alien to it. Although liberalism has obviously been successfully democratized under certain circumstances, the identification of liberalism with democracy obscures this contingent relationship and thus stands in the way of examining the conditions under which liberalism and democracy become complementary. The failure to identify this contingent relationship between democracy and liberalism, moreover, leads to a third area of weakness generally recognized in democracy promotion policies.

Democracy promotion policies are widely held to be hampered by inconsistent or half-hearted practices on the part of liberal actors. Theoretically, liberal states are expected, as we have seen, to deepen their cooperation with other liberal states and to avoid cooperation with nonliberal states. Yet, in general liberal actors regularly cooperate with nonliberal states in all policy areas. They maintain, for example, strong economic relations with China, engage in military cooperation with Saudi Arabia and political cooperation with Morocco. Liberal states as well as NGOs pour aid into Ethiopia despite its authoritarian government and systematic human rights violations (Hagmann 2012). At the same time, liberal states engage in trade wars with each other, fail to agree on the use of sanctions or military interventions as well as on the necessity or form of a legal regulation of issues ranging from the environment to criminal law. In the particular context of direct democracy promotion in all its forms, liberal actors are accused of a lack of funding, of half-hearted commitments of soldiers, and of poor coordination between different actors (UN, individual states, NGOs). In short, their actions are judged as not measuring up to the demands of liberal principles.

Instead, these inconsistencies are seen as the result of 'illiberal' pursuits. Economic cooperation with nonliberal states puts material self-interest over liberal commitments to democracy. Military and political cooperation with nonliberal states follows power political dictates rather than liberal principles. Aid for authoritarian regimes puts order over justice. The failure to commit sufficient funds or soldiers panders to public opinion rather than liberal norms. Yet, these inconsistencies clearly weaken both concrete projects of democracy promotion and the clear-cut model character of intraliberal relations and the concomitant pressure on nonliberal states. On the basis of this analysis, the only remedy to this situation lies in increasing public pressure on liberal governments to act consistently in accordance with liberal principles; and yet, though these arguments have a constant presence in liberal public discourse, that same public nevertheless generally votes for national economic stability and growth and against the commitment of large numbers of soldiers' lives to the promotion of democracy abroad.

Yet, what appears as inconsistency from the point of view of contemporary liberal theories is perfectly consistent from the perspective of Lockean theory which suggests that the democratization of liberalism is only possible once the majority of the population has acquired a positive stake in upholding liberal institutions. Hence, the maintenance and strengthening of liberal democracy requires the continued provision of material benefits to the population, that is, it requires economic growth. The foreign policies of liberal states thus have to ensure above all conditions for economic growth. Foreign policies of cooperation with nonliberal states that can make some contribution to economic growth (through resources like oil in Saudi Arabia or cheap labor in China, for example) are therefore not illiberal at all. Such foreign policies serve to maintain and strengthen (or even defend) liberalism at home. Moreover, regulating the world economy in accordance with these interests requires power and, on occasion, force. Power politics in general and cooperation with nonliberal states for its purpose in particular is therefore also an integral part of liberalism.

The Lockean theory also explains the less than systematic cooperation of liberal states with each other. Inasmuch as each liberal state needs to pursue economic growth to ensure its political survival, liberal states are competitors. Indeed, as Paris rightly points out, the liberal market economy is by definition competitive (2004: 175). Today, unlike in Locke's time, the main source of surplus value does not lie in land any longer and hence this competition between developed liberal economies does not lead to wars over land. Instead, it leads to trade wars – to conflicts in which each party attempts to ensure the establishment, interpretation, and application of economic rules and regulations in its own favor. The democratic peace thesis is thus right to note the rarity of war between liberal democracies, but mistaken in attributing this 'peace' to democratic institutions.

If such economic conflicts tend to be particularly virulent between powerful liberal states while their bilateral economic relations with weaker nonliberal states appear to unfold comparatively smoothly, this is due to the differential power relations in these cases. While economically powerful states are able to impose treaties biased in their favor onto less powerful states – and are thus happy to have these treaties enforced by their domestic courts – relatively equally matched states are direct competitors and engage in struggle over these issues. Such conflicts are, moreover, exacerbated by democracy because democratic states have to respond to the preferences of their publics and have thus less freedom to compromise. Indeed, democratic institutions and values may well 'pose additional hurdles to liberal states' submission to and compliance with international norms' (Alvarez 2001: 202).

In sum, theories that identify liberalism largely with democratic institutions and norms detect serious inconsistencies and half-hearted commitments to democracy promotion in the practice of liberal actors. This analysis is correct insofar as it argues that these practices contribute to the weakness of democracy promotion policies. What it lacks, however,

is an explanation for the persistent (half-hearted or self-interested) political preferences of liberal publics despite pervasive public debates on the
gap between democratic norms and practices. The Lockean theory suggests, in contrast, that far from being 'illiberal', self-interest based on
private property constitutes the core foundation of liberalism in general
and a matter of survival for democratic liberal states in particular. It suggests, in short, that the practice of democracy promotion on the part of
contemporary liberal democratic states is perfectly consistent with liberal principles and dynamics. Instead, it is the reduction of liberalism to
democracy in contemporary theories that fails to identify core elements
and dynamics of liberalism.

Conclusion

The end of the Cold War provided liberals with an extraordinary opportunity to proactively pursue the realization of liberal principles in
practice. One of the most prominent areas of liberal internationalist
activity lay in the area of democracy promotion. The goal of promoting
democracy was motivated by the general assumption that democracy
was the regime type best suited to the realization of the core liberal value
of individual freedom. But liberal international theories explicitly add to
this goal another one, namely the establishment of peace domestically
and internationally. Both the democratic peace thesis and the democracy transition paradigm explicitly hold that democracy has a pacifying
effect and advocate the international promotion of democracy for this
reason.

The promotion of democracy took a variety of forms in the 1990s
ranging from general diplomatic incentives and pressures to active
democracy assistance, and it played a major role in peacebuilding operations and military interventions. Yet, in all these incarnations, democracy promotion policies, at best, contributed only very little to the
establishment of democracy and/or peace and, at worst, provided institutions shoring up authoritarian governments or contributed to violent
conflict. While these policies often succeeded in changing the institutional arrangements in target states, the goal of a self-perpetuating
democratization process was rarely if ever in evidence. Similarly, while
these policies in the context of peacebuilding and military interventions
sometimes managed to remove particular perpetrators of violence, the
conflict often continued with new protagonists.

But it was the analysis of these disappointing and contradictory outcomes that really brought the failure of liberal democracy promotion
policies into stark relief. The institution of democratic elections did

not lead to democratization, it was argued, because the target societies lacked a liberal political culture which had to be generated by the introduction of further institutions. Yet, the move from the 'light footprint' of introducing elections to the 'heavy footprint' of all around state- and nationbuilding only highlighted the fact that the goal of political participation and freedom was pursued by means of political oppression and outside intervention. Instead of establishing democracy and peace, this dynamic led to authoritarian intervention and resistance. It also required substantial and long-term commitments of material resources and personnel (military as well as civilian) which in turn led to domestic pressure in the intervening states to disengage. The tensions and contradictions between liberal principles and practices thus undermined the project of democracy promotion at every stage.

Yet, while these tensions and contradictions and hence also the policy failures are usually attributed to incompetent, inconsistent, halfhearted, or even 'illiberal' practices, it is actually liberal theory focusing on political institutions that is responsible for much, if not all, of the shortcomings of these policies. Theories identifying liberalism largely with democratic political institutions, first, logically seek to foster liberalism through the introduction of democratic institutions. In the case of failure, such theories offer no other resources but the introduction of a further layer of institutions. Second, for theories identifying liberalism with democratic institutions, the resulting contradiction between freedom and oppression is not only inexplicable but also irresolvable: 'what is the "right" footprint?' (Paris 2010: 343) Meanwhile, since liberal democratic states have democratic institutions, the inconsistent or half-hearted commitment of these actors or their publics can only be explained with reference to a pursuit of 'illiberal' interests – that is, interests that have nothing to do with liberalism defined in terms of democratic institutions. In short, these theories are simply not equipped to provide either a satisfactory explanation of these tensions and contradictions or a solution to them.

The alternative Lockean conception of liberalism, however, does provide an explanation for these tensions at every stage – even if it ultimately fails to provide a satisfactory solution. Unlike the democratic peace thesis or the democracy transition paradigm, the Lockean theory suggests that the core of liberalism lies in the mutually constitutive dynamics of private property, individual freedom, and government by consent. The absence of democratic government thus suggests the lack of a liberal political culture established by individuals whose freedom is based on private property. The establishment of democracy in such situations does not require the introduction of democratic elections but rather the constitution of liberal individuals and a liberal political culture through the distribution of private property (or equivalent benefits). In the absence of such a foundation, the introduction of democratic elections and other related institutions must logically be expected to lead to precisely those paradoxical outcomes that democracy promotion policies produced: namely the expression and pursuit of interests generated by a different economic organization through democratic institutions. Hence, Carothers' injunction that in cases where the transition paradigm fitted well, the aid was not needed, while in cases where aid was needed, the paradigm did not fit (Carothers 2004: 180–1).

The very same dynamic of the constitution of liberalism also explains the coexistence of freedom and oppression that characterizes democracy promotion policies. According to Locke's theory and in line with the historical development of liberalism, the establishment of liberalism in a nonliberal environment requires the political oppression of nonliberal forces. Such a despotic liberal government can then pursue liberal policies – foremost the privatization of property – until a wider distribution of property in society (or equivalent benefits) has led to the development of a liberal political culture and makes the extension of political rights possible. In other words, freedom and oppression go hand in hand and are an integral part of the constitution of liberalism in nonliberal environments.

Finally, this dynamic accounts for the inconsistent behavior of liberal states and publics. Once liberalism is democratized, the survival of liberal governments depends on the continued provision of those economic benefits that provide the majority of the population with a stake in the liberal system. Hence, the pursuit of economic interests may be self-interested – but it is not at all 'illiberal'. And since the pursuit of those economic interests requires power, power politics is also a constitutive element of liberalism. The Lockean theory suggests, hence, that the pursuit of these interests – even if it waters down the commitment to democracy promotion – is perfectly consistent with liberalism. Such policies only appear inconsistent when seen through the lens of a partial conception of liberalism.

All three sets of tensions characteristic of democracy promotion policies thus find an explanation in the Lockean conception of liberalism. This explanation also has some constructive implications for democracy promotion policies. First, if correct, it suggests that an analysis of the socioeconomic conditions in target states may provide good indications for the prospects of democratization. Second, it suggests that policies encouraging a wider distribution of property in society may be more conducive to democratization than the introduction of political institution. Third, it highlights that democracy promotion policies inevitably involve an element of oppression, and thus provides liberal actors with a realistic assessment of the requirements and implications of these policies (to endorse or reject), and it provides target societies with realistic expectations.

In the end, therefore, the fallacy or basic problem of liberal political approaches, both in theory and practice, is indeed one of fragmentation and of misattributing the core characteristics of liberalism to one of its contingent expressions: democracy and liberal political institutions more generally. The Lockean theory, in contrast, highlights the gaping hole at the core of these theories, and hence also policies. It suggests that the economic dimension plays a constitutive role in and for liberalism, and that it is the absence of this dimension from the 'political' liberal theories today that accounts for much of their analytical and prescriptive weaknesses. Liberal theories and practices focusing on the economic dimension will therefore be explored in the next chapter.

5
Economics

Introduction

Liberal approaches focusing on political institutions, as we have seen in the previous chapter, tend to be called 'democratic' – democratic peace thesis, democracy transition paradigm – after the most important institution they identify with liberalism. In contrast, theories and policies focusing on the economic dimension of liberalism are usually clearly designated with the term 'liberal'. Hence, the last few decades have seen a return of classical liberal economic policies broadly consisting of a 'liberalization' of markets, a deregulation of trade, and the privatization of communal property – together making up 'neoliberal' economic policies. This terminology suggests that economy does indeed play a crucial – and arguably continuous – role in and for liberalism.

Neoliberal economic policies became dominant during the 1980s in the North and began to play an increasingly important role in development policies. Nevertheless, the end of the Cold War provided the opportunity of extending liberal economic principles into the planned economies of Eastern Europe and to implement them more thoroughly in the global South which had up to this point been able to retain some independence by exploiting the competition between the capitalist West and the communist East. In short, the fall of the Berlin wall provided an opportunity to realize liberal economic principles on a truly global scale. This development and its political and cultural consequences were captured by the term 'globalization' which defined not only the academic but also the political discourse of the 1990s.

The economic policies underpinning this 'globalization of liberalism' (Hovden and Keene 2001) thus focused on the institutionalization of neoliberal economic principles in the world economy at large, including their reassertion in liberal states, on the alignment of development policies with neoliberal principles and on the spread of these principles into formerly communist states. These goals were pursued, however, largely by and through political institutions. Moreover, although the immediate goals of these policies were economic – economic growth and prosperity – they were also expected to provide the basis for political stability, democratization, and international cooperation and peace. This close relationship between politics and economics is captured by the widely used term *political economy*. Yet, as we shall see, liberal theories of political economy invariably take economic assumptions as their starting point and exhibit an uneasy and often times contradictory relationship to their own political dimension, hence the title 'Economics' for this chapter.

I will first provide a brief summary of the main assumptions of liberal economic theories that underpinned the policies of the post-Cold War order. The basic assumptions of neoliberal or neoclassical economic theory can be found, as the name suggests, in classical economic theory. These assumptions came to shape development economics and they played a role in the economic strand of the democracy transition paradigm. The second part of the chapter describes the policies inspired by these theories and investigates their outcomes. Many of these policies, I will show, were vigorously, if inconsistently, pursued. The results of these policies, however, rarely lived up to expectations. Economic growth was not impressive and coupled with economic and financial crises; the gap between rich and poor individuals and states was increasing; and political stability, democratization, and peaceful cooperation remained largely elusive. These paradoxical outcomes will be analyzed in the third part. They are due, I will suggest, to two core weaknesses of liberal economic theories and policies: their failure to recognize the political basis of liberal economics as well as their failure to recognize the inherently international nature of liberal economics.

Liberal economic theories

Liberal economic theories are, like other liberal theories, divided into a rich array of different strands: classical, neoclassical or neoliberal, Keynesian, monetarist, Austrian, rational expectation, to mention just a few. Despite this variety, all liberal economic theories share a number of core assumptions that have not changed much since they were developed by classical political economists (Wolf 2004: 45; Shimko

2005: 149).[1] Moreover, it was a return to classical economic theory – most frequently called neoliberalism – that defined the post-Cold War period. Hence, I will first set out the classical assumptions of liberal economic theory and then show how these were applied to the world economy at large as well as to its three core regions: the First, Second, and Third Worlds.

'The right of all individuals to own and use property freely, subject to well-defined law-governed constraints' is the 'bedrock' of a liberal society (Wolf 2004: 25). And, as we have already seen, not only did Locke regard this as a natural right, and necessary for the constitution and reproduction of 'man' as a free human being, but he also assumed that the division of the original common into private property had already taken place in the state of nature. This property-owning individual thus provides the starting point for liberal economic theory. According to Adam Smith, this individual has the natural inclination to 'truck, barter and exchange one thing for another' (Smith 1952: 6). Individuals try to improve their lot by exchanging goods and services – that is, markets spring up spontaneously.

Within the market context, the law of supply and demand regulates prices and leads to the most efficient use of resources. That is, a product in high demand will become more expensive, thus providing an incentive to produce it while a product in low demand can only be sold for a low price thus removing such incentives. Hence, while the price and production of individual goods varies, the system itself ultimately balances supply and demand. Crucially, however, it is individual self-interest 'and not that of society' which paradoxically produces public goods: 'the study of his (the individual's, BJ) own advantage naturally, or rather necessarily, leads him to prefer that employment which is most advantagous to the society' (Smith 1952: 193). The individual is thus 'led by an invisible hand to promote an end which has no part of his intention' and by doing so promotes the good of society 'more effectually' than if intended to promote it (Smith 1952: 194). Once established, the market encourages the division of labor which enhances productivity and the most efficient use of resources; that is, it raises production and lowers prices and thus produces wealth – a wealth that ultimately benefits society as a whole.

---

[1] Core statements of liberal (political) economy can be found in Krugman and Obstfeld (2002), Friedman and Friedman (1962), Strange (1988), Gilpin (1987) and for an intellectual history of International Political Economy, see Cohen (2008).

In principle, Smith argues, the same market mechanism also works between nations. It provides consumers with the possibility of buying the cheapest product and thus provides incentives for different nations to invest in those industries in which they have an advantage. While Smith was thinking in terms of absolute advantage, David Ricardo subsequently developed the theory of relative comparative advantage. He argued that even if a country had a comparative advantage in the production of two or more products, it should nevertheless focus on the production of that product in which it has the greatest advantage. 'This simple notion of the universal benefits of specialization based on comparative costs remains the linchpin of liberal trade theory' (Gilpin 1987: 174) and establishes free trade as a core principle of liberal economic theory. 'According to this liberal and generous system, therefore, the most advantageous method in which a landed nation can raise up artificers, manufacturers, and merchants of its own is to grant the most perfect freedom of trade to the artificers, manufacturers, and merchants of all other nations' (Smith 1952: 293).

Government is thus ideally not to interfere with the market – domestic or international – since it will never be able to grasp needs and wants as well as individual consumers themselves and because any form of interference – through subsidies, tariffs and so on – will artificially increase the prices of products and thus provide incentives for inefficient production. In other words, government interference distorts the perfect workings of the market mechanism and thus harms the consumer through higher prices as well as society at large by lowering the overall production of wealth (Wolf 2004: 80–2).

Nevertheless, government has a role to play in this system. First, according to Smith, it has 'the duty of protecting the society from violence and invasion of other independent societies; secondly, the duty of … establishing an exact administration of justice; and, thirdly, the duty of erecting and maintaining certain public works and certain public institutions which it can never be for the interest of any individual … to erect and maintain; because the profit could never repay the expense …, though it may frequently do much more than repay it to a great society' (Smith 1952: 300). In other words, government has to provide a legal system that ensures the smooth working of the market as well as public goods that do not lend themselves to profit-making and external defense. Despite these important tasks of government, liberal economic theory in principle insists on the separation of economics and politics – on keeping the state out of the economic sphere as much as possible. 'Liberals believe that economics is progressive and politics retrogressive'

(Gilpin 1987: 31; Wolf 2004: 82). Yet, the progressive nature of economics can also have a beneficial effect on politics. Though classical liberal economists like Smith still reflected on the possibility of war arising out of economic competition between states (Wyatt-Walter 1996), today's liberal economists generally hold that the free market economy unites individuals and private actors through exchange and interdependence and thus has the potential to transcend political division. Indeed, free trade and an open world market are seen as a 'source of peaceful relations among nations' (Gilpin 1987: 31; Wolf 2004: 33). Similarly, as mentioned in Chapter 3, while classical liberal authors (including political economists like Ricardo) were opposed to democracy because the poor were not benefiting from liberal rules and could thus not be expected to uphold them, today a market economy is widely seen as a necessary (though not sufficient) condition for a stable and enduring democracy (Wolf 2004: xiii; Bhagwati 1992: 40; Berger 1992: 11; Huntington 1991: 30). Market economies, after all, are based on and thus support the freedom of the individual which is also reflected in the democratic system. Moreover, the prosperity produced by established market economies benefits all members of society – albeit unequally – and thus spreads the interest in maintaining liberal economic rules to all members of society.

In sum, classical liberal economic theory is based on the assumption that private property, the market mechanism, and free trade (domestically and internationally) lead to the most efficient and progressive use of resources and thus to the production of 'the wealth of nations'. In order to realize these promises, therefore, liberal economic policies need to protect and extend private property, reduce the interference of government in domestic and international markets, and provide conducive conditions for trade.

While these policies are expected to result in an increase in production and wealth for society as a whole, liberal economic theory does not promise an equal distribution of this wealth. On the contrary, in the short term the market mechanism creates winners and losers by driving 'comparatively inefficient producers out of business', by devaluing investments and costing jobs in relatively inefficient industries (Shimko 2005: 161). Despite these inequalities, however, it promises to raise the income of all members of society in the long run: economic growth and lower prices enable even poorer sections of society to increase consumption.

These core assumptions have subsequently been refined – to some extent in response to original weaknesses, and to some extent in response to historical developments in production and distribution. Thus, economists now take into account not only the cost of labor but also factors such as the availability of capital and resources as well as levels of management and technology (Gilpin 1987: 175). Recent developments have also added the issue of intra-industry and intra-firm trade, the size of markets as well as foreign direct investment and production abroad. In light of these developments, the theory of comparative advantage 'has lost some of its relevance and predictive power' and the argument for free trade, accordingly, has also become less relevant (Gilpin 1987: 178). Despite these developments, however, 'liberal economists maintain their basic commitment to the mutual benefits of free trade, to specialization based upon comparative advantage, and to the virtues of a global territorial division of labor' (Gilpin 1987: 179).

While all liberal economic theories share these core assumptions, they differ with regard to the relative weight they give to the principles of equality and liberty or, to put it economically, with regard to the extent of government intervention they tolerate. Before the recent return of classical liberal economics, economic theory and policy was dominated by Keynesianism – in response to the depression of the 1930s and its contribution to World War II. Keynes argued for a greater role of government in regulating the economy. In particular, fiscal and monetary policies were to be used to support full employment which in turn would increase demand and thus lead to economic growth. This prioritizes the principle of equality and leads to a mixed economy – based on private property, free markets, and free trade, but tolerating a greater degree of government regulation. Keynesian economics dominated the domestic policies of established liberal states and was reflected in the 'embedded liberalism' of the international economic order until the 1970s (Ruggie 1982). While the Bretton Woods Institutions (IBRD, IMF, GATT) provided incentives for a liberalization of the world economy, they tolerated government intervention, leading to the development of the welfare state or social democratic employment policies. Despite thus cushioning the detrimental effect of liberal economic policies and contributing to political stability, Keynesianism, like other liberal economic theories, is in principle 'committed to the market and the prize mechanism as the most efficacious means for organizing domestic and international economic relations' (Gilpin 1987: 27). The stagnation of the world economy in the 1970s led to a return of classical liberal economic theory – neoliberalism – from the 1980s onwards.

The logic of neoliberal economic theories demand, thus, a liberalization of the world market in order to encourage a freer flow of capital as well as trade in goods and services and free floating exchange rates. This in turn requires the deregulation of labor and capital markets within liberal states as well as the privatization of state-owned industries and services. Such policies were expected to trigger economic growth in general and raise GDP in particular countries. Albeit unequally, these gains were nevertheless supposed to trickle down to poorer nations as well as individuals within states. Politically, further integration of the world market would produce increased economic interdependence and thus contribute to international cooperation and peaceful relations.

These core assumptions of neoliberal economic theory also came to inform development economics.[2] While many Third World states had previously pursued the goal of industrialization through the protection of infant industries (or import substitution policies), such policies were now blamed for the lack of economic progress (Williams 2012: 114). From a neoliberal point of view, this government intervention was responsible for poor economic performance and compounded by the fact that developing states seemed to lack the human, administrative, and financial resources to perform even those tasks efficiently that were seen as the legitimate concern of the state: foreign policy, a legal system, administration of a monetary and financial system. The basic but powerful assumptions of liberal economic theory, it was argued, also held for developing states: Economic rationality – cost-benefit analysis – is universally valid and hence people everywhere are expected to react to price changes in the same way. Markets are expected to produce socially desirable goods. Individuals are in a better position to judge their needs than planners. And, of course, government intervention distorts the market mechanism and leads to undesirable outcomes (Williams 2012: 113).

On the basis of this analysis, neoliberal development economics called for structural adjustment in developing countries which included 'a liberalization of domestic markets by reducing price controls and allowing competition; the privatization of state-owned enterprises; reducing government expenditures; ensuring macroeconomic stability, particularly reducing inflation and government deficits; and liberalizing external trade by ending exchange rate controls and import controls' (Williams 2012: 117). These goals were to be achieved through conditional lending – that is, aid was made conditional on the commitment to implement such reforms.

---

[2] For traditional approaches, see Lal (1983), Bauer (1981), Little (1982).

In addition to these more narrow economic reforms, development theory from the late 1980s onwards called for institutional reform or 'good governance'. Recognizing that institutions can either hinder or help market transactions – and in many Third World countries institutions were thought to stand in the way of a smooth flow of market transactions – neoliberal development theory called for accountability, transparency, a greater role for civil society. And, emboldened by the end of the Cold War, bilateral donors increasingly demanded not just 'good governance' but democracy and respect for human rights as a precondition for development aid (Williams 2012: 119).

This 'political' dimension of liberal economic theory also played an important role in the democracy transition paradigm.[3] While, as discussed in the previous chapter, one strand of this paradigm focused on the establishment of liberal political institutions, another was squarely based on liberal economic theory. The introduction of liberal economic principles in the countries of the former Soviet Bloc in particular (but also elsewhere) was expected to contribute to democratization. This expectation is based on an analysis of the historical development of liberal democratic states. Originally, liberals were fiercely opposed to the introduction of democracy on the grounds that giving the vote to the poor would simply result in the plunder of the rich, and hence in the end of civilization (Plattner 2008: 64–5). Thus, both Macaulay and Ricardo were ready to extend suffrage only to those social groups 'which cannot be supposed to have an interest in overturning the right to property' (cited in Przeworski 1992: 53; Plattner 2008: 65). And yet, over time the protection of private property and the resulting technological and economic development made possible a wider spread of property within society, and consequently an extension of the franchise to wider sections of society. In other words, the history of established liberal democracies demonstrates that the liberal economy lives up to its promises of generating economic growth and leading to a wider distribution of property within society.

What is more, this history also demonstrates that such development is possible even under unfavorable conditions. While America was blessed with abundant land, a small population, and the absence of a traditional propertied class, Europe, in contrast, suffered from a comparatively limited supply of land, a large population, and the presence of a

---

[3] It is explored by Przeworski et al. (2000), Mousseau (2000), Huntington (1991), Berger (1992), Bhagwati (1992), Schmitter (1994), Acemoglu and Robinson (2006).

traditional propertied class. The more favorable conditions in America led to rapid economic development but, despite abundant obstacles, economic development ultimately also occurred in Europe. Observers conclude, therefore, that economic development is, in principle, possible anywhere (Plattner 2008: 68; Huntington 1991: 33).

The prosperity produced by such economic development is in turn conducive to democratization. The market economy is seen as the only economic system that generates a rise in incomes and thus produces an educated middle class with liberal values (Wolf 2004: 30–1). And these values in turn are conducive to and reflected in the democratic political system. In short, liberalism 'is the bedrock of democracy at home and peaceful relations abroad' (Wolf 2004: 36). The economic approach thus recognizes the constitutive role of private property, or economic development more generally, for the constitution and democratization of liberalism. 'Few relationships between social, economic, and political phenomena are stronger than that between the level of economic development and the existence of democratic politics' (Huntington 1991: 30; Przeworski et al. 2000: 273). Conversely, 'poverty is a principal – probably *the* principal – obstacle to democratic development' (Huntington 1991: 31).

The economic transition paradigm thus establishes a direct connection between core liberal economic principles and democratization (as well as peaceful international relations). On the basis of this theory, then, the spread of liberal market economies is expected to lead to economic growth and rising incomes which constitute the liberal individual who then demands (and can safely be granted) the right to political participation. The spread of this economic system into the countries of Eastern Europe and its consolidation in the Third World is thus expected to contribute to the establishment and consolidation of democracy.

In sum, the core assumptions of liberal economic theory follow quite faithfully Locke's thesis and that of subsequent liberal political economists like Smith and Ricardo. They begin with the claim that private property constitutes a natural right of all individuals who are disposed to 'truck and barter', that is exchange their various products and thus establish a market. The market, producing an equilibrium between supply and demand, is the most efficient means to organize production and distribution of material goods and thus leads to increased production and a rise in absolute incomes. This prosperity in turn constitutes liberal individuals, a liberal political culture, and hence also democracy. While government is necessary to provide the legal framework for the market as well as a few public goods, its interference in the market has to be kept to a minimum lest it distort this mechanism and result in suboptimal outcomes. Moreover, the theory of comparative advantage implies that an international division of labor and free trade – that is a free world market – can reproduce these positive effects for the international sphere where the resultant economic interdependence also leads to peaceful cooperation.

(Neo)liberal economic theory thus advocates liberalization, privatization, and deregulation as a means to free the market from undue political interference and to release its potential for economic growth and rising incomes. Liberal economic principles, moreover, are universally valid and hence such policies will produce positive results in established liberal economies, developing countries, and formerly planned economies alike. In addition, such policies make a positive contribution to the spread of democracy as well as to the development of international peace and cooperation since they provide the basis for a liberal political culture domestically and interdependence – and hence mutual cooperation – internationally.

Liberal economic policies

The general aim to restructure the world economy in accordance with neoliberal principles was widely translated into policy by liberal states from the 1980s onwards. The trigger, or opportunity, for such a restructuring arose out of the economic crisis of the 1970s when stagflation on the one hand and the debt crisis of the Third World on the other undermined the previous Keynesian settlement – for example, the Bretton Woods institutions which had been anchored in the dollar/gold convertibility. The end of this convertibility in 1971 led within two years to a return of floating currencies, and thus minimized control of capital (Rosenberg 2005: 44–5). Meanwhile, the economic crisis coupled with the oil price hikes of the 1970s meant that many developing countries were unable to repay their debts, which in turn undermined the stability of their creditors, many of them Northern Banks.

In order to confront this economic crisis, a return to classical liberal economic principles was widely advocated and politically driven in particular by the governments of Reagan and Thatcher. Despite considerable differences, the policies involved a systematic privatization of state-owned industries and public services like education, health care, water and electricity supplies, public transport; a switch from progressive to regressive taxation thus strengthening the power of private capital and a deregulation of the labor market. Internationally, the debt crisis provided the opportunity to align the policies of the IMF and World Bank with these neoliberal economic principles (Rosenberg 2005: 45).

In order to enable developing states to repay their loans, the IMF began to lend money to these states tied to stringent conditions. These 'structural adjustment' policies or loans entailed a number of key elements that were subsequently summarized under the heading 'Washington consensus', including fiscal austerity in the form of reduced government spending (or less often increased revenues), reductions of government subsidies, reduction of tariffs and other import barriers, the easing of restrictions on foreign direct investment, and the privatization of government-owned industries (Shimko 2005: 175). These policies were based on the classical liberal assumption that private property and unimpeded markets provided the most effective way to trigger economic growth and thus also increasing incomes for states and individuals alike. Accordingly, neoliberal economic policies were designed to remove political interference: to widen market mechanisms to previously state-owned sectors and to open domestic markets to international competition and investment (Shimko 2005: 176).

Yet, it was the fall of the Soviet Union that established these liberal economic principles as 'the only game in town' and provided an unprecedented opportunity to spread these principles not only to Eastern European states but also to much of the Third World. While many Second and Third World states embarked on more or less extensive reforms in order to avoid being left behind, Western liberal states took advantage of the new opportunities. Thus by 2000 the United States had signed over 300 new trade agreements 'breaking all previous records' (Rosenberg 2005: 58). More generally, the early 1990s saw the institutionalization of these principles in a variety of organizations: the EU single market (1992), the inaugural summit of APEC (1993), NAFTA and ASEAN as well as the conclusion of the Uruguay Round of the GATT and its transformation into the WTO (1994). Unmistakably reflecting liberal economic assumptions, principles, and expectations, the preamble of the WTO states that it aims to raise living standards, ensure full employment, increase incomes, expand production and trade, efficiently use the world's resources through 'the substantial reduction of tariffs and other barriers to trade' (WTO 1994). In contrast to the previous Gatt regime, the WTO includes a Dispute Settlement

Mechanism and thus the means to enforce these neoliberal policies.[4] In addition, the TRIPS agreement strengthened property rights and extended them into the sphere of intellectual property (May 2000; Sell 2003).

There is no question, then, that liberal economic principles did, indeed, inspire highly influential foreign policies world wide. These policies, moreover, especially over the longer period from the 1980s onwards, were successful in shifting power from labor to capital, in deregulating the world economy and providing it with new institutions (or old institutions pursuing new policy agendas), in privatizing vast assets and fostering the international trade of goods and services, and in extending the reach of neoliberal economic principles to the countries of the former Soviet Bloc as well as many Third World states. And yet, the widespread pursuit and institutionalization of liberal economic policies also exhibits some unevenness. While insisting on the lowering of trade barriers – especially for industrial goods and services as well as capital – liberal states, notably the EU, the United States, and Japan, were not ready to apply these principles to the agricultural sector. Thus, 'perhaps the greatest of all scandals remains the treatment of agriculture' in which rich countries pay their farmers subsidies vastly exceeding any equivalent support in developing countries resulting in a decidedly unequal playing field, and of course presenting a serious barrier to free trade in agricultural products (Wolf 2004: 215). Moreover, while such protectionist policies in the agricultural sector are particularly stark (and often highlighted because of their detrimental effect on poor countries), in fact liberal states are incredibly creative in developing a rich variety of tools – from environmental through cultural to health regulations – to protect a wide range of domestic industries. It is these tools that are at the heart of the constant 'trade wars' between the EU and the United States and which constitute much of the case load for dispute settlement in the WTO. And it is this disjuncture between policies designed to liberalize trade and their institutionalization in the world economy and systematic attempts to nevertheless protect domestic industries which advocates of neoliberal economic policies identify and decry as 'hypocrisy' (Wolf 2004: 215).

---

[4] On the WTO dispute settlement mechanism and the 'constitutionalization' of international economic law, see Cass (2001), Jackson (1997), Keohane et al. (2000).

Moreover, the success of neoliberal economic policies must be measured by the extent to which these policies achieve their stated economic and political goals. Concretely, these policies are supposed to lead to economic growth and rising incomes. These economic achievements in turn are expected to contribute to political stability, democracy, and peaceful cooperation.

Economically, the early 1990s saw considerable growth, for example in capital flows: a sixfold increase in private finance (Rosenberg 2005: 50). Moreover, the opening up of markets in the former Soviet Union, Eastern Europe, China, and India gave a boost to trade as well. However, these developments did not necessarily lead to the expected economic growth: instead, overall economic growth rates in the period from 1980 to 2000 actually slowed down (Berry and Sevrieux 2006). This growth, inasmuch as it did take place, moreover, did not result in a general – albeit unequal – rise in incomes.[5] Instead, while the income of the rich has risen remarkably during that period, the income of the vast majority of the population has stagnated or declined – within and between states. While observers differ considerably on how to measure inequality, even advocates of economic 'globalization' attest to the growing inequality: while gaps in living standards 100 years ago were 10:1, by 2004 they had grown to 75:1 (Wolf 2004: 314). In general, the results range from some highly successful to apparently hopeless cases. Income disparities are rising and it seems to be very difficult in some cases to break 'the bonds of poverty' (Przeworski et al. 2000: 277). Indeed, so pronounced has this increasing inequality become that it has led, even in rich countries, to political resistance in the form of the Occupy movements.

Similarly, instead of contributing to the transfer of technology, making intellectual products available through the market mechanism, the TRIPS agreement is widely seen as a 'rent-extraction device' that undermines the ability of (not only poor) states to educate their population and to provide for public health (Wolf 2004: 216–7; Bhagwati 2004: 183–5). Indeed, the fact that generic drugs especially for the treatment of AIDS/HIV under the TRIPS rules had become too expensive for poor countries eventually led to the negotiation of exceptions to the normal patent rules.

More broadly, neoliberal economic policies triggered one economic crisis after another – some of them national like the Swedish and Finnish

---

[5] Observers widely agree that there has been a slight decrease in absolute poverty rates which, however, is almost entirely due to the economic growth of China and India and does not reflect rising incomes more generally.

banking crises of the 1990s or the Mexican economic crisis in 1994, some regional like the Asian financial crisis in 1997, and some global like the recent financial crisis and global recession since 2008. In response to these crises, governments now widely scramble to re-regulate economic, and especially financial, markets, hence attributing these crises to precisely those neoliberal policies that had previously been offered as a solution. Moreover, liberal economists concur with this assessment by insisting on the centrality of the state for economic globalization (Wolf 2004: 16) and calling for a complex set of new policies and institutions to manage 'globalization' (Bhagwati 2004: 239).

Overall, then, while liberal economic principles were indeed widely translated into policy and institutionalized in the world economy, liberal states themselves tend to engage in protectionist policies in certain key areas. Instead of leading to sustainable economic growth, these policies have triggered a wide array of economic and financial crises culminating in a global recession (Blond 2008). And while they were indeed successful in raising the income of some individuals and societies, this did not as expected lift the overall income levels. Instead, in rich and poor countries alike the incomes of the vast majority of the population have either stagnated or fallen over this period. While these policies have indeed created employment in some areas, their price all too often was unemployment in others. In light of these polarizing economic results, moreover, neoliberal economic policies did not contribute to political stability and cooperation either but instead in many cases led to resistance and political upheaval.

These decidedly uneven results of neoliberal economic policies for the world economy as a whole, moreover, are perfectly in line with those of neoliberal development policies. Though conditions for structural adjustment were widely written into IMF loans, these policies were often not, or only partially, implemented by recipient states (Williams 2012: 121) and in those cases where they were implemented, the results were disappointing. Assessing its own structural adjustment policies, the IMF lists growth rates of 1.5 percent during the 1980s, followed by 0.3 percent in the early 1990s and 1 percent by the mid-1990s. Meanwhile, the World Bank found 'no evidence for a direct effect of structural adjustment on growth' and other studies even link these policies to a reduction of growth (Shimko 2005: 184). Even if one adopts the IMF's own assessment, therefore, the economic aim of structural adjustment policies – economic growth and rising incomes that would enable developing states to repay their loans – has not been achieved. Indeed, a comparison between countries that adopted these policies with those that did not suggests that IMF conditions at least on occasion had a detrimental effect on the economic recovery of client states. Hence, during the Asian financial crisis Thailand, South Korea, and Malaysia all experienced problems in paying back loans. While the former two accepted an IMF loan and implemented adjustment policies which led to a decline in GDP and rising unemployment, Malaysia refused and subsequently resolved its problems without suffering a similar fate (Shimko 2005: 184). In sum, the application of neoliberal economic principles in development policies hardly achieved even their narrowly defined economic goals.

In addition, structural adjustment policies were widely criticized for their detrimental impact on the environment, on indigenous populations, and on women in particular and they came to be seen as a serious meddling of multilateral or bilateral donors in the internal affairs of developing states. In light of these criticisms and their poor results, structural adjustment policies were increasingly seen as illegitimate. Analyzing these problems, especially in Africa, the World Bank came to the conclusion that indigenous cultures and political institutions stood in the way of the kind of rational economic actions presupposed by liberal economic theory. It thus developed a 'good governance' agenda that required 'participation, accountability, legitimacy' or, in short, a liberal public sphere as a precondition for development aid (Williams and Young 1994: 88; Williams 2008). With the end of the Cold War, moreover, prior strategic reasons for development aid had vanished. In order to rally support for continuing development aid, therefore, 'proponents reinvigorated the crusade to use aid to spread deeply rooted American ideals about democracy, liberty and good government' (Moore and Robinson 1994: 143). Similar arguments underpinned the bilateral development agenda of other states. In Britain, 'ethical foreign policy' tied foreign aid to good governance which variously included respect for human rights, democracy, low military expenditure while Germany exploited the vagueness of this definition by adding market-oriented economic policies to the list (Moore and Robinson 1994: 146–9). In short, the failure of structural adjustment policies that were focused on the economic sphere was now seen to have its roots – perfectly in line with liberal economic thought – in the imperfections of the political environment and institutions. The end of the Cold War opened up the opportunity to transform political institutions in the Third World in line with liberal principles and hence the promotion of market democracy came to dominate the agenda: democratization, the liberalization of the public sphere and civil society became conditions for economic aid; the introduction of market democracy was hailed as the answer to civil wars and conflict and played a crucial role in UN peacekeeping operations during the 1990s (Paris 2004).

Yet, the outcome of these policies was, again, rather mixed. First of all, liberal states did not consistently provide aid to 'well governed' states but continued to support strategic allies and/or engage in large arms sales even though this undermined the 'good governance' agenda. Secondly, while many countries scrambled to introduce democratic elections, these rarely led to stable liberal democracies. The majority were soon either backsliding into authoritarianism or became 'illiberal democracies' (Carothers 2002; Zakaria 1997). Thirdly, in those cases in which civil conflict was rooted in economic grievances, the focus on political institutions was unable to resolve the conflict and instead simply pushed violence from the public into the private sphere (Paris 2004: 114–33). In other cases, the push for democratization and a liberal public sphere played an important role in exacerbating or rekindling conflict (Paris 2004: 56–7). Finally, there is no indication that 'good governance' leads to economic growth as the World Bank implied. Indeed, none of the East Asian countries that achieved impressive economic growth and a successful integration into the world market did so on the basis of 'good governance'. On the contrary, the governments of China, Taiwan, South Korea, Singapore clearly did not live up to the criteria of 'good governance'.

Liberal economic theory also played a tremendously important role in the transition of the former communist states to market democracies. The end of the Cold War and the interests of Eastern European states not only in catching up economically but also in aligning themselves politically to the West meant that their transition to market democracies were strongly influenced by liberal economic policies. In order to achieve this aim, Eastern European states, including Russia, had to privatize government-owned industries, establish stock exchanges and capital markets, relax exchange controls, cap inflation, reduce state expenditure, and modernize their banking systems (Russell 2001: 48). Such policies are obviously perfectly in line with liberal economic principles and they were strongly encouraged by the West, not just politically but also economically. All Eastern European countries, including Russia, received huge IMF loans in support of these policies, and the latter was even invited to join the G7 (Russell 2001: 49).

This opening up of the Eastern European economies to liberal economic principles was in many ways, at least at a first glance, successful: none of these countries has returned to the planned economy of the past and all have been, to a greater or lesser degree, integrated into the liberal world economy as well as, in many cases, into particular Western institutions like the EU or NATO. However, much of the production of the former communist states lacked competitiveness on the world market and hence this transition was fraught with difficulties. While it opened up these economies to Western goods and services, it hardly allowed them to sell their own products on the world market, thus establishing more dependency than interdependency. Consequently, living standards during the first decade after transition fell, unemployment was high at the same time as previously taken-for-granted social services were scrapped. Despite the introduction of democracy, inequality was increasing in Eastern European countries. Liberal economic theory suggests, however, that such weaknesses may disappear in the longer run (Gradstein and Milanovic 2004).

At closer inspection, however, most of these countries now constitute mixed economies and there are profound asymmetries both within and between them. While some Eastern European states have more liberal market economies than Western states, others retain considerable elements of the prior planned economies. While some sections of society in those states have become incredibly wealthy, others have been economically and socially marginalized. Despite these social costs, however, on the surface, these states appear to have made a successful transition to democracy. Yet this transition has arguably as much to do with push as with pull factors. That is, the desire of the Eastern European countries to extricate themselves not just from the economic but more importantly from the political 'embrace' of the Soviet Union/Russia and hence their aim to join the EU and/or NATO has no doubt played a crucial role in keeping their development in the direction of market democracies largely on track. Indeed, even with these push/pull factors in place, a number of these countries – currently Romania, Hungary and Bulgaria – clearly 'strain to build democracy' and raise concerns in EU circles (Bilefsky 2012). Where this offer of joining Western institutions was not available or desired, namely in Russia itself, the introduction of a liberal market economy has led to extreme economic inequality and to an 'authoritarian democracy' that does not live up to the expectations of liberal theory. According to Freedom House data, Russia is in 2012 categorized as 'not free' and 54 percent of the population of Central and Eastern Europe and Eurasia live under unfree regimes (Freedom House 2012).

In sum, then, (neo)liberal economic theory was widely translated into policies from the 1980s onwards and the end of the Cold War provided an opportunity to spread these policies to wider regions of the world and to implement them more thoroughly in the domestic and international context. Nevertheless, such policies were generally pursued in an inconsistent manner: neoliberal rules were widely implemented and pursued in and through international organizations even while liberal states themselves continued to engage in protectionist policies and developing states implemented these policies only in a patchy manner. Moreover, their economic goals – growth and rising incomes for individuals and states alike – were not generally achieved. Economic growth was slow over that period and accompanied by a series of economic and financial crises. Moreover, income inequalities within and between states were increasing. The political aims of stable democratic domestic regimes and peaceful cooperation internationally were also largely elusive. While many states introduced elections, these often came to play a supportive role for authoritarian regimes and at times contributed to internal conflict. Internationally, moreover, neoliberal economic policies do not appear to have contributed much to more peaceful and cooperative international order. Domestic instability, civil wars in many parts of the world, including Europe, UN peacebuilding operations, the wars in Iraq and Afghanistan, the war on terror, and the concomitant securitization of international trade and travel suggest instead a rather volatile international order. The reasons for these disappointing results of neoliberal economic policies must therefore now be explored.

Analysis

Not only opponents but also advocates of neoliberal economic policies widely acknowledge and analyze the weaknesses or failures of these policies. These analyses are themselves based on the core assumptions of liberal economic theory. And yet, I will now show, instead of providing a satisfactory explanation of (or even solution to) these problems, they ultimately highlight core contradictions in liberal economic theory and policy itself. I will first elaborate these contradictions and subsequently show how they play out in a number of contexts.

Most damaging, in terms of liberal economic theory, is of course the fact that the policies of liberalization, deregulation, and privatization failed to lead to economic growth in general and to rising, if unequal, incomes for individuals and states alike. Liberal economists argue that this failure has its roots in the inconsistent implementation of these policies. Third World states, as we have seen, did not systematically implement the structural adjustments demanded by the IMF or the

World Bank and even liberal states themselves are accused of continued engagement in protectionist policies (Wolf 2004: 215). Subsidies for
European, American, and Japanese agriculture provide a perfect example for the negative consequences of government intervention in the
market: they raise the prices of agricultural products for consumers in
the rich states and keep their cheaper counterparts from the developing
countries out of the market, thus contributing to poverty there. But not
only in the sphere of agriculture do liberal states fail to live up to the
rules they impose on others. The inclusion of the TRIPS agreement into
the WTO is also widely seen as a case of liberal governments undermining market forces on behalf of certain sectors of their domestic economy
(Bhagwati 2004: 182). TRIPS is nothing but 'a rent-extraction device'
for certain companies with 'potentially devastating consequences' for
public health, education as well as technological innovation in poor
countries (Wolf 2004: 216–7) who are suddenly supposed to 'pay for
patents they had been accessing freely until then' (Bhagwati 2004: 183).
In light of the general support for neoliberal economic policies and the
push on the part of liberal states to implement these rules in international economic organizations as well as in individual developing
countries through the IMF, World Bank, or bilateral trade agreements,
these protectionist policies on the part of rich states are denounced as
a 'grotesque hypocrisy of the high-income countries' driven by greed
(Wolf 2004: 219).

But it is not just rich states that undermine the potential of free
market policies to deliver economic growth and rising incomes. International economic organizations like the IMF are seen as multilateral
tools of the G7, the United States, Wall Street whose policies constitute
intrusive interventions in the running of poor countries (Wolf 2004:
289, 294). Indeed, the very purpose of the IMF – namely to rescue failing economies as well as their creditor banks from the consequences of
their actions, that is, from bankruptcy – undermines the market mechanism that depends on such failures as a trigger for much needed reforms
(Shimko 2005: 180).

In sum, these analyses suggest in most general terms that what
accounts for the failure of liberal economic policies is the political fragmentation of the world (Wolf 2004: 316) and hence the interference
of political institutions in pursuit of particular interests in the market.
Market failures are rooted in the 'hypocrisy, greed, and stupidity that so
often mar our own politics in both developing and developed countries'
(Wolf 2004: 320). This hypocrisy, greed, and stupidity in turn has its
roots in the vested interests of private actors that successfully manage

to get states and other political actors to pursue policies in line with these interests. That is, particular industries (for example in the case of TRIPS) push the state into rent-seeking policies; particular domestic constituencies co-opt the state into pursuing short-term advantages (such as immigration control) in spite of their long-term economic disadvantages. Liberal economic theory suggests, in short, that market failures have their roots, as Adam Smith already noted, in the 'prejudices of the public' and, 'what is much more unconquerable, the private interests of many individuals' who irresistably oppose the freedom of trade (Smith 1952: 201).

Persistent inequality is thus not produced by economic globalization but by 'the refusal (or inability) of some countries to participate' (Wolf 2004: 140). The failure of neoliberal economic policies to produce economic growth and a general increase in incomes is not due to too much but to too little, to the 'still limited integration of the world economy' (Wolf 2004: 320). The solution to the problem, accordingly, is a further reduction of government interference in the market (Wolf 2004: 82). This analysis implies, then, a continuation and more systematic implementation of policies of liberalization, deregulation, and privatization for liberal states, multilateral economic institutions, and poor states alike.

However, liberal economists recognize that such policies, at least in the short term, can have detrimental effects: letting inefficient industries, financial institutions, or even states 'fail' clearly leads to hardships for the workers and citizens affected by these failures. A further intensification of these policies thus has to be accompanied, it is argued, by a complex set of new policies and institutions able to cushion the blow of global financial and economic developments at the domestic level (Bhagwati 2004: 235, 239). 'Indeed, policies and capacities of states remain central to any understanding of how economic globalization works' (Wolf 2004: 16). Hence, the liberalization and integration of the world economy requires precisely the kind of institutions and the policies – the (welfare) state and regulation of the market – that liberal economic theory identifies as the root of the problem.

Herein, then, lies the core contradiction of liberal economic theory which blames the interference of political institutions, predominantly governments, for the failures of the market but then demands that precisely these institutions be available to address the integral downsides of market economies, which consist in people who work or have invested in inefficient sectors of the economy losing their livelihood through no fault of their own.

While liberal economic theory cannot resolve this fundamental contradiction, the Lockean theorization of liberalism can and does account for it. Historically, rich landowners and merchants were interested in protecting their property from government interference, representing (at least in principle) the 'commonwealth'. Yet, this goal required the separation of private property from common property and it constituted both property holders and workers as autonomous individuals, freed of the rights and obligations previously established through common property. This move could only be accomplished, however, through political power, that is through legislation which codified these new arrangements and thus reconstituted society as a conglomerate of private interests. Since only a small section of society could have an interest in these reforms, however, the vast majority of the population had to be excluded from government.

Contradictory interests, moreover, did not only attend and shape the constitution of such a 'liberal' society and government. Rather, once freed from political regulation, the market mechanism kept producing fundamentally contradictory interests between those who, at any one time, benefited from unregulated competition and those who did not. Highly productive industries benefited from competition while those going out of date had an interest in protection; labor shortages benefited laborers while at other times a surplus of labor benefited employers. To be sure, the beneficiaries of this system changed from one time to another, from one location to another. Overall, however, the market economy is based on the principle of competition and thus continuously (not only in the short term) produces winners and losers (Inayatullah and Blaney 2004: 129–59). Moreover, it is not the case that in these shifting circumstances the fate of individuals – over the long term – was relatively evenly divided. The cards were clearly stacked in favor of propertied individuals since, as Locke had famously announced, 'the Grass my Horse has bit; the Turfs my Servant has cut; and the Ore I have digg'd ... become my *Property*' (Locke 1994: 289). In other words, the propertied individual collects the surplus value not only of his own work but also of that of his horses, servants, or other investments, while the latter have nothing but a right to subsistence. Although the market mechanism is in principle perfectly capable of wiping out such accumulated riches, this danger is much smaller for a rich man than it is for a poor one. The former, after all, can weather the ups and downs of markets for some time and thus also gets a chance to redeploy his assets – or simply to live off them. Meanwhile, the poor man is in danger of losing his very livelihood at the slightest change of market forces.

Such centrifugal interests and forces had the potential to undermine the entire system, that is, to lead to revolution. Hence, government was accorded the task of mitigating the detrimental effects of the market mechanism sufficiently to avoid revolution.

In contrast to liberal economic theory, this Lockean account shows that the self-interested individual or private actor is itself the product of a liberal market economy – constituted through its separation from common property and subsequently entirely dependent for survival on the single-minded pursuit of its self-interest. Indeed, this (incorporated) person is the quintessential liberal individual hailed by Adam Smith whose pursuit of private interests, as we have seen, is expected to produce public goods or even 'moral virtues' (Wolf 2004: 57).

Furthermore, in pursuit of its interests, this individual needs the state: it needs to secure rights to its property, it needs to push through legislation in favor of its short-term economic interests – which may shift from free trade to protectionism – and it needs the state to mitigate the worst economic inequalities in order to stave off the ultimate fragmentation of society, that is, revolution or civil war. The Lockean account thus confirms the recognition of liberal economists that political institutions in general and the state in particular play an integral role in a liberal market economy. But it also shows that the liberal state is constituted with a contradictory remit: of upholding private property rights and free markets on the one hand and of providing such regulation as is politically necessary to mitigate the detrimental consequences of the market on the other. In other words, it is in the very nature of liberal states to respond to a variety of decidedly contradictory private interests; indeed, the modern liberal state is constituted for precisely that purpose. Yet, this contradictory remit has its roots not, as liberal economic theory suggests, in extra-economic political interests but in the very failure of the market mechanism itself. For while the market economy is indeed highly productive, left alone it fails to deliver rising incomes for all. And it is this tendency that polarizes society economically and hence also politically and thus necessitates state intervention.

This economic fragmentation, moreover, does not only give rise to the state and its contradictory purposes; it also engenders the political fragmentation of the world. The problem of the contradictory tendency of market economies – of privatization and free market exchange undermining political stability and with it the necessary political framework for a market economy – could be solved by pursuing privatization and trade abroad. In this way, the economic benefits of privatization and marketization could be imported while its detrimental political effects remained outside the domestic political sphere. Hence, Locke advocated, indeed campaigned for, colonialism and offered the vast tracts of land in America as a resource for appropriation. While Locke still thought in terms of land, such policies were subsequently pursued in a variety of ways. Hence, the British textile industry was established not on the basis of comparative advantage, which was originally held by Indian weavers, but by deliberately destroying the Indian textile industry through three core policies: first, a wide range of protectionist measures that kept Indian cotton off British markets; second, once British rule had been established in India, the harassment of Indian weavers; and finally, once British cotton had the comparative advantage, the opening up of the Indian subcontinent through the construction of railways and the subsequent flooding of the Indian market with cheap textiles from Lancashire (Pomeranz and Topik 1999: 218, 230).[6] Alternatively, in the Congo the Belgian rulers wanted to use the domestic population as a cheap labor force. Hence, rivers were poisoned to destroy their independent livelihoods followed by a demand for taxes to be paid in money, which could only be earned by taking (extremely badly paid) jobs (Russett et al. 2000: 413). On the one hand, these policies, by undermining or destroying some economies and providing capital for the development of others, created serious economic inequalities across the world; on the other hand, they required and produced international political fragmentation: they could only be pursued by denying foreign political communities equal political rights, rights to sovereignty, and with these political they also lost their economic rights. Just as private property and individual liberty in the domestic sphere were constituted through their separation from a prior commonwealth, so sovereignty entailed the strict separation of political communities. And in both cases the rights of the newly established entities were prioritized over those of the old. Historically, this political fragmentation allowed the appropriation of property abroad and thus the mitigation of the failures of liberal economics at home – in the long run providing the basis for economic and technological development as well as democratization in the dominant states of the system.

In contrast to the claims of liberal economic theory, therefore, not just the self-interested private actor and the state but also the political

---

[6] Pomeranz and Topic provide an excellent overview over the (often violent) means by which trade was established as well as the destruction of indigenous economies all around the world as a precondition for the economic development and the industrial revolution in Europe (1999).

fragmentation of the modern international system is a direct product of the internal contradictions of liberal market economies.[7] The
'multiplicity of countries and divergent historical experiences' that are
identified as standing in the way of global public goods produced by
economic globalization (Wolf 2004: 316) are not so much remnants
of a pre-liberal age that need to be overcome in order for liberal market economy to work its magic; they are in their modern form instead
largely the product of liberal market economy and its internal contradictions. Both economic inequality and political fragmentation and in
many cases the very existence, shape, and form of sovereign states in the
current international order – from European settler states like the United
States, Canada, Australia, New Zealand through virtually all states on
the African continent – are the direct product of liberal market contradictions and their political implications. The Lockean account suggests,
then, that the liberal market economy has never been a purely domestic economy; instead the international or transnational sphere played
a constitutive role in its development. The liberal market economy, in
other words, requires the constitution of *homo oeconomicus*, that is individuals based on private property (at the very least) in their bodies,
which are produced by separating them from constitutive social and
political (i.e. common) ties, and it requires the political institution of
the modern state, providing the glue between these private individuals
by backing their economic interests abroad, thus leading to a politically

---

[7] Obviously, other forms of political fragmentation preceded the sovereign states
system and the latter was grafted onto or transformed the former. Economic
interests, moreover, were also an integral part of such earlier systems with war,
conquest, annexation a major means for appropriation. Yet the liberal fragmentation of the international order differs from its predecessors precisely in separating
politics and economics, in enabling the pursuit of private economic interests
internationally while restricting political responsibility to the domestic sphere.
This is the core difference between the Spanish and the British empire in the early
modern period, with the former establishing political control over the natives
in order to enable economic exploitation while the latter simply appropriated
their property in land, leaving the natives – now deprived of their traditional
livelihood – to their own devices. This distinction between economics and politics could, of course, not be upheld in the long term. Native resistance ultimately
led private actors to enlist the state in defense of their investments – in America
leading to the 'Indian wars'. Similarly, as John Stuart Mill noted for India, the
activities of the East India Company undermined the economic and political stability of native Indian states to such an extent that Britain ultimately had no
choice but to pick up the pieces and directly govern these territories (Mill 1984:
119–20).

fragmented international system based on the modern conception of sovereignty.

These processes constitute the core dynamics of liberal economics and they are by no means restricted to the historical origins of liberalism but continue to play a crucial role today, for example in the solutions to the shortcomings of recent neoliberal economic policies. In general, as we have seen, liberal economists advocate a wider and deeper integration of the world economy – more rather than less globalization and a roll-back of self-interested political intervention in the world market. More concretely, they often identify immigration control as a detrimental political intervention in the operation of the market. While states allow the free flow of goods and services across borders, they prevent an equivalent free flow of people. This protection of domestic labor markets harms workers from poor countries by preventing them from relocating to areas with better paid jobs and it also harms the consumers in rich countries who have to pay more for goods produced by 'expensive' workers. The free movement of labor is thus expected simultaneously to trigger economic growth and enhance equality in the world (Wolf 2004: 315).

There are, however, two preconditions for economic migration: the first is economic inequality without which there would be no incentive to migrate; and the second is that the potential migrant has to be detached from social and political ties. Hence, Bhagwati argues against critics of female migration in particular that 'it is more likely that many women in the global care chain are better off rather than suffering from emotional "deficit" and distress. The migrant female worker is better off in the new world of attachments and autonomy; the migrants' children are happy being looked after by their grandmothers, who are also happy to be looking after the children; and the employer mothers, when they find good nannies, are also happy that they can work without the emotionally wrenching sense that they are neglecting their children' (Bhagwati 2004: 77–8). A radically unequal set of rights is here recognized for the migrant nanny on the one hand and the 'employer mother' on the other. Only when the migrant female worker is detached from her own familial, social, and political ties, conceived as an 'autonomous' individual without 'emotional deficit and distress' over the separation from her family and wider community, does she become available as cheap labor and thus in turn 'free' the employer mother for better paid economic pursuits. But this is not the whole story. For in Bhagwati's vision the employer mothers are endowed with 'an emotionally wrenching sense that they are neglecting their children' even if they just leave them to go to the office during the day. Unlike the female migrant worker, then, the employer mothers are recognized as constituted through intimate emotional ties to their children and hence also a wider social and political community. It is the denial of such ties to some sections of the world's population that makes them eligible as a source of economic growth for others whose social and political ties are recognized. And it is in defense of these political rights that liberal economists themselves claim that 'enlightened immigration policies' must be accompanied by a lot of regulation (Bhagwati 2004: 218), thus reproducing the political fragmentation of the world. And this fragmentation in turn plays an important role in the justification of economic inequality for, as Bhagwati argues, it is 'lunacy' to compare household incomes in different parts of the world because these households do not belong to the same society and therefore do not compare themselves with each other (Bhagwati 2004: 67). And yet, in order for economic migration to take place – and to play its dedicated role as a source of economic growth through the provision of cheap labor – the potential migrant needs to compare household incomes, otherwise they would not migrate at all. This conception of migration, in short, faithfully repeats all the steps familiar from Locke's arguments – starting with the production of the 'autonomous' individual and ending with the reproduction of political fragmentation and its contradictory yet necessary role in enabling as well as restraining liberal markets.

In precisely the same way, Locke had argued that '*Land* that is *common* in England ... is left common ... by the Law of the Land, which is not to be violated. And though it be Common, in respect of some Men, it is not so to all Mankind; but is the joint property of this Country' (Locke 1994: 292). England, here, is recognized as a political community and as such it has the right also to common property. In contrast, the Amerindians were denied this right as a political community and provided only with the individual right to subsistence; and hence their land was common to all 'mankind' and could be appropriated. Yet another 200 years later, John Stuart Mill as well argued that 'barbarians have no rights as a *nation* ... The only moral laws for the relation between a civilized and a barbarous government are the universal rules of morality between man and man' (Mill 1984: 119). In each case, the denial of political rights dissolves the community into individuals whose property – whether in land or labor – is then available to generate economic growth for those who have the power to assert their own political rights and to appropriate this property.

It is these decidedly international political roots of a market economy based on private property that are obscured by the methodological
nationalism characteristic of liberal economic thought which until
recently 'conceived development as a project linked to national economic and political independence' based on national cultures, political
traditions, national industries and local markets (Przeworski 1992: 55).
This methodological nationalism serves two core purposes. First, it hides
the fact that such national economies were the product of international
politics enabling the appropriation of property abroad while denying
political responsibility for its consequences. Bhagwati, again, provides
a perfect example for this oblivion when he claims that migration has
only become politically contentious now that it flows from poor to rich
countries and not, as in the past, from old to new (Bhagwati 2004:
209). This claim simply fails to register that the very territories Locke
offered for settlement and appropriation were in fact already occupied
by indigenous societies, whose resistance suggests, indeed, that they
did consider the migration from 'old' to 'new' as problematic. In fact,
these migrations resulted not only in the loss of land (and hence livelihood) and political independence for numerous societies; they were
also accompanied by massacres, ethnocide, genocide.[8] Second, methodological nationalism allows liberal economists to cite the impressive
economic development within liberal economies as evidence in support
of the claim that a market economy does indeed lead to general, albeit
uneven, growth; that it ultimately raises the incomes of even the poorest
members of society – in contrast to alternative systems whose economic
woes are equally presented as home-made and regularly cited as proof
for the superiority of the liberal version (Smith 1952: 1; Inayatullah and
Blaney 2004, 2012). This assumption underpins the claim that 'market
failures are nearly, though not always, domestic in origin' (Wolf 2004:
87). Here, the exclusion of the international dimension of liberal economics hides the fact that much of this 'liberal' growth is based on
the expropriation and exploitation of 'foreigners' which in turn plays
a crucial role in producing their economic misfortunes.

Unlike liberal economic theory, then, this Lockean account does provide a satisfactory explanation for the mixed results of recent neoliberal

---

[8] The Spanish migration to America, albeit not liberal, for example, is estimated
to have cost 70 million indigenous American lives within the first 50 years – that
is, 17 percent of the entire world population at the time – through diseases, drop
in living conditions and massacres (Jahn 2000: 73).

economic policies. Economically, as we have seen, these policies failed to generate considerable growth. The Lockean reflections on the origins of liberal economics suggest that economic growth slows down if and when international opportunities for appropriation are not any longer readily available. While the opening up of markets in Eastern Europe, China, India, and other Third World states in the wake of structural adjustment policies and the end of the Cold War did, for a short time, provide a boost to markets, once these economies are in principle integrated into the world market and hence also (after decolonization) endowed with political sovereignty, economic growth is naturally constrained by the level of inequality that is politically sustainable – in individual states (rich or poor) as well as in the system as a whole. In other words, the very success of spreading the principles of market economy across the entire globe removes that sphere 'outside' the liberal economic system in which appropriation could be pursued with relative political impunity, that is, in which economic and political inequalities could be translated into vast resources for profit and economic development. Since the end of the Cold War, however, the very integration and globalization of the liberal world economy means that the political fall-out of liberal economic policies now threaten the system from within – whether this threat concerns individual political units within the system as is the case in civil conflicts, secessionist policies, the Occupy movements, or the global system in the case of outrage over the consequences of intellectual property rights for health and education. And it is this pervasive and now to a great extent globalized threat of political 'intolerance' that ultimately puts limits on the possibility of economic growth.

The Lockean account highlights, moreover, that political intervention is necessary in order to mitigate the inherent tendency of the market to produce winners and losers. It thus explains the rising inequalities within and between states as a direct result of the reduction of political regulation which lies at the core of neoliberal economic policies. The growth that did occur, in other words, did not lead to generally rising incomes because it is not the market mechanism that leads to a 'trickling down' of such growth but rather political mediation between winners and losers, political redistribution, that generates such an effect where it occurs.

The same market mechanism, moreover, explains the inconsistent behavior of private actors, states, and multilateral institutions – their commitment to the principles of free trade on the one hand and their pursuit of protectionist policies on the other. Unlike liberal economic theory, these actors, Locke's work shows, are themselves the product of the internal contradictions of the market economy. Being based on private property, this economy requires the separation of the individual from common property and thus constitutes the self-interested individual or private actor whose survival depends entirely on the short-term pursuit of its particular interests.

Similarly, it is the internal contradictions of the liberal economy that constitute the state with the contradictory remit of simultaneously upholding liberal principles of private property and free trade and constraining their operation in order to ensure political stability. Liberal states are therefore set up to respond to, and be co-opted by, private interests (whether protectionist or not) as well as to put limits on them. While the necessary level of political intervention may change from time to time, the fact of it as well as its contradictory nature is determined by the operation of liberal economics. These contradictory demands, as Locke's work shows, have made use of and transformed the political fragmentation of the world which enables private actors to pursue their economic interests abroad while ensuring political stability at home. The propensity of rich and poor states alike to protect their economic and political interests – through the protection of domestic agriculture, industries, or labor markets or the failure to implement structural adjustment programs – even while they call for open markets on the part of others is thus not 'hypocritical' but rather perfectly in line with the demands of a liberal economy.

The failure of neoliberal economic policies to fulfill their core economic promises – namely a general, albeit uneven, increase in incomes – also accounts for the mixed results of their political promises. While these policies according to liberal economic theory are expected ultimately to contribute to internal political stability as well as democratization, these expectations were only partially met. Inasmuch as neoliberal economic policies managed to reduce political intervention, they resulted in an exacerbation of the integral economic tendencies of this system: in the production of economic inequality and hence also political confrontation. These opposing political forces in turn account for much of the political instability produced by these policies. In many rich countries, increasing inequality was directly addressed by the Occupy movements, by mass demonstrations, and occasionally even contributed to secessionist movements (in Spain, for example) – a clear expression of the centrifugal tendencies of the market mechanism. In poor countries this production of inequality, instead of producing stability, often exacerbated civil conflict (Paris 2004). In other cases, the resultant polarization provided support for authoritarian regimes (Carothers 2002). Hence, 'foreign economic penetration and coercive government may reinforce each other as local governments become ever more dependent on foreign military assistance ... to maintain control over the social unrest that economic developments have created' (Russett et al. 2000: 433). In addition, the dependency of poor countries on development aid made their governments more responsive to international donors than their own population – thus in turn undermining the prospects for democracy (de Waal 1997: 628). The introduction of liberal economic principles in Eastern Europe, too, produced serious economic inequalities and in some cases – despite the pull factor of EU membership – a decidedly half-hearted development of democracy. In short, the market mechanism produces economic inequalities and thus confrontational politics instead of political stability and democratization.

Moreover, in contrast to liberal economic theory and its methodological nationalism which insists on the domestic sources of market failures, the Lockean account acknowledging the constitutive role of the international sphere for such markets in the first place also explains the less than impressive results of neoliberal policies in the international sphere where they were supposed to contribute to mutually beneficial cooperation and peace. Though relations between the West and Eastern European states have, on the whole, clearly improved since the end of the Cold War, elsewhere inequality, the failure to cooperate and even aggression continue to characterize international politics. With the demise of the Soviet Union and the elevation of liberal economics to the 'only game in town', the power differentials between rich and poor states had suddenly become greater, and perfectly in line with the Lockean account, rich states immediately moved to exploit these power differentials to mitigate the detrimental effects of the liberal economy for the domestic sphere. First, instead of paying a 'peace dividend' in the form of development aid, the latter initially declined simply because the political need to forestall 'revolution' had radically diminished. Secondly, development aid could now be more explicitly tied to political conditions that clearly undermined the political rights of developing states to nonintervention and sovereignty. Thirdly, rich states moved to develop and codify liberal economic principles in and through multilateral economic organizations in which developing states do not enjoy the same rights – either because of weighted voting or, in the case of the WTO, because their markets are simply too small to provide them with sufficient leverage (Weiss 2005). This political inequality provided rich states with the opportunity to protect their own industries and markets while imposing free trade and market principles onto poor states. These policies, in short, do not establish mutually beneficial and cooperative relationships between different states – including between rich states. Hence, trade rounds are stuck, trade wars are pervasive, protectionism continues and even economic cooperation within the EU is lately at stake. Moreover, as the war in Iraq showed, neither is political cooperation between liberal states a foregone conclusion nor are leading 'neoliberal' states (like the US and the UK) particularly peaceful in their foreign policies. Yet, while such policies run counter to the expectations of liberal economic theory, they are perfectly in line with the dynamics of liberalism sketched by Locke.

Conclusion

Even though classical liberal economic theory had already in the 1980s informed economic policies, the end of the Cold War provided the opportunity to widen and deepen these policies: to implement them in the societies of the former Soviet Bloc and to push them through more thoroughly in countries of the Third World that had hitherto been able to retain more control over their policies by exploiting bipolar competition. The very absence of alternative models also allowed for a firmer implementation and enforcement of those rules at the international level through multilateral economic organizations.

Neoliberal economic policies were thus widely – if inconsistently and unevenly – translated into practice. Despite such auspicious circumstances, however, the outcome of these policies did not meet expectations. Instead of considerable economic growth and increasing incomes, these policies led to slow growth, rising inequality within and between states as well as serious economic and financial crises. The failure to produce the expected economic benefits in turn meant that their political aims also remained largely elusive. Instead of contributing to domestic stability, widespread democratization, and international cooperation and peace the post-Cold War period was characterized by political unrest, civil conflict, the spread of illiberal democracies and trade wars, civil wars, and interventions at the international level.

Instead of providing a satisfactory explanation for, or solution to, these disappointing policy results, liberal economic theory reveals a fundamental contradiction in its approach. Market failure, it claims, is caused by political interference in the market – by the self-interested pursuit of particular and short-term interests of private actors, states, and multilateral institutions. Without such intervention, according to liberal economic theory, the market mechanism would produce not just 'global public goods' but even 'moral virtues' such as prosperity, environmental protection, justice, and the welfare state (Wolf 2004: 57). As a solution to the problem, liberal economic theory thus advocates the continuation of economic globalization and the further restriction of political intervention in the economy. And yet, in order to cushion the detrimental effects of such policies, it calls for precisely those institutions and policies that it blames for causing the problem in the first place.[9] Liberal economic theory thus offers neither a satisfactory explanation of nor a consistent solution to the problem.

In contrast, Locke's work shows, in spite of his own commitment to liberal principles, that all the institutions accused of undermining the workings of the liberal market economy and held responsible for its failings – the self-interested private actor, the state, and the political fragmentation of the world – are themselves the product of the inherent contradictions of a liberal market economy. They are constituted by the core principle of liberal economy, competition, whose very raison d'etre lies in producing winners and losers. And it is these contradictory results of the liberal market economy that require political institutions tasked with the mediation between opposing forces. The roots of the much-decried 'hypocrisy' – of pursuing particular (economic) interests while subscribing to and preaching supposedly universally valid economic principles – thus do not lie in the political institutions: they arise from the fact that the liberal market economy itself constantly produces and serves particular rather than universal interests. The root cause of 'hypocrisy', in other words, lies not in political practice that is inconsistent with liberal economic theory; it lies instead in liberal economic theory that is inconsistent with the history and nature of its own subject matter – in a theory which excludes the inherently political and international dimension of liberal economics and is, by doing so, able to expunge its contradictory and particularist nature from the record.

And it is this methodological nationalism which accounts not only for the contradictions in liberal economic theory itself but also for the weaknesses of policies based on this theory. Oblivious of the fact that liberal economic growth has, right from the start, depended on economic

---

[9] Moreover, the fate of liberal economics itself frequently leads to a shifting of position amongst liberal economists. Hence, Martin Wolf who has been cited in this chapter widely in defense of globalization has, in light of the increasing crisis of the late 2000s, veered back toward more Keynesian positions.

opportunities abroad and treating international factors impacting on domestic economic development as a recent and historically unprecedented phenomenon (Przeworski 1992: 55; Acemoglu and Robinson 2006: 347–8), liberal economic policies focus on the reform of domestic markets and economic policies. They are based on the assumption that 'market failures are nearly, though not always, domestic in origin' (Wolf 2004: 87). Such policies, for example in the case of structural adjustment, however, are bound to fail if access to international markets is not readily available or profits are needed to pay off international debts.

Similarly, it is the international dimension of liberal economics which shows that domestic economic development where it occurred was intimately tied to expropriation in the international sphere and hence that the market mechanism always produces winners and losers and thus also political friction. Oblivious of this international dimension, however, policies based on liberal economic theory miss the fact that economic growth is dependent on such international opportunities and hence require policies that exploit and inscribe such inequality in the international order. The implementation and enforcement of liberal economic principles in the world economy where the size of the market ensures political influence and hence also the opportunity to export free trade (or even rent-seeking) policies while protecting home industries constitutes a direct continuation of this dynamic, which explains a lack of opportunities for weaker economies. While such policies are perfectly in keeping with, indeed constitutive of, the liberal economy, they appear as a stark contradiction or 'hypocrisy' to an economic theory framed in terms of a single domestic economy.

Moreover, it is oblivion to the political basis of liberal economy – the fact that it is produced and reproduced against (more or less) widespread resistance and thus requires political power – which draws into focus the potential political limits of economic growth. In other words, in both the domestic and the international sphere the extent to which potential 'losers' are able to resist privatization, liberalization and deregulation defines limits for liberal forms of economic expansion and thus contributes to the unexpected low growth rates. What is more, these limits are themselves the product of the neoliberal policies of the post-Cold War era which deepened and widened economic inequality (as well as producing economic crises) to the point at which political intervention became necessary.

Thus, the disjuncture between liberal economic theory and practice has its roots not in the 'imperfections' of individuals, states, and other political institutions and particular interests. The latter, as we have seen, are actually the product of liberal economics and their 'imperfections' or contradictions are simply a faithful reflection of the 'imperfections' of the liberal economy itself. The disjuncture between theory and practice has its roots instead, in a theory which explicitly excludes two major and constitutive dimensions of liberal economic practice from its core assumptions and thus justifies policies that instead of leading to general economic growth, rising incomes and political cooperation reproduce economic and political inequality both within and between states.

6
Norms

Introduction

Liberal norms like individual freedom and equality play, of course, a role in the political and economic liberal theories and policies discussed in the previous two chapters. The political institution of democracy and the organization of economies based on private property and free markets are thought to embody and help realize the norms of individual freedom and equality. Although normative liberal approaches of course aim to realize the same core liberal norms, they approach this task in a different way and thus deserve independent discussion.

While political and economic approaches generally aim to establish particular political and economic institutions that are in turn expected to lead to the realization of liberal norms, normative approaches begin with the liberal norms themselves; they treat these norms as guiding principles for the reform of actors, institutions, and practices. Hence, normative liberal theories tend to elaborate the rationale of liberal norms in the abstract, identify ways to realize such norms, and advocate the necessary policies. This approach explains some of the subtle – though by no means exclusive – differences between normative and other liberal approaches. Since liberal norms in the abstract are always conceived as universal and since these norms are seen as the source and inspiration for change, normative theorists tend to focus on 'universal' institutions for the implementation and realization of liberal principles. Hence, normative approaches tend to advocate the reform of international law in light of liberal principles, or the integration of liberal principles of distributive justice into the international economic order at large, or the strengthening of human rights in the rules, institutions, and practices of the global order. This focus on global institutions and practices does not, of course, exclude the advocacy of liberal norms for particular actors like states, just as the focus on particular actors and institutions of the political and economic approaches does not exclude support for a liberal reform of global institutions. Nevertheless, while the political and economic approaches in principle adopt a bottom-up approach to the realization of liberal norms (from the particular to the universal), normative theorists tend to adopt a top-down approach (from the universal to the particular).

This chapter hence focuses on the theories and policies that adopt such a top-down approach with regard to the realization of liberal norms. I will first introduce some of the normative liberal theories that have played a prominent role in the post-Cold War era: the cosmopolitan democracy project, proposals for distributive justice, and projects for the reform of international law, as well as, more specifically, the legalization of humanitarian intervention. The second section explores the fate of these projects in practice. It shows that many of these projects were never seriously taken up by political actors, and those that were arguably translated into policies were pursued inconsistently and with, at best, mixed results. The gap between theory and practice in the case of normative liberalism is arguably even wider than in the case of political and economic liberalism. The analysis of these approaches in the third section shows that these disappointing results have their roots in the abstraction of liberal norms from their constitutive practices – which leaves them either devoid of the means to translate these norms into practice or forces them to identify particular actors, institutions, and practices as bearers of these norms – with the result of providing normative justifications for the reproduction of highly particular or unequal international relations.

Normative liberal theories

Like other liberal theories, normative theories, too, tend to cover the political, economic, and normative (in the sense of substantive norms) dimensions of liberalism – but usually with a focus on one of them to the detriment of the others. This section will thus introduce a range of examples with the cosmopolitan democracy project addressing the political realm, theories of distributive justice the economic realm, and theories concerned with international law, human rights, and humanitarian intervention the realm of norms and rules.

Explicitly encouraged by the 'transition from one international system (the Cold War) to another', the cosmopolitan democracy project sets out to 'build a political project for a different world order' (Archibugi 1998: 199).[1] Taking stock of the given conditions, cosmopolitan democracy authors identify challenges arising from globalization. Increasing interdependence undermines the ability of individual states to control their political, economic, cultural, and even natural environment – and this in turn undermines the political autonomy of the citizens who have no say in many decisions that directly affect their lives (Archibugi 1998: 204–5). The liberal norm of individual freedom thus demands an extension of democracy not just into individual states but into the international system at large. Apart from more fully realizing the principle of individual autonomy, democratizing the international system is here seen as a method of ensuring 'civilized coexistence' which allows communities 'to democratically address problems that also involve others' and thus to contribute to peace and nonviolence (Archibugi 1998: 205).

This democratization of the international order, inspired by Kant's third definitive article on cosmopolitan law, entails the institutionalization of political participation of individuals and civil society actors in the transnational and international realm. In addition to the inclusion of these subnational actors, supranational actors are also expected to participate in international democratic decision making (Kant 1957: 20, 32; Held 1996: 227ff). In other words, cosmopolitan democracy authors advocate the globalization of democracy and thus the democratization of globalization (Archibugi 2004: 438).

For purposes of realization, the cosmopolitan democracy authors point out that 'those communities which enable policy and law to be shaped by their citizenry' have most closely realized the ideal of universal political participation and the EU can even count as an 'international example of cosmopolitan democracy' (Held 1996: 232; Archibugi 1998: 201, 220, 215f; Linklater 1998: 204). Hence, these states are seen as an avant-garde, 'an association of democratic nations which might draw in others over time' (Held 1996: 232). In addition, 'the cosmopolitan model entrusts civil society as opposed to national governments with the task of "interfering" in the domestic affairs' of other states with the goal of increasing political participation (Archibugi 1998: 218).

In sum, this project advocates the promotion of democracy not only in individual states (like the democracy transition paradigm and the

---

[1] Key contributions to this project include Daniele Archibugi and David Held (1995), David Held (1996, 1997), Richard Falk (1995, 1998), Barry Holden (2000), Antonio Franceschet (2002), Bruce Morrison (2003), Daniele Archibugi (1998, 2003), and Andrew Linklater (1998).

democratic peace thesis) but also in the decision-making structures of the international system as a whole. And in this latter context, it is rather radical in advocating the extension of political rights to individuals, civil society organizations, and supranational organizations if and when they are affected by particular decisions. Special responsibility for this promotion and extension of democracy falls to civil society associations as well as the EU as a model for emulation and extension.

Normative liberal theories that focus on the economic sphere, on questions of inequality, poverty, hunger, or distributive justice, take the blatant material inequalities of the contemporary international system as a starting point and develop arguments for the requisite reforms of that system.[2] Based on utilitarian arguments, some authors hold that the rich have a duty to prevent the suffering of the poor up to the point where their own sacrifices reach the same level as that of the currently poor (Singer 1972). Others conceive subsistence rights as basic security rights and consequently posit a positive duty to ensure their realization (Shue 1996). Rawls, in *The Law of Peoples* (2001), argues that rich liberal states have a duty to assist 'burdened' societies – though no duty to prevent inequality in the international system. Relatively radical implications for global income distribution and environmental protection arise from the concept of 'justice as impartiality' that holds that the rejection of rules (concerning inequality, environmental protection, and so on) has to be based on impartial arguments – arguments that do not favor the interests of some over those of others (Barry 1995). Similarly radical, Thomas Pogge's analysis suggests that the rules and institutions governing the global economic order – such as the WTO – are fundamentally biased and actively contribute to the production of poverty and inequality. Even just the 'negative' moral duty of doing no harm thus requires the fundamental reform of these institutions (2002). An early and very influential example of such normative theorizing in International Relations is the work of Charles Beitz. In effect, Beitz provides a cosmopolitan application of John Rawls' *Theory of Justice* (1971) by arguing that the latter's 'difference principle'[3] developed for domestic societies would also be adopted by states in the international system.

---

[2] Prominent authors in this field are Beitz (1979), Pogge (2002), Barry (1995, 2005), O'Neill (1986), Singer (1993), and Shue (1996). For an overview and discussion of this literature, see Brown (1997) and Tan (2010).

[3] The 'difference principle' suggests that rules leading to material inequality in society are only just insofar as they benefit the weakest members of society more than others.

Moreover, Beitz holds that the contemporary interdependent or global-ized world actually constitutes one society, and thus a proper framework for the Rawlsian principle (1979, 1983: 595).[4] The application of this principle to the international sphere would have serious redistributive consequences – for example, with regard to natural resources.

There is agreement amongst all these theories, however, that poverty and material inequality are a matter of moral concern and must be addressed. The suggestions range from a rather mild duty to engage in charitable acts to fairly radical calls for a fundamental reform of the rules and institutions of the world economy. For the most part, these theories are concerned with establishing the moral duty of such poli-cies and hope that relevant actors will endorse and realize those duties. And 'relevant actors' in this context are logically rich societies that have the means to provide help, powerful states that are capable of shaping the rules and institutions of the international economic order, as well as liberal actors who already embody liberal principles of justice. In prac-tice, of course, these three characteristics often go together. Thus, Beitz distinguishes between three types of states: those 'whose institutions conform to appropriate principles of justice', namely the rights of indi-viduals; those which are likely to become just 'if left free from external interference'; and those which are 'neither just nor likely to become just' (Beitz 1979: 91f). The two former types of states enjoy the right to non-intervention while the latter can be intervened in – and such inequality is justified if it provides goods which rational members in the original position must be assumed to choose (Beitz 1979: 91f, 100). In other words, these goals are to be realized by providing liberal states with the right to impose the necessary norms and policies on nonliberal states.

In sum, then, normative theories quite widely engage with and advo-cate reforms to the international or global economic order. But the realization of these reforms is dependent on a prior endorsement of the moral duties underpinning them. And while such moral duties are considered to be universally valid and thus expected to be endorsed by all individuals, particular responsibility falls on liberal actors, including states, partly because they embody the right principles of justice and partly because they tend to have the power to undertake such reforms.

Given that normative theories are generally interested in the devel-opment and spread of liberal norms, it is not surprising that they also

---

[4] Beitz subsequently based his theory on Kant since Rawls' work is not easily extended into the international sphere (1983).

address questions of international law and international organization. Hence, John Rawls takes on the challenge of developing just principles of international law in *The Law of Peoples* (2001). As in his previous work inspired by Kant, Rawls uses a hypothetical social contract, first, in order to establish 'the liberal political conception of a constitutionally democratic regime' followed by a hypothetical social contract between liberal peoples choosing the principles of the law of peoples, and finally a social contract between liberal and decent peoples agreeing on the law of peoples. The outcome is a reasonable society of peoples identified with Kant's pacific federation (Rawls 2001: 10, 59f, 126). This society excludes outlaw states and 'burdened societies' – the former because they are by definition lawbreakers and the latter because they lack the (material) capacity to fulfill their rights and obligations under this international law. While 'burdened societies' are entitled to assistance, outlaw states do not have to be tolerated and can be 'forced to change their ways' (Rawls 2001: 90, 81). Neither outlaw states (or their peoples) nor 'burdened societies' have a voice in the social contracts establishing the law of peoples.

Similarly, but more narrowly, it is sometimes argued that a right to democratic governance is emerging (Franck 1992). Such a right implies that the voice of nondemocratic states does not have 'the same legitimacy-conferring power as the consent of individuals' (Buchanan 2003: 171). In other words, a reform of international law and international organization would need to recognize differential rights for democratic and nondemocratic states – and hence make full rights of sovereignty dependent on democratic regimes.

Alternatively, guided by the democratic peace thesis which posits high levels of cooperation as well as a lack of aggression in the relations between liberal states, Anne-Marie Slaughter argues that such cooperation is visible also in the legal field. Private actors develop soft law rules, substate actors cooperate across borders, and liberal states vertically integrate international into domestic law. Yet such cooperation does not occur in relations with and between nonliberal states. In pursuit of liberal values as well as peace, therefore, Slaughter advocates the adoption of a new model of international law 'normatively applicable to all States even if positively descriptive of only some' based on individual self-regulation, transnational regulation, and the vertical enforcement of international agreements (Slaughter 1995: 39). This model challenges the traditional divide between public and private international law and promises to serve the contemporary international order better. In other words, peace and cooperation can be achieved by adopting the rules, regulations, and practices of intra-liberal behavior as universally valid international law.

Finally, liberal norms at the international level are most prominently embodied in the concept of human rights. These rights cover individual freedom, political participation, private property, and hence liberal principles in all their core dimensions. Human rights are thus both an exceptionally attractive object of liberal theorization and a core means for the realization and extension of liberal norms in the international order. Hence, the literature on human rights in general is vast, and its review goes well beyond the scope and focus of this study. The end of the Cold War, however, provided an opportunity to pursue the spread and enforcement of these rights more proactively, a goal which has been explicitly developed in the literature on humanitarian intervention on which I will therefore focus here.[5]

The advocacy of humanitarian intervention is based on the claim that there exists a moral obligation to come to the rescue of people in need – often derived from the hypothetical case of a drowning child (Wheeler 2000: 49). The recognition of this universal moral obligation, however, is of relatively recent origin. In the past, it is argued, humanitarian sensibilities were less developed and/or moral obligations were restricted to the boundaries of particular political communities. According to the former view, 'violent conflicts', 'acts of genocide', and 'crimes against humanity' were in the past 'considered normal' (Müllerson 2009: 136). According to the latter, justice was considered an 'internal norm' and force an 'external rule' – 'with acts of generosity toward the foreigner embodying an exception' (Elshtain 2003: 64). Thus, 'non-interventionism is a doctrine of the past' (Tesón 2003: 128) based on an 'insistence on sharp and morally decisive distinctions between citizens and aliens' (Linklater 2000: 483). And it is this limitation of moral obligations to members of one's own political community that has become embodied in the political and legal structure of the international system – primarily through the legal norm and political institution of sovereignty.

This historically particularist conception of moral obligations has over time, however, gradually become more universal, albeit unevenly. In Europe in particular, the experience of the holocaust (Wheeler 2000: 302) led to a universalization of this sense of moral obligations which

---

[5] Key texts on humanitarian intervention include Hehir (2010), Wheeler (2000), Holzgrefe and Keohane (2003), Tesón (2005), Chesterman (2001), Coady (2002), and Lang (2001, 2003).

has now become embodied in European states (Linklater 2000: 484, 486). Other parts of the world, meanwhile, remain wedded to a more restricted understanding of moral obligations reflected in the principle of sovereignty, which still underpins the international political and legal order and its traditional sharp moral distinction between citizens and aliens (Linklater 2000: 492). According to this account, the gradual universalization of moral obligations in some parts of the world has not been matched by a similar development of the political and legal principles of the international order and thus produces a tension between politics and morality. This clash between a universalist morality and a particularist political order thus requires reform of the latter 'in the name of cosmopolitan conventions whose time may have come' (Linklater 2000: 493). In other words, the 'good international citizen must come to the assistance of the victims of institutionalized cruelty' but in this quest has to 'resolve the tension between legalism and progressivism in a new legal order that alters the relationship between order and justice, citizenship and humanity, and sovereignty and human rights' (Linklater 2000: 493).

Conversely, defense of the principle of sovereignty or the right to nonintervention is presented 'as the one doctrine whose origin, design, and effect is to protect established political power and render persons defenseless against the worst forms of human evil' (Tesón 2003: 129). The failure to recognize interventions with humanitarian outcomes as such attests to the 'moral bankruptcy' of those wedded to principles of sovereignty and nonintervention (Wheeler 2000: 296) and, of course, to the 'immoral' character of the international order based on sovereignty. What is needed, then, is a 'moral transformation' that makes governments in the West see that humanitarian intervention 'is both morally permitted and morally required' (Wheeler 2000: 310). Respect for, and defense of, human rights thus requires the legalization and practice of humanitarian intervention which is equated with morality and counterposed to the political and legal principles of sovereignty and nonintervention as standing for particularist and hence immoral interests.

This literature aims to convince readers that the legalization of humanitarian intervention constitutes a moral obligation. Yet, the resistance of 'nonliberal' states to such moves does not only provide a barrier for the legalization of humanitarian intervention but arguably also provides a barrier for its practice in cases of serious human rights violations. In order to address that problem, Buchanan and Keohane advocate a reform of the UN which will enable the legal practice of humanitarian intervention while simultaneously preventing abuse of this license. The proposal includes two parts: the first is the development of an accountability system under existing UN auspices; the second is based on the claim that democratic states meet the standard for 'comparative moral reliability' (Buchanan and Keohane 2004: 19). On this basis, Buchanan and Keohane advocate the establishment of a coalition of democratic states willing to undertake humanitarian interventions with the rights and privileges to overrule a deadlocked UN Security Council.

Normative liberal theories, in sum, aim to spread all three core dimensions of liberal norms either separately or in combination. Hence, the cosmopolitan democracy project advocates a democratization of the international system, theories of distributive justice more or less wide ranging reforms of the international economic order, legal theories the reform of international law in line with liberal norms and practices, and the literature on humanitarian intervention the spread and protection of human rights worldwide. While there is, to be sure, a difference in focus between all these theories, they are not at all mutually exclusive. Hence, the democratization of the international order is expected to lead to a better protection of human rights as well as increased economic justice; the reform of the international economic order is frequently described as a matter of human rights; legal reform is expected to enhance the protection of individual rights, of political participation, and of economic cooperation; and the protection of human rights clearly entails political and economic rights. Moreover, in every case, the realization of these liberal norms is also expected to contribute to cooperation and peace.

According to normative theories, these norms are themselves the source of their subsequent realization. That is, the endorsement and internalization of these norms provides political actors with a goal that shapes their policies. Hence, inasmuch as normative liberal theories explicitly engage with the question of translating these norms into practice, they tend to identify relevant actors in world affairs as protagonists for the extension and realization of liberal principles. The EU, for example, embodies liberal principles in general and provides sub- and suprastate actors with decision-making power. It is thus presented as a model for, and protagonist of, cosmopolitan democracy. Liberal individuals, companies and civil society associations widely engage in transnational cooperation and are hence seen as leading forces in the development of a liberal international law breaking down the distinction between public and private. Rich, powerful, and liberal states or societies have the material ability, the political power, and endorse the liberal principles necessary to provide economic help to poor societies and to reform the rules of the international economic order in line with liberal principles. Liberal states, moreover, do comparatively well in protecting human rights at home and are therefore expected to play a leading role in extending this protection across borders.

Conversely, nonliberal actors are not expected to exhibit such progressive policies and still need to be convinced – and in some cases even forced – to adhere to these principles. Normative liberal theories, in short, expect liberal actors to provide, at a minimum, a moral and political example for nonliberal actors and, at a maximum, provide these actors with legal rights and obligations that are denied to nonliberal actors for purposes of extending liberal principles. Hence, we now need to investigate in how far these expectations have been realized in the post-Cold War period.

Normative liberal policies

The promotion of democracy has been, as we saw in Chapter 4, an integral part of liberal foreign policies albeit with less than impressive outcomes. Yet, the cosmopolitan democracy project goes further than political democracy promotion and propagates the inclusion of individual, sub-, and suprastate actors into international decision making at large. And, indeed, NGOs have played an increasingly important role within liberal states as well as within international organizations. Relevant NGOs and other nonstate actors (such as the PLO, for instance) have been granted observer status at the UN, the IMF, the WTO, and other international organizations. They are widely consulted in areas of their expertise. NGOs are, moreover, quite regularly financially supported by states who delegate the implementation of some policies (like support for democratization abroad) to these actors. There can be no doubt that all these activities have provided NGOs with an increasing influence in world affairs.

These developments, however, do not necessarily amount to the democratization of world politics envisaged by the cosmopolitan democracy project. First of all, despite their rising involvement in world politics, NGOs are generally not provided with a formal voice in decision-making processes – either in the context of international organizations or within states (Archibugi 2004: 450). The same holds for individuals and other substate actors. And inasmuch as suprastate actors like the EU or international organizations themselves have the right to vote on particular issues, such rights are generally held in lieu of individual states that constitute the membership of these organiza-tions, and they have not been systematically extended after the end of the Cold War.

Secondly, the growing role of NGOs – even without decision-making powers – in the world today does not necessarily amount to democrati-zation in the substantive sense of providing individuals and communi-ties affected by certain decisions with influence on the decision-making process. This is so because NGOs are not actually democratically elected representatives of individuals or groups affected by certain decisions. Though the members of environmental NGOs, for example, may well be affected by decisions concerning climate change, they neither represent all people affected by those decisions nor represent all positions on these issues. In other cases, moreover, the membership of an NGO may well be largely drawn from a constituency that is precisely not directly affected by the issue at question. Since amnesty international, for example, is rarely tolerated under brutal regimes, its membership is largely made up of citizens of states that have a relatively good (if not perfect) record in respecting human rights – leaving the views and policies of those affected by severe violations of human rights unrepresented. Thirdly, the particular policies of an NGO are generally not even decided by its own membership. Instead, most NGOs represent a particular political posi-tion and subsequently recruit like-minded members. Finally, although the vast majority of civil society associations and NGOs have their roots in liberal states, such organizations have also sprung up in non-liberal states, are funded by nonliberal institutions, and operate across borders – thus undermining the assumption that such institutions are of a particularly liberal nature (Sørensen 2012: 163–4; Adamson 2005).

There is then not much evidence of a developing cosmopolitan democracy. States and international organizations make no move to pro-vide individuals, sub- or suprastate actors with voting rights on issues that affect them. Instead, they tap into the expertise of these actors and delegate the implementation of some policies. In combination with the undemocratic nature of these actors and their largely Western prove-nance, thus, NGOs do not contribute to the democratization of world politics – though they do provide a link between states, interest groups, and transnational policies. Indeed, notes Archibugi, 'for the first time in history, states with democratic regimes are concentrating an amount of economic, technological, military, ideological and political resources sufficient to ensure control over the entire world. Despite this, military force once again rules international politics. Cosmopolitan democracy will be nothing more than a miserable consolation if it proves incapable of restraining the consolidation of this increasingly hegemonic power' (2004: 466).

Theories of distributive justice, at a minimum, hold that liberal principles demand charity toward less advantaged people(s). And there is no question that charity is provided. Many charities as well as international organizations regularly provide aid in food and clothing, technical expertise, medical services, and so on. In addition, charity is widely forthcoming in cases of natural and humanitarian disasters. And yet, despite the fact that these charitable activities have been ongoing for decades, there is no indication that they play a major role in the abolition of poverty or the creation of a more equitable distribution of material resources in general. Moreover, nonliberal states and publics are also widely involved in providing charity suggesting that this moral obligation is not solely generated by liberal values.

There is, in addition, also clear evidence of a systematic provision of material assistance to poor or 'burdened societies'. Development policies and development aid are an integral feature of world politics, and states as well as international organizations explicitly recognize the need for providing such assistance. The provision of development aid is widely institutionalized in states as well as international organizations in the form of development agencies and ministries, the UNDP, the IMF, the World Bank, and so on. Yet, these policies and institutions began to be developed shortly after World War II and became more important during the period of decolonization. Though over this period, we have seen changing strategies of development aid, in contrast to the expectations of normative theory, the hoped-for 'peace dividend' at the end of the Cold War has proved illusory (Thomas and Reader 2001). Instead of increasing, development aid actually decreased after the end of the Cold War (Archibugi 2004: 438). Indeed, the shifting strategies of development assistance generally attest to the fact that these policies did not achieve their aims (though it may have made a positive contribution in individual cases) of systematically putting an end to poverty and inequality – hence the frequent need for new approaches. On the contrary, it has been suggested that target countries became dependent on aid, subject to the vicissitudes of the world market, locked into an inequitable system of exchange, and burdened with debt – with the result that donor states earned more in interest than they provided in aid (de Waal 1997). While there is no question that some countries have successfully lifted themselves out of poverty, there are no strong indications that development aid has played an important role in making this possible. Overall, after more than half a century of systematic development assistance, the gap between rich and poor in the world has widened.

In addition, the assumption that it is specifically liberal values that generate a moral obligation to provide development aid is undermined by the fact that many nonliberal states – from Saudi Arabia through China to Cuba – also systematically provide such assistance.

Finally, the more radical theories of distributive justice hold that the structure of the international economic order itself is productive of inequality and poverty and thus requires reform. Though there is ample evidence for the first part of this claim, there is hardly any for the realization of the latter. A good example is the TRIPS agreement which resulted in seriously narrowing access to intellectual products from academic texts for students across the world through HIV/AIDS medication for millions of patients in poor countries. These cases generated such an outrage concerning the decidedly 'immoral' implications of these policies that alternative arrangements were subsequently negotiated – mediating the worst consequences of these policies. However, these settlements are explicitly defined as exceptions while leaving the general rules that led to these excesses in place. And just as there is no indication of a radical reform of the basic principles of the TRIPS agreement, there is no indication of such reforms of the rules, regulations, and structures of the international economic order in general. Despite long-standing complaints from developing countries, the United States and the EU for example continue to subsidize agriculture. Even the Millennium Development Goals are systematically scaled down (Pogge 2004).

Policies of distributive justice, in general, thus take the form of charity or development aid – and these policies are indeed well established and an integral part of liberal societies, states, of many international organizations, and, indeed, of the post-World War II international order itself. Though they may provide help in individual cases, these policies do not achieve their aim to systematically remove poverty and inequality from the international economic order. The end of the Cold War, moreover, has not had a systematic impact on the nature and extent of these policies which are, in any case, not restricted to liberal actors. More radical implications of liberal norms demanding the reform of the structures of the international economic order itself are not at all being taken up by liberal actors – though more systematic demands for such reforms are frequently voiced by developing (including nonliberal) states. The expectations of liberal distributive theories are thus only partially met by policy initiatives and rarely at all in regard of their outcomes.

In the area of international law, liberal theories expect the development and realization of liberal principles in the relations between liberal states and other actors as well as a systematic exclusion of nonliberal states from such developments. In practice, liberal states as well as companies do, of course, widely cooperate with each other, and the latter are also active in the development of 'soft law' for the regulation of transnational interaction (Slaughter 1995, 2000; Cutler 2003). Yet, liberal states themselves do not necessarily stand out in their commitment to, and vertical enforcement of, decidedly liberal principles of international law. The United States, for example, does not 'permit the enforcement, in its local courts, of most human rights treaties' (Alvarez 2001: 194). Moreover (as already noted in Chapter 4), liberal states often fail to reach agreement even on issues of common interest, such as enforceable treaty rights in the area of investment (Alvarez 2001: 199). Such legal cooperation and its vertical enforcement, in contrast, is often highly successful between liberal and nonliberal states (Alvarez 2001: 196). Similarly, while it is the case that individual nonliberal states are on occasion defined as 'rogue' or 'outlaw' states and thus excluded from a range of rights and privileges (through diplomatic, economic, or even military sanctions), the vast majority of nonliberal states enjoy legal equality with liberal states. What is more, liberal states actively cooperate with these nonliberal states diplomatically, economically, and militarily – in bilateral as well as multilateral contexts. The expectation of a systematic distinction between liberal and nonliberal states in the area of international law is thus not borne out in practice.

An exception to these rather inconclusive developments, however, lies in the area of human rights. Here, the end of the Cold War enabled the reform of what is now the UN Human Rights Council which also provides individuals with the possibility of submitting complaints. In addition, humanitarian disasters have increasingly led to the demand for military interventions. In the justification of these interventions, whether authorized by the UN Security Council or not, humanitarian issues have gradually begun to play a role. Moreover, the idea of a 'concert of democracies', an 'alliance of democracies', a 'democratic league' that plays a leading role in world politics above and beyond traditional institutions based on the concept of sovereignty irrespective of regime type, for example advocated by the Princeton Project (Ikenberry and Slaughter 2006), has also been taken up by politicians – of both parties in the United States (Clark 2009). And it may be argued that some of the interventions that have taken place in recent years, Kosovo and Iraq, were justified precisely by such a self-selected coalition of leading liberal states circumventing the Security Council. Finally, the adoption of the Responsibility to Protect is widely taken to indicate an integration of core liberal values into international law.

These developments, too, however, do not unequivocally amount to a realization of the expectations of normative liberal theories. Though the reform of the UN Human Rights Council and especially its reports on individual countries are widely seen as an advance on the previous situation, and human rights increasingly constitute a major reference point for international politics, 'the direct impact of international human rights law on practice in most of the world remains weak and inconsistent' (Cassel 2001). Even liberal states frequently and prominently violate human rights, especially in the course of the war on terror – and not just abroad (in Guantanamo Bay, Abu Ghraib or Bagram) but also in the domestic sphere (Roberts 2004). Moreover, the application of human rights law where it occurs, it turns out, can have detrimental effects on the rights of vulnerable populations. Israeli courts, for example, increasingly use human rights law instead of international humanitarian law to advance the interests of settlers over those of the Palestinian population in the occupied West Bank (Gross 2007).

Similarly, the protection of human rights through humanitarian interventions on closer inspection presents a rather mixed picture. First, observers differ on whether any, and if so which, interventions may qualify as humanitarian. This problem arises partly because interventions with humanitarian outcomes are not necessarily justified and/or undertaken with that aim. In this category fall the interventions by India in East Pakistan, by Vietnam in Cambodia, and by Tanzania in Uganda (Wheeler 2004; Tesón 2005). The problem also arises because humanitarian aims, even if they are specified, usually go hand in hand with other interests and justifications. In the case of Kosovo, for example, Tony Blair made it abundantly clear that national interests of various kinds were a precondition for intervention (1999). Moreover, as it later turned out, NATO's need to construct a new raison d'etre for its continued operation after the end of the Cold War for which it was originally created also played an important role in the decision to intervene (Ong 2003).

Secondly, and partly as a consequence of the requirement for some 'national interest', interventions to end humanitarian disasters are pursued in an extremely inconsistent manner. Some interventions are not undertaken at all (Chechnya, Darfur, Syria), others, infamously in Rwanda, are undertaken much too late (Wheeler 2000: 208–41; Hehir 2010: 179–200), and in yet others like Kosovo the end of the war led to the widely asked question: 'where are the bodies?' (Ignatieff 1999), indicating vastly exaggerated claims about the extent of the supposed humanitarian disaster that justified the intervention.

Thirdly, the conduct and outcome of such interventions raises serious questions regarding their effectiveness in pursuit of the protection and enforcement of human rights. After the end of the Cold War, one of the earliest cases falling into that category was the intervention in Somalia whose primary aim was to provide food aid to a starving population. And yet, it has been argued that by the time of the intervention this aid was no longer needed and, more generally, that there is no indication that the intervention had any impact on mortality rates in the country (de Waal 1994). In addition, the US forces became drawn into the civil war in the country and subsequently withdrew quickly. Today, Somalia is one of the most 'burdened' countries on earth: subject to continuing internal divisions, economic deprivation, interference from its neighbors as well as rich (and often liberal) powers who exploit the lawlessness to fish in Somali waters and dump their (poisonous) garbage there.

We find a similarly sketchy record in the case of Bosnia, where intervening troops stood by as thousands of citizens were killed (Ignatieff 2003: 316; Tesón 2003: 122); in the case of Kosovo, where half the victims of ethnic violence were killed after the intervention in the form of airstrikes had begun (Charney 1999: 834–41; Hehir 2010; Wheeler 2000) as well as in the cases of Afghanistan and Iraq where human rights had also played a role in the justification of the interventions – which were however overshadowed by other goals (as discussed in Chapter 4).

Fourth, while liberal states often took the lead in these interventions and did cooperate with each other, including in acting outside (or above) Security Council authorization, a 'concert of democracies' was never institutionalized. What is more, in many cases, liberal states did not act in concert: France and Germany objected to the Iraq intervention, Germany did not participate in the Libya intervention. At the same time, nonliberal states do undertake interventions – like Vietnam in Cambodia – they do contribute troops to multilateral interventions and regional organizations like Economic Community of West African States (ECOWAS) have intervened in Liberia and Sierra Leone.

Whether and in how far these interventions achieved their aim of protecting and enforcing human rights cannot be authoritatively decided, since we don't know how the situation in these countries would have developed without intervention. What is clear, however, is that liberal states do not systematically protect human rights through interventions, that they do not automatically cooperate, that they have not institutionalized particular privileges for themselves, that such interventions generally pursue mixed and not just humanitarian goals, and that nonliberal states are equally capable and willing, on occasion, to undertake such interventions.

The adoption of the Responsibility to Protect by the General Assembly, finally, does not necessarily indicate a step toward the legalization of humanitarian intervention. Formally, General Assembly resolutions have no standing under international law. More importantly, however, the text that was ultimately adopted emphasizes the primary responsibility of states for the protection of their population which only devolves to the international community if and when a state is unable or unwilling to fulfill this obligation. It thus affirms the principle of sovereignty – albeit in a slightly watered down version – and provides the international community with arguments against intervention (Bellamy 2005).

In sum, roughly three different types of outcomes of 'normative' policies can be identified in practice. In the first case, normative principles are not at all translated into practice. There is no indication of radical reforms of the international economic order, for example, or of a developing cosmopolitan democracy. In the second case, normative principles are practiced but without the progressive or emancipatory effects envisaged by normative theory. Hence, charity and development assistance are systematically provided – and have been so for many decades – yet without leading to a more just or equitable system of distribution. Similarly, NGOs and private actors clearly play an increasing role in international law and politics – but their activities appear to complement or even strengthen the existing political and legal arrangements rather than to undermine them. In the third case, liberal norms are actively pursued but often fail to achieve their aims or lead to counterproductive outcomes. Thus, interventions frequently fail to stop human rights violations; the application of human rights law may contribute to the violation of the fundamental rights of the most vulnerable populations; and the outlawing of 'rogue' states violates the principle of legal equality.

Moreover, the core expectation of normative theories that liberal actors, institutions, and practices will systematically adhere to liberal principles and cooperate with each other in contrast to nonliberal actors is not borne out. Whether at home or abroad, liberal actors do not consistently adhere even to such basic liberal principles as human rights, and even less do they pursue the democratization of the international order or a more egalitarian economic order. Similarly, liberal actors do not systematically cooperate with each other regarding either economic arrangements or military interventions, and they frequently fail to vertically integrate international law. At the same time, however, they regularly cooperate with nonliberal actors in all areas of international politics and economics, and the latter also contribute to a range of 'liberal' projects such as charity, development assistance, transnational NGO activity as well as 'humanitarian interventions'. In short, while there is evidence for individual aspects of normative liberal thought in practice, its overall claims regarding the emancipatory potential of liberal norms and the structure of liberal–nonliberal relations find hardly any support. This radical disjuncture between normative liberal theory and practice thus calls for analysis.

Analysis

Normative liberal theories are, in some sense, more radical than their political and economic counterparts. The latter identify political 'backwardness', economic 'underdevelopment', or 'traditional' cultures in nonliberal societies as a major factor for the unsatisfactory realization of liberal principles in the world – though liberal actors bear some responsibility, too, for their failure to analyze these conditions and their implications properly as well as for organizational and political shortcomings in addressing them. Normative liberal theories, in contrast (though not exclusively), focus largely on the responsibility of liberal actors for the unsatisfactory realization of liberal principles in the world. Since they assume that liberal norms are the mainspring of liberal practices and institutions, the primary responsibility for realizing liberal principles lies with those actors that already embody liberal norms – at least to some extent. These actors, hence, are expected to engage in the realization of liberal principles; and normative theories often ruthlessly expose and criticize the gap between liberal principles and practices.

And yet, the policies inspired by normative liberal theories do not tend to realize this radical potential. On the contrary, they frequently are not pursued at all and where they are, they either are an integral part of the existing order or even advocate systematic legal and political inequality within the international system; an inequality in which the very liberal actors who are so scathingly criticized for failing to live up to liberal norms are accorded with special rights and privileges. This contradiction, I will show now, has its roots in the abstraction of liberal principles from the particular context of their constitution and the dynamics of their development. And it is this abstraction that leads to a reductionist conception of liberalism and obscures the internal tensions of liberalism even while it reproduces them in practice. From a

Lockean point of view, I will show, this dynamic is perfectly intelligible – if ultimately not resolvable.

The aim to democratize the international order itself, as we have seen, was hardly taken up at all by liberal actors. In response to these failures, Archibugi highlights the need to develop a conception of democracy in line with the contemporary globalized world that does not rely on the traditional democratic states for the realization of a cosmopolitan democracy. Instead, global public opinion (expressed in the huge demonstrations against the Iraq war) is identified as a likely protagonist for the project. In addition, it is necessary to determine more clearly which kinds of 'norms, or soft law, are more likely to influence the decisions of states and of international organizations' (Archibugi 2004: 465). And finally, the cosmopolitan democracy project has to identify concrete and realistic policies that can contribute to a gradual development of cosmopolitan democracy (Archibugi 2004: 465–6).

All three weaknesses of the initial approach identified here concern the relationship between theory and practice: which actors do in practice embody the theoretical principles? How do these principles have to be formulated in order to be taken up in practice? And which concrete policies serve the realization of the theoretical principles? While the cosmopolitan democracy project had failed to provide a satisfactory account of the relationship between the theoretical norm of cosmopolitan democracy and liberal democratic states, the Lockean theorization of liberalism and its historical development does provide such an account. It shows that the political right to consent to, and participate in, government was a tool for the realization of liberal norms and policies more generally and as such this right was explicitly accorded only to those sections of society, or those societies, that were seen as bearers of these norms and denied to 'nonliberal' groups and societies. Hence, the democratization of liberal states themselves, that is the introduction of universal suffrage, could only ensue once the majority of the population had become bearers of such liberal norms – which in turn had been made possible through the denial of political and economic rights to other societies. This inequality allowed liberal states to widen the population's economic stake in the system and subsequently also their political participation. The norm of *liberal* democracy thus emerged as a result of the establishment of the sovereign state which in turn is based on the denial of rights of sovereignty to other communities.

In light of this account, the failure of the EU or other liberal states to pursue policies of cosmopolitan democracy is not surprising since the norm of liberal democracy is constituted through the state. As long as the distinction between the domestic and international sphere contributes to the maintenance of liberal democracy domestically, therefore, liberal states cannot pursue the goal of cosmopolitan democracy without jeopardizing their own liberal character. In other words, the moral norm of cosmopolitan democracy stands in contradiction to and potentially undermines liberal democracy in practice.

Moreover, this account suggests that world public opinion does not present a more likely protagonist for policies of cosmopolitan democracy than the EU. After all, once democratized, liberal states are dependent on public opinion and the latter is constituted by and through these states: while there may occasionally exist a temporary disjuncture between public opinion and the government (as in the case of the Iraq war in Spain and Britain, for example), in a democracy such a gap, if it concerns fundamental norms, cannot persist for long. In other words, the counterposition of liberal states (pursuing statist goals) and public opinion (pursuing cosmopolitan goals) fails to take into account their mutually constitutive as well as particular rather than universal nature. Indeed, in the case of the demonstrations against the Iraq war, the public demanded above all Security Council authorization – and hence legal backing – for the war. This demand thus did not entail a principled objection to the use of military force, and it affirmed precisely the kind of undemocratic international organization – in the form of the Security Council – which the cosmopolitan democracy project sets out to reform.

The failure of the cosmopolitan democracy project thus does not lie at the level of identifying the correct bearers of liberal norms. Instead, its weakness lies in its normative starting point – in the abstraction of norms from the particular practices that constitute such norms in the first place. The result of this abstraction – a universal (cosmopolitan) conception of democracy – must, for the purposes of realization, be linked back to real actors, institutions, and practices, which, however, happen to be constituted as bearers of particular rather than universal norms. Hence, the EU and other liberal states pursue the particular statist conception of liberal democracy and so does public opinion – even if it finds itself occasionally in agreement with that of some other publics. Such agreement does not constitute a world public opinion or global civil society.[6]

---

[6] For a more thorough critique of this notion, see Brown (2001) and Walzer (1997).

Moreover, the need to identify particular actors, institutions, and practices as protagonists of universal norms establishes a hierarchy between these and other actors, institutions, and practices and provides at least a temporary moral justification not only of their particular policies but also of their inequality in the international system in general. Hence, the assumption that the EU as a 'post-Westphalian' political entity actually does embody more universal norms than other states provides the basis for according it with rights of intervention in 'solidarist' or 'puralist' states (Linklater 1998), and the assumption that liberal civil society organizations embody and advance norms of cosmopolitan democracy provides the basis for justifying their rights to intervene in less advanced societies (Archibugi 1998: 218). In the same vein, deriving the notion of a world public opinion from the temporary agreement of some public demonstrations on a particular issue necessarily elevates these publics and their position over others that may not have taken much interest in the matter or even demonstrated some support for it (like American public opinion).

In sum, the abstraction of liberal norms from their constitutive practices explains all three of the standard outcomes of normative theory in practice. As long as liberal norms remain at the level of abstraction and are not linked to concrete practices, they remain politically sterile. Inasmuch as such a link between abstract norms and concrete practices is established through the identification of norm-bearing actors, institutions, and practices, normative theory helps to justify and reproduce existing (and necessarily particular) policies – and thus fails to achieve its emancipatory goals. Finally, the attempt to salvage the emancipatory potential of normative theory by providing these norms-bearing actors, institutions, and practices with the rights to actively impose these principles on others ultimately tends to undermine those very goals. In this case the realization of the particular rather than universal norms embodied by relevant actors, institutions, and practices undermines the principle of (political) freedom or self-determination as well as the principle of legal equality.

Similar dynamics operate in the area of distributive justice. While theories of distributive justice demand, roughly, the provision of charity, or of systematic aid, or of a radical reform of the structures of the international economic order, in practice only charity and aid provision play a role. Why is the radical potential of theories of distributive justice not translated into politics? Following the Lockean exposition, liberal actors are constituted through private property – and the institution of private property introduced inequality (already in the state of nature).

Inequality is thus a fundamental feature of a liberal economic system. Its justification lies in the claim that private property is more productive than common property and will thus eventually benefit all people – albeit not equally. Historically, however, this inequality in the domestic sphere created political instability and thus had to be managed carefully. This management was made possible by the distinction between the domestic and the international sphere that allowed for the differential allocation of the costs and benefits of this economic system: that is, for the import of economic benefits and the export of its costs – thus mediating domestic inequality to some extent. The liberal economic order thus did not just produce inequality in the domestic and the international sphere, it also constituted a hierarchy of moral obligations – with the domestic sphere taking precedence over the international. This account suggests that there are not only economic and political but also moral reasons for the failure of liberal actors to pursue a radical reform of the international economic order.

Economically, the exploitation and in some cases deliberate destruction of indigenous economies in the colonial world thus played a constitutive role for the economic development and subsequently also domestic democratization of liberal states (Russett et al. 2000: 413). Though there is considerable debate on the impact of these historical developments on contemporary economic inequality, there is no doubt that developing countries today are deeply penetrated by, and dependent on, industrial (largely liberal) states and the world economy shaped by these states (Russett et al. 2000: 416). While this dependency of poor countries is widely recognized and discussed, the reverse – namely the continuing dependency of rich liberal states on this system – is less thoroughly explored. In strictly economic terms, poor countries are, indeed, 'vulnerable' in their relations with rich countries and the world market in general, while the latter are for the most part only 'sensitive'. Yet, these economic measurements do not take into account their political implications – the fact that the political survival of a democratized liberal state depends on the continued provision of economic opportunities and benefits to the majority of the population. As long as the provision of these benefits is thought to require an unequal distribution of the costs and benefits of the liberal economic system, therefore, rich liberal states are politically 'vulnerable'; that is, dependent on the continuing inequality of this international system in order to maintain domestic liberalism.

These political and economic reasons for resisting radical reform are, however, not devoid of a moral dimension. Residents of developed countries are often 'offended' by the suggestion that they have a moral obligation to reform the international economic order and instead point to the moral need to take care of the domestic poor before helping foreigners (Russett et al. 2000: 421). This moral obligation to address inequality within particular communities first is a result of the distinction and inequality between the domestic and international spheres necessitated by the internal contradictions of liberalism. In other words, liberal subjects are not just economically but also morally constituted in and through relations of inequality. Abstracted from this context, the universal moral obligation to establish distributive justice thus stands in contradiction to real existing particular moral obligations established over a long time in and through a rich density of social and political relations of redistribution within the domestic sphere – made possible by its distinction from the international sphere.

Moreover, this account helps make sense of the fact that charity and aid do constitute an integral part of the liberal international economic order, which they help to reproduce instead of challenge. Charity and aid provision are necessary and flexible tools to manage and mediate economic inequality. In the domestic sphere, both charity and more systemic aid (or welfare) arrangements were and still are used to soften the worst excesses of economic inequality, to provide even the poor with a stake in the system (thus preventing revolutions), and to uphold the moral claims of the system itself – if and to the extent that such management proves politically necessary. Charity provides recipients with temporary relief, but it also creates dependency in the long term. Systematic investment and aid in poor countries often stimulate growth in the short term, but are then followed by a repatriation of profits, debt payments, and ultimately also dependency (Russett et al. 2000: 418). The latter is most visible in the widespread use of conditionality. By relieving short-term needs, these policies help to prevent political upheaval and to firmly integrate poor countries into the world economy.

Charity and aid differ radically from systemic reforms in that they constitute entirely voluntary – and thus flexible – political tools in the hands of donors. And it is the political nature of these tools that explains why the widely expected 'peace dividend' after the end of the Cold War proved illusory (Thomas and Reader 2001: 87). While superpower competition during the Cold War had required the provision of aid in order to prevent poor countries from firmly associating themselves with the enemy camp, this political danger disappeared with the end of the Cold War and the widely hailed monopoly of the liberal political and economic system. In addition, poor countries found themselves suddenly competing with the former Soviet republics or allies for aid (Russett et al. 2000: 429).

And yet, this does not mean that charity and aid do not play a moral role. They are of course often provided out of a genuine desire to help. Yet, one-sided as they are, they constitute donors as free, benevolent (moral), and capable (quintessentially liberal) agents in relation to incapable (economically and politically) and dependent recipients. Hence, they do not just contribute to the reproduction of the liberal international economic order, and provide it with a moral dimension, they also reproduce the particular morality embodied in liberal actors.

Radical policies of distributive justice, in sum, are not taken up by liberal actors because the latter are not just economically and politically but also morally constituted through inequality. The political, economic, and moral management of this inequality, however, requires charity and aid as flexible tools which therefore contribute to the reproduction of the system. This particularity escapes normative theories and policies that abstract from the historical constitution of liberal norms themselves.

Of the policies inspired by liberal norms, it was humanitarian intervention for which the end of the Cold War provided the most significant opportunity. Yet, the record of such interventions has been rather mixed. In some cases of relatively clear-cut humanitarian disasters, interventions were not undertaken. In those cases where they were undertaken, the goal of ending humanitarian disasters and protecting human rights was at best partially achieved; at worst such interventions have been criticized for providing cover for continued violations of human rights. And the move to legalize humanitarian interventions through the adoption of the Responsibility to Protect has arguably not strengthened the obligation to intervene.

Analyzing this situation, advocates of humanitarian intervention argue that the failure to intervene is caused by a lack of moral commitment on the part of liberal states. These states fail to accept that 'humanitarian intervention is both morally permitted and morally required' (Wheeler 2004: 310); they follow their self-interest instead of protecting the liberal norms of human rights and hence are not 'good international citizens' (Linklater 2000: 493) or even supporters of 'the worst forms of human evil' (Tesón 2003: 129). In response to these failures, normative theories demand a 'moral transformation' (Wheeler 2004: 310) and dedicate their energies to demonstrating the validity and necessity of these moral norms.

The same lack of moral commitment, according to these theorists, is ultimately also responsible for the partial or mixed outcomes of those interventions that were undertaken. Hence, in the case of Bosnia or Rwanda the interventions came too late because liberal states were not ready to commit troops and material resources in time to stop the worst excesses; that is, they put their own material and political interests before the moral obligation to protect the victims of human rights violations. Conversely, in the case of Somalia the intervention was abandoned before its goals could be achieved because of the unanticipated fatalities amongst the (American) intervention forces (Wheeler 2004: 207). In the case of Kosovo, the intervention provided cover for the continued violation of human rights because interveners first withdrew the OSCE observers and then, in order to avoid fatalities amongst their own troops, decided to proceed via high altitude bombing instead of sending ground troops (Wheeler 2004: 239; Charney 1999: 840). This 'risk transfer militarism' (Shaw 2002) shifts the cost of the intervention on to the very people whom it is supposed to protect. The failure to plan for, and commit material resources to, post-conflict reconstruction or statebuilding similarly attests to self-interest trumping moral obligations (Wheeler 2004: 207, 282). In light of this analysis, advocates of humanitarian intervention return to the claim that these weaknesses can and must be resolved by clarifying the moral obligation entailed in liberal norms and hence getting liberal actors to embrace them over and against their particular interests.

Yet, why does this moral commitment appear to remain so weak despite abundant and high-quality arguments in its support – not just in the academic literature but also in public discourse? The problem, following the Lockean account, lies in the separation of norms and practices, or the counterposition of morality and politics. The very term 'humanitarian intervention' distinguishes these acts from other interventions that are seen as political, that is in pursuit of particular rather than universal interests and hence illegal. Humanitarian interventions, in contrast, are justified on the grounds that they aim to realize universal moral principles in the form of human rights and are therefore presented as inherently nonpartisan and defensible (Hehir 2010: 12). The historical development of liberal norms, including human rights, however, followed particular interests – those of propertied men who aimed to protect their property and independence from interference by the state – and became subsequently institutionalized within particular liberal states. Liberal norms, the Lockean account suggests in contrast to contemporary normative theories, therefore, are not the source of liberal institutions and practices. Instead, they are the abstracted and universalized conception of particular interests and their political aspirations. The realization of these aspirations thus leads to the establishment of particular political institutions like the state that embody those norms and principles. Particular interests and institutions are therefore a necessary means for – rather than a barrier to – the realization of liberal norms like human rights. And it is this constitutive relationship between particular interests and institutions and liberal norms that explains why liberal states only engage in humanitarian interventions when these do not undermine the interests underpinning the liberal rights of their own populations. It also explains why the conduct of interventions that are undertaken in terms of material and political commitments as well as military strategy is always tempered, always limited by the need to uphold all dimensions – material benefits, political consent, individual rights – of liberalism at home. In other words, humanitarian interventions do not pitch crass and immoral self-interest versus lofty moral obligations; they pitch the particular human rights of one community versus those of another.[7]

In practice, this is clearly recognized even by normative theorists who distinguish between obligations to fellow citizens and obligations to outsiders: Humanitarian interventions do not have to be undertaken if they are expected to bring 'substantial harm' to 'fellow citizens' (Elshtain 2003: 74–5) and 'states are not required to sacrifice vital interests (…) for the sake of helping others' and even soldiers' lives do not have to be sacrificed 'in large numbers' (Wheeler 2000: 49). There are, to be sure, disagreements on the extent of the sacrifice that can be required of fellow citizens and soldiers (Cook 2003: 150–1; Elshtain 2003: 75). Yet, in all cases the obligations toward its own citizens and soldiers provide the state in general (not just the liberal or modern state) with moral standing. Hence, the universal moral obligation is explicitly recognized as not 'absolute' (Tesón 2003: 127), as 'an imperfect duty' (Nardin 2003: 23).

Once particular institutions like the state are, in practice, seen as embodying moral principles, however, a response to humanitarian disasters cannot any longer be depicted as an epic struggle between politics and morality. Instead, it requires negotiating between competing (and often times even the same) moral principles embedded in different political institutions and practices. This involves the weighing of lives saved versus lives lost through the application of military force as well as the 'moral' benefits of establishing rights respecting institutions in target states versus the 'immoral' consequences of adding to the permissible

---

[7] For a more thorough discussion of humanitarian intervention, see Jahn (2012a).

causes of war in the international system (Hehir 2010: 161, 163; Tesón 2003: 117–8; Miller 2003: 237; Coady 2002: 17; Jackson 2000: 291). Hence, a variety of political institutions – amongst them the legal rules of the international system – are recognized as having moral standing. And even protagonists of humanitarian intervention acknowledge that 'these are cases where whatever we do we will end up tolerating a violation of *some* fundamental rule' (Tesón 2003: 110). The decision to be made is therefore not one between politics and morality but requires '*moral-political* considerations' (Tesón 2003: 127; emphasis added). Hence, the fact that humanitarian intervention is 'something far more talked about than done' (Farer 2003: 55) is not necessarily a sign of 'moral bankruptcy' (Wheeler 2000: 296); it may well be the result of precisely such 'moral-political' considerations. And the necessity of these considerations also explains the difficulties of actually identifying humanitarian interventions. After all, if the humanitarian or moral dimensions of these acts cannot be clearly separated from particular interests and institutions, then the very notion of humanitarian intervention as opposed to other interventions becomes questionable.

Moreover, the fact that morality and politics, or human rights and particular interests and institutions, are not actually separate and contradictory forces explains both the failures and the unintended consequences of normative theories. These theories, as we have seen, commit themselves to provide sophisticated conceptions and justifications of liberal norms such as human rights with the aim to convince actors on the ground to internalize and realize those norms. Yet, the limited and sometimes counterproductive outcomes of attempts to realize these norms in practice are attributed to a lack of (the right kind of) moral commitment – and hence to the failure of normative theories to present a sufficiently compelling conception of these norms (thus sending scholars back to the drawing board). And, indeed, if norms are constituted through particular interests, practices, and institutions, then normative theories are unsuccessful because they elaborate and advocate norms abstracted from these particular circumstances. Conversely, where such norms are taken up, their realization logically takes the form of particular interests, institutions, and practices – and hence does not live up to the expectations generated by abstract universal norms.

Yet, the need to link these abstract norms to particular circumstances is widely recognized among normative theorists who therefore elaborate the particular conditions under which human rights are likely to be violated and those which are conducive to their protection. Cited among the causes of systematic human rights violations are the 'attempt to align the boundaries of the state and the boundaries of the nation' which leads to ethnic cleansing (Linklater 2000: 484) or regime types like 'anarchy' and 'tyranny' (Tesón 2003: 96–7). Here, the causes of systematic human rights violations are seen as 'deeply rooted in the political, economic, and social structures of societies' (Wheeler 2000: 306).

Solutions are accordingly found in alternative political arrangements. Ethnic cleansing requires the reconfiguration of 'political systems that violate fundamental moral principles' (Linklater 2000: 486), that is, the establishment of states 'which are more universalistic and more sensitive to cultural differences' (Linklater 2000: 484). The solution to anarchy and tyranny lies in the constitution of a liberal state (Tesón 2003: 96). And the means for implementing these solutions in the context of humanitarian intervention generally lie in war which is itself recognized as a highly political tool (Elshtain 2003: 68; Heinze 2009; Chesterman 2001; Coady 2002: 16; de Waal 2007).

In order to make norms relevant to practice, therefore, normative theorists identify those actors, institutions, and practices in the real world that embody these norms comparatively well and provide them with the rights and privileges necessary to extend these moral institutions – while denying similar rights to morally less advanced political systems. This goal of universalizing particular political systems runs up against the political and legal norms that explicitly protect the political, economic, and cultural pluralism of the current international system and thus requires 'a new legal order' (Linklater 2000: 493; Wheeler 2000: 310). Accordingly, the world's states are divided into those whose political institutions are already – to some extent – in accordance with the realization of human rights and those that are not. Liberal (modern, universal, European, democratic) states are seen to meet the standard for 'comparative moral reliability' (Buchanan and Keohane 2004: 19) and are thus charged with the responsibility to safeguard individual rights at home and abroad (Tesón 2003: 127). These states become the 'custodians of the global human rights culture' (Linklater 2000: 486).

Concrete proposals to this end include 'a treaty based coalition among liberal democratic states' with the right to override a deadlocked Security Council on questions of humanitarian intervention (Buchanan 2003: 171; Buchanan and Keohane 2004; Ikenberry and Slaughter 2006),[8] a call for 'gradations in sovereignty' (Keohane 2003; Paris 2004),[9] right up

---

[8] For an overview and critique of such proposals, see Clark (2009).
[9] For a discussion of the internal contradictions of this position, see Jahn (2007b).

to the establishment of a new imperialism on the grounds that 'the weak still need the strong and the strong still need an orderly world' (Cooper 2002: 5). The result of this reasoning is an international order no longer based on the principle of equality. 'State-majoritarianism, under current conditions in which many states are not democratic cannot be viewed as having the same legitimacy-conferring power as the consent of individuals' (Buchanan 2003: 171). The theoretical linkage of moral principles to particular sets of political institutions thus leads to an identification of the latter with morality and a simultaneous denial of moral standing to alternative political arrangements. Most importantly, however, normative theories thus end up advocating the principle of inequality in international law and politics – a principle that stands in direct contradiction to the universal and abstract core liberal norm of (legal) equality. In other words, the abstraction of universal liberal norms like human rights in normative theory either makes them sterile in practice or else, ironically, leads liberal theory to provide moral justifications for policies that directly violate universal liberal norms. There is no clearer example for this dynamic than the application of human rights law by Israeli courts in the occupied territories. While traditional humanitarian law recognizes the special conditions of occupation and sets out to protect the vulnerable population in occupied territories, human rights law entirely disregards this context and can thus be used to justify the destruction of Palestinian houses in order to protect the freedom of religion of Israeli settlers (Gross 2007) – that is, to provide a legal justification for already existing unequal power relations.

This inequality is even more pronounced, indeed it constitutes the defining feature of policies aiming to reform international law itself. International law is seen here as a major tool for the realization of the entire range of substantive liberal norms (democracy, distributive justice, human rights), and the core mechanism to achieve this goal consists in establishing legal inequality between liberal and nonliberal actors, institutions, and practices. This takes the form of denying nonliberal actors the traditional right to participate in the making of, and consent to, international law – that is, to deny these actors the status of full subjects of international law or full sovereignty – while simultaneously designating liberal actors, institutions, and practices as full subjects of universally applicable international law. Concretely, the voices of nonliberal states (and 'burdened' societies) are excluded from the (imagined) agreement on international legal norms between 'liberal' and 'decent' states – but nevertheless subjected to these norms, if necessary by force. Nondemocratic states are denied the right to consent to decisions on intervention yet subjected to such decisions made by democratic states. The soft rules and regulations arising from interaction between liberal (state as well as nonstate) actors are to be applied universally, that is, also to nonliberal actors that had no part in their development.

Yet, these visions are only partially realized. While soft rules and regulations clearly often do apply to nonliberal actors, they do not necessarily embody a systematic distinction between liberal and nonliberal actors. The latter may be involved in developing such rules; inasmuch as these rules pertain to nonstate actors, they do not challenge the full sovereignty of nonliberal states. Most importantly, however, where nonliberal states are indeed 'forced' to accept such rules against their will, this force rests on inequalities of economic and political, not legal, power. Similarly, although the nondemocratic nature of specific states – like Iraq under Saddam Hussein – clearly help to justify intervention, such interventions also occur in democratic states (like Serbia in the context of the Kosovo intervention). Most importantly, however, there is no sign of a systematic denial of full sovereignty rights to the vast majority of nondemocratic states in the world. On the contrary, such states often actively participate in the making of international law (for example, in the constitution of the ICC) while democratic or liberal states may well remain outside such legal developments (the United States and Israel, for example). Albeit the idea of a 'democratic club' trumping the Security Council in matters of humanitarian intervention has been widely taken up and discussed, there have been no serious moves to establish such a privileged institution. The picture that emerges is thus familiar: the more radical proposals – those that aim for a formal institutionalization of legal inequality – are not realized, and the occasional distinction between liberal and nonliberal states does not fundamentally challenge the status quo. Most paradoxically, however, liberal international law is essentially identified with the establishment of legal inequality – in radical contradiction to the association of liberalism with equality before the law.

And yet, historically legal inequality is constitutive of liberalism itself as well as of its norm of legal equality. In light of the fact that liberal norms – constituted through private property – were not widely held in society, the law was indeed used to realize such norms. Such law could, however, only be established through the denial of political rights – the right to participate in, and consent to, legislation – to 'nonliberal' sections of society. The subsequent development of legal equality in such unequal societies, in turn, was made possible by the establishment of legal inequality between societies – by an international law that accorded full political and economic, or sovereign, rights to some communities and denied it to others. This unequal international law provided liberal states with the opportunity to appropriate the resources necessary in order to establish the preconditions for legal equality in the domestic sphere.

The establishment of legal equality in the domestic sphere was thus based on the creation of nonliberal actors – actors that were simply designated as not deserving of equal rights (yet). Hence, Locke excluded indigenous communities in the Americas from equal political and therefore also economic rights just as 19th century international lawyers justified the restriction of sovereignty to European (settler) or 'civilized' states. Today, this impetus finds its most visible expression in the attempt to designate certain states as 'outlaw' or 'rogue' states. As in the past, however, this designation does not reflect practice but is rooted in an abstract conception of liberal norms. In practice, as I have shown in Chapter 3, Locke was unable to provide logically or empirically compelling differences between indigenous and English societies that would justify the exclusion of the former from equal rights – which was ultimately simply based on the fact that European states *could* – had the power to – deprive them of these rights. Similarly, 19th century international lawyers were unable – try as they might – to identify logically and empirically convincing *systematic* differences between European and non-European societies (Anghi 2007) which would justify the inequality of international law in the age of imperialism. Such unequal international law could nevertheless be codified because European (settler) states had the power to impose it. The most recent attempts to establish a distinction between liberal and nonliberal states suffer from the same theoretical weakness: calling these actors 'outlaws' suggests that they act outside the law, break the law. In fact, however, most states obey international law most of the time. This rule is independent of regime type: while nonliberal states indeed obey most of international law most of the time (and even play a constructive role in developing that law), liberal states themselves clearly (and famously) break that law on occasion. Hence, nonliberal states are 'found deficient for what they are rather than what they have done'; they are 'ontological outlaws' (Clark 2009: 566). Indeed, neither do these states place themselves outside the law (except for particular and clearly circumscribed instances which we also find in liberal foreign policies), nor does the misleading designation as 'outlaw' states liberate them from the law's shackles. In practice, 'outlaw' states are subjected to a variety of legal measures – such as sanctions (weapons), inspections – that are not visited upon other members of the system (Simpson 2001, 2004). Hence, while 'outlaw' states are excluded from the rights of international law, they are nevertheless subjected to its obligations, and more intensely so than other state – an arrangement that is only possible on the grounds of unequal power relations.

The failure of liberal reform projects in the post-Cold War order ultimately has its roots in the abstraction of liberal norms from practice which leads to an 'ontological' conception or designation of actors, institutions, and practices that simply misses their particular nature. Having severed the link between practice and theory, normative approaches can only grasp practice through the abstract norms which provide their starting point. Consequently, concrete actors, institutions, and practices are defined by the abstract or universal norms they embody, or lack. Liberal states are defined through the universal liberal norms that their constitutions are built on – and expected to behave accordingly: to provide private actors with a voice in legal and political decision making, to cooperate with other liberal states, to integrate liberal international norms into domestic law – and to refrain from such engagements with nonliberal actors. Conversely, nonliberal actors are defined through the absence of liberal norms and thus expected to deny private actors a political and legal voice, to resist cooperation with other states, to refuse integrating international into domestic law, or even to break the former.

What this 'ontological' conception of actors, institutions, and practices overlooks is that both liberal and nonliberal actors were historically constituted with reference to each other: that liberal constitutions and norms in some communities were based on the denial of these rights to others. Hence, each of these actors embodies and pursues particular rather than universal norms: liberal states tend to respect the human rights of their own citizens, but not necessarily those of outsiders (Guantanamo); nonliberal states may deny rights to their own citizens, yet act in accordance with international law in their dealings with other states. Moreover, in realizing their own goals, each of these actors is dependent on the other. Just as the United States depends on relations with China, Iran depends on relations with the (largely liberal) West – irrespective of whether its aim is to build a nuclear bomb or to feed its population. And it is this intimate relationship that accounts for the rich and dense relations that constitute and link these actors and shape their policy decisions – and which runs directly counter to the normative expectation that such actors behave in accordance with abstract principles that pitch historically mutually constitutive entities against each other.

Most importantly, however, the attempt to implement legal inequality fails because its normative protagonists overlook the dynamic relations between these mutually constituted actors. While the realization of liberal international law in the past, as we have seen, could only succeed in situations of decidedly unequal power relations, it simultaneously produced resistance on the part of the disenfranchised which eventually led to decolonization – and aided by the competition between the Soviet Union and the United States during the Cold War to a relatively egalitarian international law (an exceptional period in the history of modern international law). The normative interpretation of the end of the Cold War as ushering in the *ideological* monopoly of liberalism (Fukuyama 1989) gave rise to the idea that unequal international law could now be reestablished. This interpretation failed to recognize not so much the power of nonliberal ideas and forces (as Huntington, for example, suggests in the 'Clash of Civilizations', 1993) but rather the fact that the very attempt to institutionalize legal inequality – between democratic and nondemocratic, liberal and nonliberal, human rights respecting and human rights violating states – constitute the latter in opposition to the former and galvanize resistance. In other words, it was the proactive pursuit of liberal inequality itself – from the construction of 'rogue' or 'outlaw' states through high-handed interventions lacking Security Council approval to ideas of 'conditional' sovereignty, especially on the part of the United States – that ultimately led to widespread resistance and found expression, for example, in the systematic use of the veto in the Security Council as well as in widespread support for the development of the ICC as a means to counter US interests (Schabas 2004).

In sum, projects to reform international law in light of liberal principles are characterized by the justification of (more or less extreme) legal inequality based on a systematic theoretical distinction between liberal and nonliberal actors, institutions, and practices (Cohen 2004). This core of liberal international law is entirely in line not only with the Lockean arguments but also with the development and practice of international law subsequently. However, the distinction between liberal and nonliberal actors underlying these projects is based on liberal norms abstracted from practice and thus misses their particular and mutually constitutive nature in practice. Oblivious to this connection, moreover, these reform projects are unaware of the dynamic relations between these actors – of the fact that the very pursuit of a liberal international law necessarily constitutes others as nonliberals and triggers their resistance to policies explicitly designed to deprive them of rights held under previous international law (see, for example, Bishai 2012).

Nevertheless, some of the features of liberal international law are being taken up in practice: not all but a few states are clearly designated as 'outlaw' states and treated as such; democracy and respect for human rights play a much more important, conditional, role at least for weak states; and there is no doubt that soft law regulations do affect actors that have not consented to them. Yet, these developments do not fundamentally challenge traditional international law. Instead, they are expressions of existing inequalities.

Conclusion

The aim to realize liberal norms and principles in international affairs is, of course, a long-standing one and, as we have seen in the previous two chapters, was pursued with particular vigor after the end of the Cold War through attempts to transform particular political and economic institutions. Yet, the demise of the Soviet Union was also interpreted from a normative point of view as ushering in the ideological monopoly of liberalism and thus to provide an opportunity for the implementation of liberal norms at the level of global institutions. Thus, a variety of normative theories advocated the democratization of the international system at large, that is, cosmopolitan democracy; the pursuit of distributive justice through reforms of the international economic order; the global protection of human rights and an alignment of international law with liberal norms and practices.

Some of these projects, notably radical reforms of the international economic order or the democratization of the international order, were hardly taken up in practice. Meanwhile others like the global protection of human rights through humanitarian interventions or the introduction of 'gradations' of sovereignty conditional on democratic or other liberal credentials in international law have been taken up in practice, but in an inconsistent and ad hoc manner. While interventions in cases of humanitarian disasters have taken place, they neither covered all or even the most serious cases, nor were systematically justified with reference to human rights or generally authorized by the Security Council. Consequently, there has been no integration of the concept of humanitarian intervention into international law in general. Similarly, while some nonliberal states were indeed designated as 'outlaw' states curtailing their rights at the same time as increasing their obligations under international law, such legal inequality was certainly not introduced systematically for all nonliberal states. On the contrary, the vast majority of nonliberal states continues to enjoy full rights of sovereignty and cooperates with liberal states in all areas of international politics. Moreover, even in those cases where reform projects were indeed translated into political practice, the results did not necessarily live up to expectations. In many cases, interventions failed to prevent what was generally considered as avoidable human rights violations and in some even seemed to contribute to them. Similarly, moves to make sovereignty conditional on the institutionalization and practice of liberal norms like democracy or human rights has arguably not widened the realm of liberal law but generated resistance to it.

These weaknesses of normative projects are due to the fact that the liberal norms elaborated by normative theory are lost in the process of translation into practice. In order to ensure the emancipatory power of liberal norms, normative theory elaborates these norms in abstraction from practice. And, indeed, the resultant universal conception of liberal norms serves to highlight the gap between liberal theory and practice and thus provides guiding principles for reform. Yet, the realization of such principles requires a reconnection to practice. Taking its starting point from abstract liberal principles, however, normative liberal theory has no choice but to grasp practice through the lens of these principles – concretely, to try and identify particular actors, institutions, and practices that embody such principles and can serve as their avant-garde in practice. Hence, democratic states are seen as proponents of a universal principle of cosmopolitan democracy, liberal states and societies are committed to liberal principles of distributive justice and hence identified as protagonists for global economic reform, liberal states largely respect human rights and are hence seen as 'custodians' of these rights globally, and liberal states or private actors respect liberal principles in their legal interactions and are thus expected to spread them through their implementation in international law. Yet, it is not just particular actors but also the development of international politics itself that is interpreted through abstract liberal norms, hence Fukuyama's famous claim that the demise of the Soviet Union resulted in an *ideological* monopoly of the liberal world view and hence the possibility of realizing its political, economic, and normative principles worldwide.

These expectations were largely frustrated in the post-Cold War era simply because the various protagonists identified as bearers of liberal norms did not, or at least not systematically, behave in accordance with these norms. Democratic states did not champion the extension of decision-making rights to sub- and suprastate actors; though continuing to provide charity and development aid, instead of working for a more fundamental reform of the international economic system, liberal states vigorously resisted calls for such reforms; they also resisted a general obligation to intervene abroad for the protection of human rights; liberal actors continued to cooperate widely with nonliberals thus providing the latter with full legal standing under international law; and the assumption of a liberal monopoly at the end of the Cold War had exaggerated the power of liberalism and underestimated that of alternative world views (Huntington 1993). In short, the assessment of international affairs through the lens of abstract liberal norms produced an inaccurate picture.

The roots for this disjuncture between liberal norms and practice lie, as Locke's work shows, at the very heart of liberalism. It arises from the need to justify norms based on particular interests as universally valid. In practice, however, the realization of these norms led to the establishment of highly particular actors, institutions, and practices: to the restriction of political rights to property owners, to the exclusion of communities from property rights, to the codification of these inequalities in law, to the restriction of this law to particular communities (that is, to the establishment of states), and ultimately to the restriction of the rights of states to those communities powerful enough to successfully claim it. In other words, the history of the realization of liberal norms is a history of successive fragmentation, of the constitution of particular entities in which liberal norms could only be realized if they were not universally shared.

This history from which normative liberal theory abstracts accounts for the inconsistent behavior of the particular liberal actors, who cannot pursue the universal realization of liberal norms without undermining their own liberal constitution. That is, the protection of human rights abroad may well entail the violation of such rights (of soldiers, for example) at home. It also explains the continuing and rich engagement with nonliberal actors whose constitution was and remains instrumental for the establishment and reproduction of liberal actors. Hence, economic cooperation with nonliberal states provides the material basis for domestic liberalism. Most importantly, however, it highlights that the active attempt to realize liberal norms is itself productive of nonliberal actors, institutions, and practices as well as of resistance to this establishment of inequality.

In sum, while the abstraction of liberal norms from their particular and often unsavoury historical roots is supposed to produce a pure, untainted, and universally valid conception that exposes the shortcomings of existing international relations and serves as a guiding principle for reform, this very act of abstraction leaves these principles disconnected from practice – whence they either lose their relevance for practice entirely or need to be reconnected to practice. Yet, once the mutually constitutive relationship between theory and practice has been severed, reestablishing this linkage is a one-sided affair: an identification of supposedly universal norms in particular institutions. Hence, the particular institution of the democratic state which appears wanting in light of the universal norm of democracy suddenly becomes the bearer of this norm; liberal states that do not live up to notions of universal distributive justice are suddenly seen as the natural protagonists of this norm; states that restrict their respect for human rights largely to the domestic sphere suddenly become the custodians of the universal protection of human rights; and states that restrict the rights and obligations of liberal law to the domestic sphere become the avant-garde of a liberal international law. The very institutions who clearly fail to live up to abstract liberal norms are designated as its protagonists. And in this role, normative liberal theory elevates these institutions over others, provides them with superior moral standing, and more often than not also with the legal and political means to impose their norms, institutions, and practices onto others. The distinction between theory and practice, in short, turns the critical motivation and potential of normative theory into a moral justification of unequal power relations. Or, as Rob Walker has aptly put it, 'the abstract attempt to apply ethics to politics, truth to power, or universality to particularity simply conjures away the very specific ways in which these apparent opposites are already mutually constitutive of the modern state' (Walker 2010: 129).

7
Conclusion

Introduction

In light of the unexpected fate of liberal policies in the post-Cold War era, and given that liberal theories fail to provide a satisfactory explanation for these developments, this study set out to develop a conception of liberalism capable of accounting for the dynamics and paradoxical outcomes of these policies. Circumventing the contemporary fragmentation of liberal thought and practice, I have gone back to the reflections of John Locke which theorize the relationship between the different dimensions of liberalism and make explicit the policies as well as the theoretical claims necessary to realize liberal principles in practice. The Lockean argument suggests that:

Liberalism is a political project that aims to establish individual freedom through private property and to protect and extend this freedom through government by consent. It pursues this goal through the privatization/expropriation of common property and hence requires the production and reproduction of unequal power relations domestically and internationally. And it provides a philosophy of history that presents this inequality as the result of natural and differential levels of development.

This conception entails all the core elements generally associated with liberalism: the individual rights to life, liberty and property or human rights; liberal political institutions like government by consent (today largely equated with democracy); economic policies favoring private property, the market and free trade; as well as a meliorist or optimistic conception of history (Evans 2001; Gray 1986; Doyle 1997). In addition, however, it also provides an explicit statement of the co-constitutive nature of these elements of liberalism and hence of the dynamics generated by their pursuit. Such dynamic relations develop across four core dimensions: between theory and practice; between economic, political, and normative issue areas; across space; and across time. In conclusion, it is now possible to explore the implications of these dynamics of liberalism, first, for liberal theories, second, for its role in history and, third, for liberal (foreign) policies.

Liberal theory

Liberal theories, as we have seen in Chapter 2, fall into a variety of different strands. This diversity is frequently presented, on the one hand, as testifying to the richness of the liberal tradition and, on the other, as precluding a common definition which in turn also stands in the way of an analysis of liberalism per se. In light of this diversity, it is argued, the best we can aim for are analyses of particular strands or aspects of liberalism in theory and practice. The first contribution that the revised conception of liberalism makes is to explain this diversity of liberal thought, and, indeed, more widely the plurality of approaches within International Relations in particular and the fragmentation of the modern social sciences more generally. Secondly, however, it also suggests that the fragmentation leading to this diversity is itself a core dynamic of liberalism. Inasmuch as contemporary liberal theories take this fragmentation for granted and reproduce it, they play a major role in the – conscious or unconscious – ideological justification and reproduction of this political project. Yet, by recovering the core dynamics of liberalism, thirdly, this conception opens up the possibility of a more comprehensive analysis of liberalism in theory and practice.

Locke, as the historical and biographical context suggests, did not analyze the workings of an already existing 'liberalism'. Though he picked up on what was later identified as core 'liberal' ideas and interests that had some currency in the socio-political context of the time, his work largely consisted in developing a systematic account of these ideas and interests and a program for their realization. Locke, in short, developed a *political* program and provided a complex and sophisticated conception of history as a framework within which that program made sense. And it was indeed as a political program that his work was already during his lifetime taken up by the Whig party and subsequently by other political actors – notably in America (Arneil 1996). Yet, since these ideas and interests were not widely shared, their realization – through privatization/expropriation – required political power and thus generated tensions whose management led to the development of the

separate spheres of economics and politics, each over time developing its own norms, actors, institutions, and practices characteristic of
the modern liberal state. This transformation of traditional political
communities into modern states, however, also implied the separation
between different political communities and thus led to the constitution
of domestic and international politics as separate spheres – each again
with their own norms, actors, institutions, and practices. The inequalities enshrined in and between these different spheres – voting rights
for some but not for others, rights of sovereignty for some but not for
others, (a measure of) redistribution in the domestic but not the international sphere – finally, were justified with reference to differential levels
of historical development. The realization of the liberal political project,
in other words, gradually constituted a world of separate spheres for politics, economics, and ideas, for domestic and international politics, and
for history and theory.

The result of this historical process of fragmentation is reflected in the
fragmentation of the modern social sciences into different disciplines –
politics, economics, law, international relations, history, philosophy – as
well as in the fragmentation of disciplines like International Relations
and that of liberal theory itself. Historically, the fragmentary dynamics of liberalism produce, as we have seen, nonliberal forces which
have generated their own competitive theories based on a critique of
liberalism – Marxism in the 19th century and fascism in the 20th
century. Within the discipline of International Relations, in addition,
realism is an offspring of liberalism (Shilliam 2007). Unlike liberalism,
Marxism, and fascism which offer a (more or less) comprehensive model
for the organization of domestic and international society, realism offers
at best a very few ground rules for the conduct of international politics.
This paucity suggests that realism is not, in fact, a competitive political
project but rather a product of the exclusion and subsequent system-
atization of the essential role of power politics within liberalism. Since
power politics does not chime well with liberal norms and promises, the
separate theorization of the power political dimension of liberal world
politics helps to present and promote liberalism as a genuine alternative
to 'realist power politics'. Hence, the two approaches are systematically
formulated and developed with reference to each other, though it is
liberalism that not only shaped the modern international order but
also first developed systematic reflections on its nature and dynamics
(Long and Schmidt 2005) and realism which responds to the contradictions between liberal theory and practice by fully endorsing its internal
fragmentations – between issue areas, space, time as well as theory and

practice. Hence, realism focuses (at least originally) strictly on the political to the exclusion of economics and morality; on the international to the exclusion of the domestic; on a timeless present thus excluding past and future; and it is firmly based on practice in contrast to norms (on how things 'are' rather than how they 'ought to be'). All of these defining characteristics of realism provided critics with ample ammunition: it has been widely accused of ignoring the important role of economics and not just lacking but even justifying the irrelevance of ethics in international affairs; it has been accused of ignoring the importance of domestic politics for international relations, of logically excluding any possibility of systemic historical change, and of deriving its core assumptions from a conception of human nature without regard to the theoretical lenses through which this nature is constructed (famously, Ashley 1988). This paucity of realist theory arises out of, and maps perfectly onto (Boucoyannis 2007), the contradictions of liberal theory and practice and helps to reproduce it by monopolizing liberalism's 'dark side'. In short, realism is a product of the internal tensions of liberalism and their competitive relationship in fact complements, justifies, and helps reproduce the former.[1]

This dynamic of a competitive complementarity also defines the diversity of the liberal tradition itself. While Locke, writing before the historical consolidation of liberalism, explicitly theorizes the co-constitutive nature of politics, economics, and norms, these spheres become gradually separated in subsequent liberal theory. Although classical liberal thought generally engages with the political, economic, and normative dimensions of society, the analysis of their respective internal workings gradually leads to a separation of political economy (Adam Smith, David Ricardo, Friedrich List) and political philosophy (Immanuel Kant). Though engaging with all three dimensions, John Stuart Mill, by the mid-19th century, devotes a separate book to each of them: *Considerations on Representative Government* (1998b) to political institutions, *On Liberty* (1998a) to the question of norms, and *Principles of Political Economy* (1994) to the economic sphere. The separation of these spheres is, finally, reflected in the different actors, institutions, and practices that provide the focus of analysis in different strands of contemporary liberal theory: economic liberal approaches largely investigate firms, producers, consumers, markets, costs, and prices; political

---

[1] Hence liberal theories frequently state a competitive as well as complementary relationship to realism (Moravcsik 1997: 513, 522, 542; Deudney and Ikenberry 1999: 196).

liberal approaches focus on individuals and states, political regimes, international organizations, and cooperation; while normative liberal approaches analyze norms, morality, law and identify their (potential) bearers and practices. Domestic liberal theories focus on the vertical relations between individuals and governments (Hoffmann 1987: 405) while international liberal theories focus on the horizontal relations between states or private transnational actors. While empirical liberal approaches investigate the historical development and practice of liberalism, normative theory develops its norms and projects them into the future.

Yet, the diversity of liberal approaches is not restricted to such functional differentiation. Since liberalism is a political project, its realization is dependent on, and requires adjustment to, a variety of conditions in different times and places leading to significant variations in liberal thought and practice. Hence, where liberalism was largely driven by private enterprise – as in America and England – it became associated with Adam Smith's night watchman State (Smith 1952),² while the state was seen to play a crucial role for the development of liberalism in France giving rise to a much more 'statist' version of liberalism (Saint Simon 1975). British economic and imperial power led to a strong association of liberalism with free trade (Howe 1997) while the international economic pressure on Germany and its need to catch up led to the development of a more protectionist version of liberalism (List 2013). While French and British imperial power engendered a missionary and expansionist liberalism captured in the 'white man's burden' and the 'mission civilisatrice' (Mill 1998b; Tocqueville 1994; Jahn 2000; Pitts 2005), the French expansionist drive on the European continent led in Italy and Germany to the development of a nationalist version of liberalism (Mazzini 2009; Shilliam 2009); the interventionist liberalism of Burke and Paine and the noninterventionist liberalism of Kant (Walker 2008; Jahn 2012a). While American liberalism was able to solve its internal tensions through expansion and the appropriation of indigenous land, lacking these opportunities a 'new liberalism' of a more social variant developed in Europe (Boucher 1994; Clarke 1978; Weiler 1982). This last example shows, moreover, that these variations did not just arise

---

² Whether and in how far Smith actually advocated the noninterventionist state is contested (Wyatt-Walter 1996) but that it came to play an important role in English and American liberalism is not. The situation changed gradually in England after World War I and seems, if early interpretations of the 2012 American election result are correct, slowly on the decline there, too.

between different states but also within states and over time. Hence, propertied sections of society may, on the whole, develop a Hayekian (Hayek 2001, 2011) or Nozickian (Nozick 1974) conception of liberalism while property-less sections of society may tend toward a more social or Keynesian interpretation of liberalism (Keynes 2006). Moreover, with changing circumstances, particularly with shifting power relations, conceptions of liberalism change – hence increasing domestic (often in combination with international) political pressure forces a previously anti-democratic liberalism into a democratic liberalism (Acemoglu and Robinson 2006); increasing political pressure in the colonies gradually transforms an imperialist liberalism into an anti-imperialist and subsequently even into a multicultural or postcolonial liberalism (Kymlicka 1995; Ivison 2002).[3]

A comprehensive conception of liberalism thus not only confirms the claim that liberalism is a rich and diverse tradition of thought, it also explains this diversity as the result of social and political fragmentation generated by the attempt to establish liberalism in a variety of nonliberal environments. Simultaneously, however, this explanation undermines the assumption that the diversity of liberal thought precludes a common conception of liberalism and its assessment in theory and practice as well as the explicit or implicit assumption that this diversity offers genuine alternatives. After all, the dynamic of fragmentation that leads to a plurality of liberal theories has its roots ultimately in the disjuncture between theory and practice. For it is the absence of a majority of individuals whose freedom was established through private property and guaranteed through government by consent – the absence of a liberal society – that establishes the need to create such a society more or less from scratch. And it is the means to this end – political emancipation and oppression, economic appropriation and expropriation, cultural/historical elevation and denigration – that produces the tensions which liberalism manages through separation. In other words, the plurality of liberal actors, institutions, practices, and theories is internal to liberalism and together constitutive of it. Despite their diversity,

---

[3] The gradual nature is nicely illustrated by the move from the imperialist liberalism of John Stuart Mill to the more paternalist liberalism of John A. Hobson (2006) and ultimately to the largely anti-imperialist liberalism of today. Institutionally, this movement is neatly matched by colonial rule in the 19th century followed by the mandate system in the first part of the 20th century and finally decolonization and a pluralist international system in the second half of the 20th century.

therefore, liberal theories tend to express not only the internal tensions of liberalism but also their co-constitutive nature across all four dimensions.

Hence, economic theories from Smith (1952) to Bhagwati (2004: 233) blame government intervention (politics) for the failure of market economics even while they recognize these interventions as rooted in economic interests (Smith 1952: 201) and call on government to manage market failures (Bhagwati 2004: 239). Moreover, such markets are justified in moral terms as producing common (Smith 1952: 193) or even global (Wolf 2004: 36) moral goods in the long run (time) even while those goods fall prey to self-interest in the short term (Wolf 2004: 215). Meanwhile, free trade is in the general international interest, but only as long as it does not undermine domestic advantages (Smith 1952: 197–8; Bhagwati 2004: 218, 235). In all these dimensions, the separation of politics and economics, of economics and morality, of the domestic and the international, of past, present, and future actually plays a constitutive role for liberalism itself, accounting for its shortcomings on the one hand and promising a solution on the other. The same is true for normative and political liberal theories. In one form or another, liberal theories contain the constitutive separation between issue areas, across time – from the classical stage theory of political economy (Smith 1952; Blaney and Inayatullah 2010) through Mill's stages of political development (Mill 1998b; Jahn 2005b) to contemporary distinctions between a pluralist, solidarist, and post-Westphalian level of moral and political development (Linklater 1998); across space – from rights to common property within the state and their denial to outsiders (Locke 1994) through liberty and representative government for Europeans and 'despotic rule' for non-Europeans (Mill 1998b; Jahn 2005a) to full rights of sovereignty for liberal or democratic states and their denial to nondemocratic states (Slaughter 1995; Keohane 2003; Rawls 2001); and between theory and practice – from Kant's distinction between a moral/legal and a natural path to perpetual peace (Kant 1957) to contemporary normative versus empirical approaches (Long 1995; Moravcsik 1997).[4]

---

[4] It is these unresolved tensions within liberal theories that give rise to heated debates about the 'correct' interpretation of classical liberal authors. The question whether Kant is best interpreted as a statist or a cosmopolitan, whether Smith was really in favor of laissez-faire economics or considerable government intervention, whether Mill was actually arguing for or against intervention reflects the presence of the internal tensions of liberalism in the writings of these authors.

In sum, then, the diversity of liberal theories is itself a product of the core liberal dynamic of fragmentation which is, moreover, reproduced within and through these theories. Inasmuch as these theories reflect the fragmentation of society, they provide sophisticated and often highly detailed analyses of the workings of their respective spheres. At the same time, however, inasmuch as they take the results of liberal policies – a world fragmented into such different spheres – as their starting point, they fail to grasp or analyze the core dynamics of liberalism that lead to this fragmentation. By treating the outcome of liberal policies as the result of independent historical developments, liberal theories obscure the root of liberalism's internal tensions and contradictions and contribute to their reproduction, that is, they contribute to liberalism as a political project. While the diversity of liberal theories thus indeed offers a range of choices – between more or less statist, more or less interventionist, more or less social policies – these choices do not signify the difference between a liberalism based on selfish and material interests and one based on moral and civic virtue (Hoffmann 1995: 174), a grassroots liberalism or a liberalism of privilege (Richardson 2001), a liberalism of restraint or a liberalism of imposition (Sørensen 2012), an offensive or a defensive liberalism (Miller 2010) because they are mutually constitutive, each developing in response to the shortcomings of another.

Moreover, this analysis implies that the diversity of liberalism cannot be interpreted as a sign of its gradual maturation or realization. Liberalism has an extraordinary potential to engender historical change which is reflected in the diversity of liberal theories. Change, however, is not to be equated with progress. The move from antidemocratic liberalism to a democratic liberalism does not occur because 'the philosophy of liberalism contains within itself the seeds of its own democratization' (Plattner 2008: 60) but rather because the inequalities and tensions produced by liberalism became unsustainable and this shift in power relations requires the introduction of democracy (Acemoglu and Robinson 2006), suggesting that future shifts in power relations are also capable of reversing that process. Hence, different versions of liberalism coexist not only at any one time but often even within the writings of any one author. J. S. Mill advocated representative government for Europeans and despotic rule for non-Europeans just as some liberals today advocate colonial rule for the 'weak' and full sovereignty for the 'strong' (Cooper 2002; Mill 1984) or at least recognize and investigate the intimate relationship between 'liberal order' and 'imperial ambition' (Ikenberry 2006). The diversity of liberalism, in sum, offers a variety of alternatives within liberalism but not a choice between liberalisms. It attests to liberalism's powers of transformation – both of its environment and itself – but not to its potential of progressive realization.

Instead, insofar as the diversity of liberal theory takes for granted, reflects, and reproduces its core fragmentary dynamics, it contributes to the political project of liberalism. In this sense, 'liberal theory' is, in fact, a contradiction in terms. Inasmuch as such approaches are 'liberal', they are more accurately described as ideologies. In this, liberal approaches are of course neither alone nor, indeed, necessarily worse than other approaches that entail the propagation of comprehensive political models. Rather, liberalism has played a decisive role in shaping modern world politics for centuries now and it is, for the moment at least, 'the total exhaustion of viable systematic alternatives' (Fukuyama 1989; Plattner 2008: 24) to liberalism which calls for a thorough analysis of the latter. The conceptual account of the core dynamics of liberalism, finally, provides the crucial first step toward the possibility of such a comprehensive assessment of liberalism's role in history and practice.

Liberalism in history

The end of the Cold War, as we have seen at the beginning of this book, gave rise to two different conceptions of the emerging liberal world order. The first of these conceptions was based on power: it held that the hegemony of liberalism, its triumph over alternative ideologies or political projects, did indeed establish a liberal world order. The second and equally wide spread conception of a liberal world order was, in contrast, based on the universal realization of liberal norms and principles: in this sense, the world order emerging after the end of the Cold War was not yet properly liberal at all because it was still populated by nonliberal actors, institutions, and practices. In Fukuyama's words, 'the victory of liberalism has occurred primarily in the realm of ideas...and is as yet incomplete in the real or material world' (Fukuyama 1989: 4). Despite widespread criticisms of Fukuyama, these two conceptions of a liberal world order can be found, more or less explicitly, in liberal approaches more generally. On the one hand, the liberal world order exists because much of this order is shaped by the actions of 'leading liberal states' (Sørensen 2012: 23). On the other hand, the existence of 'weak and failed states' (and liberalism's awkward responses to such nonliberal forces) works against 'any aspiration for a stable liberal world order' (Sørensen 2012: 116). And it is this distinction between a liberal order based on power and one that extends to the realization of liberal principles which has given rise to the association of a proper liberal order with the relations between liberal actors only – a liberal subsystem (Deudney and Ikenberry 1999) – and to their proactive liberal policies designed to realize liberal principles in the as yet nonliberal spaces of the world.

These contradictions, I will now show, have their roots in the fragmentary dynamics of liberalism properly understood. The concept of liberalism which accounts for these dynamics, moreover, provides a clear guide to the assessment of liberalism in world history and it resolves the contradiction between these two conceptions of a liberal world order.

The first of these trajectories of fragmentation concerns the separation of the political, economic, and normative spheres, and with it the constitution of differentiated actors in each of these spheres. Narratives about the role of liberalism in history usually focus on the development of liberal political actors, predominantly liberal states (for example, Ikenberry 2011). Yet a comprehensive conception of liberalism draws attention to other liberal actors, in particular private actors or companies and civil society actors or 'norm entrepreneurs'. Apart from states, such actors have indeed played a tremendously important role not only for the constitution of core liberal states themselves but also for the projection of liberalism abroad. To begin with, it was private actors like Locke's own employer, the Earl of Shaftesbury, whose interests, including his extensive overseas interests, were reflected in the development of liberal principles. The same is true for Grotius whose treatise *De Praedae* was written in defense of the capture of a Portuguese ship by the Dutch East India Company and chapter XII of this book was published as *Mare Liberum* – which subsequently came to play an immensely important role for liberal overseas policies and international law – on behalf of the Dutch East India Company (Armitage 2001: 109). Locke's own investment in, and involvement with, the slave-trading Royal Africa Company, the Company of Merchant Adventurers to trade with the Bahamas, and the East India Company draws attention to the fact, first, that these private actors played a crucial role both for the development of liberalism within Europe itself and for its impact far beyond the borders of individual European states. Indeed, it was these companies that paved the way for the subsequent establishment of colonial empires; and it was these companies, too, that did not only employ but also inspire later liberal writers such as James and John Stuart Mill.

In addition, the separation between church and state in Europe – to which Locke also contributed with his *Letter Concerning*

Toleration – gradually turned churches and their missionary societies into what we would now call civil society organizations. These organizations functioned just like contemporary 'norm entrepreneurs' both domestically and internationally. They played, for example, a crucial role in the anti-slave trade movement (Porter 1999; Hall 2002). Moreover, in a bid to protect the natives from encroaching settlers and the resultant dispossession, missionaries in Africa advocated 'explicitly imperial solutions', that is colonial rule (Stanley 1990: 132). In return for such protection, however, the local population was expected not just to take on Christianity but to commit themselves to a 'civilized' and 'industrious' way of life, that is, to adopt the social, economic, and cultural norms and practices of the colonial power (Igarashi 2013). Just like private companies, then, such civil society organizations played a crucial role for the development of liberalism itself as well as, simultaneously, for its spread.

The comprehensive conception of liberalism developed in these pages suggests, then, that such actors, institutions, and practices have to be included into any proper assessment of liberalism's role in history. This inclusion, in turn, considerably widens the time frame relevant for an assessment of liberalism's role in world politics – all the way back to the activities of private 'liberal' actors before the establishment of liberal states. It also widens the relevant spatial framework for it shows that liberalism is not the result of an endogenous development in individual liberal states which was then gradually extended into the international sphere. Instead, the establishment of liberal states in Europe occurred simultaneously and in relation to the transformation of communities abroad. This means that all the areas in which liberal – state or nonstate – actors were active need to be included in a comprehensive assessment of liberalism's role in history.

The second trajectory of fragmentation is already anticipated in the previous reflections: it occurs across space and leads to the distinction between the domestic and international spheres – to the pursuit of power politics in the latter in the quest to establish and protect liberal achievements in the former. These inter- or transnational policies of liberal actors are therefore to be considered as a part of liberalism and inasmuch as they shaped other actors in the international sphere – including nonliberal actors – they must be included in a systematic assessment of liberalism's role in history. And once this co-constitutive nature of the domestic and international spheres is recognized, the spatial scope of liberalism's power and operations changes dramatically. In other words, the definition of liberalism can then not any longer

be reduced to its 'non-empire related' activities like voluntary bar-
gains, rule-based systems, frameworks of cooperation (Ikenberry 2011:
70).[5] Instead, colonialism, imperialism, and more generally the power
political practices characterizing these policies become an integral and
constitutive part of liberalism.

Recognizing the third trajectory of temporal fragmentation – that is,
the presentation of contemporaneous societies as occupying different
stages of historical development – as a product of liberalism draws attention to the historical contemporaneity both of different iterations of
liberalism itself and of liberal and nonliberal actors, institutions and
practices. It undermines an interpretation of history as a progressive
realization of liberal norms and principles and draws attention both to
the simultaneous and mutually constitutive production of liberal and
nonliberal actors, institutions, and practices and to the intimate connection between the progressive and regressive dynamics of liberalism
in history. Hence, both in theory and in practice antidemocratic and
democratic liberalism, colonial and anticolonial liberalism, laissez-faire
and welfare liberalism, interventionist and noninterventionist liberalism tend to occur together and are mutually constitutive of liberalism.
Locke could only extend political rights to some sections of society
because he simultaneously denied them to others and, indeed, the
demand for political freedom was historically coterminous with its sup-
pression by liberalism (Di Muzio 2012); just as contemporary authors
still argue that liberalism does not necessarily require democracy (Sartori
1995) and liberal actors today promote democracy in some places even
while they fail to recognize, or even attempt to undermine, it in others.
Similarly, the granting of sovereignty rights to some communities is consistently combined with its denial to others. Hence, Locke granted these
rights to powerful states and denied them to weak indigenous communities (Locke 1994: 292), Mill defended the right to sovereignty for
'civilized' European states while justifying colonialism for 'uncivilized'
non-European communities (Mill 1998b; see also Bell 2006a, 2006b),
and today the assertion of sovereignty rights for 'liberal' states frequently goes hand in hand with the denial of full rights of sovereignty
(at least temporarily) for 'nonliberal' states – both in theory and in
practice (Rawls 2001; Cooper 2002; Ignatieff 2003; Paris 2004).

---

[5] And the foreign policies of Bush then do not constitute a break with liberal
internationalism (Ikenberry 2011: 265) but rather an integral part of it (Desch
2007; Moses 2010; Dodge 2009).

These inequalities are consistently justified, in the past as well as today, with reference to different levels of development. Weak indigenous communities in America lacked political rights because, unlike the Europeans, they had not left the state of nature yet (Locke 1994: 289); humanity went through stages of economic development – from hunters and gatherers through pastoral, agricultural to commercial society – and the higher levels of development conferred more rights than the lower ones (Meek 1976); humanity passed through stages of political development – from savagism through slavery, barbarism to civilization – the latter morally obliged and politically and legally empowered to tutor the former (Mill 1998b); and today these temporal distinctions map onto the economic levels of 'least developed', 'developing', and 'developed' countries or the moral-political levels of 'pluralist', 'solidarist', and 'post-Westphalian' (Linklater 1998) development. Indeed, we are told, 'in terms of historical time, countries can be a thousand years apart. Historically, Afghanistan and millions of villages scattered across the underdeveloped (let alone the undeveloped) areas today are about where most of Europe was in the Middle Ages' (Sartori 1995: 104). 'Historical time' is thus not 'time' – for in terms of the latter 'Afghanistan' and 'the millions of villages scattered across the underdeveloped' world clearly coexist with the 'developed' world in the present. 'Historical time' refers instead to a substantive philosophy of history that, by relegating some communities to the past, explains differences as the result of an independent historical trajectory and justifies a hierarchical order between them. Yet, recognizing this temporal fragmentation as a core dynamic of liberalism draws attention to the co-constitutive nature of 'development' and 'underdevelopment', 'modernity', and 'tradition'. The continuity of these temporal distinctions within liberalism, first of all, undermines the claim of a progressive development of liberalism itself. The changes that occur over time are largely changes in terminology that make no difference to the core function of subordinating 'barbarism' or 'tradition' or 'underdevelopment' to 'civilization', 'modernity', or 'development'. Secondly, it draws attention to the fact that liberalism tends to put the historical cart before the horse by presenting developmental stages like 'modernity' as the result of a 'natural' historical trajectory that independently confirms the validity of liberal principles and provides them with 'global reach' and 'durability' (Ikenberry 2006: 146). Recognizing temporal fragmentation as a core product of liberalism suggests, in contrast, that both 'modernity' and 'tradition', 'development' and 'underdevelopment' are a product of liberalism. A comprehensive assessment of liberalism's role in history thus has to include its relations to, and production of, differential levels of development.

Finally, recognizing the fragmentation of theory and practice as a product of liberalism draws attention to the mutually constitutive relations between the two – and with it to the crucial role of power politics in and for liberalism. It was because liberal principles were neither widely shared nor reflected the social and political practices on the ground that they had to be abstracted from these realities and derived from a hypothetical state of nature. In this theoretical form they could henceforth function as guiding principles for political action designed to transform 'deviant' realities. Yet, the attempt to align reality with theory can only be achieved through the exertion of power. Power politics, however, has unintended consequences. While the gap between the realities and liberal theory compels liberal forces to accumulate power and establish unequal power relations, these policies simultaneously generate resistance. This contradictory dynamic plays a crucial role in the history of liberalism. Ironically, therefore, the triumphs of liberalism are invariably followed by liberal crises. In other words, a comprehensive assessment of liberalism's role in history has to include attention to liberal power politics and their contradictory outcomes.

Taken together, these four trajectories of historical dynamics allow for a reassessment of liberalism's role in world history and its standing today. Such an assessment, they suggest, needs to take into account the practices of liberal states as well as private and civil society actors and, most importantly, the policies of nonliberal actors inasmuch as they are a product of, or dependent on, liberal policies. Viewed in this light, liberalism was not established in particular societies and then gradually expanded into the international sphere. It is instead a political project pursued right from the start by private actors whose success led to the transformation of existing political communities – the establishment of modern states – and with them the establishment of the modern states system. Yet, given that these private actors operated not just domestically but also internationally, this process was coterminous with the transformation of societies in the international sphere through political, economic, and normative engagements which ultimately led to a colonial world order (Pomeranz and Topik 1999). Viewed in this light, at the latest by the end of the 19th century, with the colonization of Africa, virtually all societies around the globe were, to a greater or lesser degree, shaped by or dependent on liberalism. In spatial terms, then, the 'globalization of liberalism' had already been completed by the end of the 19th century (McDonald and Sweeney 2007).

This triumph of liberalism gave rise to an optimism not at all dissimilar to the one marking the beginning of the 1990s: industrial production and free trade were destined to solve the remaining material problems and war, at least between the major liberal powers, had become obsolete (Angell 1910) – a notion that was not systematically held by classical liberal thinkers (Hont 2005). What this optimism overlooked, however, was the fact that having reached the limits of spatial expansion, the contradictions and tensions of liberalism now played themselves out inside this liberal world order. Within liberal states resistance to economic exploitation and political oppression had been growing throughout the 19th century and led to the development of socialist and communist as well as, after World War I, fascist movements; competition between liberal states was rising and colonialism triggered the beginnings of liberation movements. These internal contradictions ultimately blew up in two World Wars and a 'twenty years crisis'. This crisis and the rise of the Soviet Union split the liberal world order apart.

During the Cold War, liberal policies – though actively pursued – were for the most part constrained in geographical terms to the Western zone of influence and tempered by the need to ensure internal political stability. The fall of the Soviet Union at the beginning of the 1990s ushered in a second liberal world order which was greeted with as much optimism as the first. Yet, again this triumph of liberalism brought its internal tensions and contradictions to the fore. It freed the liberal impulse to extend and deepen the reach of liberal norms, institutions, and practices and it did so by reproducing the core contradictions of liberalism: the spread of freedom through military means and political oppression; the production of prosperity through large-scale expropriation and exploitation; the protection of human rights through their violation. And it is these internal contradictions which quickly led to what Ikenberry calls a 'crisis of authority', of 'rule and governance', that is, a crisis internal to the liberal world order (Ikenberry 2009: 80).

The current world order is indeed a liberal one, but a comprehensive conception of liberalism suggests that it is by no means 'incomplete'. This liberal world is not just based on power awaiting the universal realization of liberal principles in practice – the latter are themselves constitutive of power politics. Hence, the nonliberal actors, institutions, and practices that inhabit this order are themselves the product of a realization of liberal principles and hence an integral part of the liberal world order. The contradictions of this liberal world order, in other words, are the contradictions of liberalism itself. Despite its comprehensive nature, however, this liberal world order does not signify an 'end of history' in which political and 'ideological struggle' which calls forth 'daring, courage, imagination, and idealism' is replaced by 'economic calculation' and the 'endless solving of technical problems' (Fukuyama 1989: 18).[6] Such a vision can only arise from a 'normative' conception of liberalism that has relegated all its contradictions and tensions into practice. Rather, a conception of liberalism which accounts for its internal tensions and fragmentary dynamics draws attention to the fact that many of the political struggles of the past 500 years were already struggles generated by liberalism – internal struggles. It also draws attention to the fact that these internal struggles have, in principle, the power to split a liberal world order apart, as they did in the mid-20th century. The current 'crisis of authority' within the liberal world order confirms this dynamic since it has its origins largely in the contradictory nature of liberal policies during the 1990s themselves which undermined the belief in, and generated resistance to, liberal norms, institutions, and practices.

In sum, a proper conception of liberalism which integrates its fragmentary dynamics attests to the power of liberalism as a historical force: to its ability to transform the natural as well as social context in which it operates and to its ability to adapt to these changing contexts. Yet, this power is at once greater and smaller than generally acknowledged within liberal approaches. It is greater inasmuch as its power to constitute liberal actors, institutions, and practices extends to the production of nonliberal actors, institutions, and practices; its power of establishing modern liberal states is accompanied by the creation of the modern international system; its ability to instigate development (political, economic, normative) is coupled with the production of underdevelopment. But it is smaller insofar as none of these powers amount to a progressive realization of liberal norms and principles. The power of liberalism in history is driven by its contradictions and fragmentary dynamics, not by the universal validity and gradual realization of its principles – it is, in short, both beneficial and destructive (Weber 2010).

Liberal policies

Despite the auspicious circumstances produced by the end of the Cold War and the proactive pursuit of liberal policies during the 1990s,

---

[6] See Melzer et al. (1995) for critical discussions of Fukuyama's conception of history.

'liberal values, practices and institutions are on the defensive; the profound optimism of the post-Cold War 1990s is a thing of the past' – not least because the liberal foreign policies of that period led to 'economic crisis, frail and wilting democracies…and a flagging support for liberal values' (Sørensen 2012: 167). In short, these policies are widely seen to have missed their goal of successfully spreading economic prosperity, liberal political institutions, and values. And yet, the conception of liberalism developed in this study suggests that this assessment is at least partly misleading. Its implications for liberal policies are threefold. First, it explains the nature and the outcome of liberal policies during the post-Cold War period. Secondly, it provides the basis for a realistic assessment of the limits and possibilities of liberal policies more generally. Finally, it allows for a more accurate identification of the challenges facing liberal policies.

To begin with, the conception of liberalism developed in these pages explains the 'impulse' to spread liberal norms, institutions, and practices that came to characterize liberal policies during the post-Cold War period. This impulse arises from the internal contradictions of liberalism which lead to the constitution not just of liberal but also of nonliberal forces. Yet, the very existence of such nonliberal forces – poverty, unfreedom, inequality – stands in contradiction to the universal promises of liberalism. While the existence of such nonliberal forces during the Cold War could be attributed to apparently external obstacles like the Soviet Union, the latter's demise provided not just an opportunity to spread these principles more widely but, more importantly, also an urgency to prove the power and validity of these principles. After all, in a liberal world order the continued existence of nonliberal actors, institutions, and principles undermined the universal promises of liberal principles. Hence, at the end of the Cold war the identification of the main obstacle to the realization of liberal principles shifted immediately from the power of the Soviet Union and its alternative model of society to weak and failing states, defined by the absence of 'liberal' qualities and a lack of 'development' (David 1992/3: 131). Such weak and failing states do not, however (for the most part), present a serious material (economic, political, military) threat – they are weak, after all. Instead, it is the very existence of these nonliberal spaces that constitutes a threat to the promotion of 'political and economic progress' as promised by liberal principles (Sørensen 2012: 5) and compels liberal actors into policies designed to transform them – as quickly and thoroughly as possible.

The 'failures' of these policies during the 1990s, as we have seen in Chapters 4, 5, 6, were variously attributed to inconsistent behavior on the part of liberal actors themselves. Yet, these inconsistencies arise out of the four core dimensions of fragmentation produced by liberalism – the fragmentation of issue or policy areas, its spatial fragmentation, its temporal fragmentation, and the separation between theory and practice. The separation of the political, economic, and normative realms constitutes a range of different actors, institutions, and practices – companies, states, and 'norm entrepreneurs' like NGOs – within liberalism. These actors are, moreover, internally divided in terms of their particular interests and functions. Hence, some economic sectors are interested in free trade and others in protection; political actors are divided into different ministeries tasked with the pursuit of economic, development, foreign, domestic policies; civil society actors generally devote themselves to particular issue areas like distributive justice, the environment, human rights and so on. The fragmentary dynamics of liberalism thus do indeed lead to a 'disaggregated state' (Slaughter 1995). In addition, liberalism is divided into separate liberal states, each in turn embodying a (slightly) different version of liberalism and pursuing its spread by different means. Hence, US conceptions of democracy differ from European ones and the former are more willing to use military means while the latter tend to rely more on international organizations and law (Kagan 2002). The fragmentary dynamics of liberalism thus account for the diversity of liberal policies in terms of their goals, their protagonists, and their practices.

These dynamics also explain the widely noted lack of 'coordination' that weakened liberal policies in specific cases. Though a better 'coordination' between these policies is of course possible in specific instances, it can ultimately not overcome the contradictory goals pursued by these actors which are, after all, constitutive of liberalism itself. Hence, liberal economic actors pursued both free trade and protectionist policies during the 1990s. Yet, it was the push for the former that generated the need for the latter and thus militates against 'consistent' economic policies. Moreover, these contradictions are mediated through the constitution of a separate domestic sphere and its distinction from the international. This spatial fragmentation thus explains the tendency of liberal policies to impose free trade on other states while protecting domestic economic actors. In other words, 'consistent' free trade policies cannot be undertaken without jeopardizing the constitution and political stability of domestic liberalism.

The same dynamic operates within the political sphere where the constitution and maintenance of a domestic (and democratic) liberal order depends on the continued provision of economic benefits from the international sphere and hence also the favorable political power relations on which the former are based. In other words, liberal actors can pursue the spread of democracy only where it does not undermine the economic and political interests constitutive of domestic liberal democracy. Hence, democracy was proactively promoted in cases where it advanced the political and economic interests of liberal states – that is, in weak and failing states as well as in Eastern Europe. It was decidedly half-heartedly pursued in cases where domestic liberal stability depended on the continuation of smooth economic and/or political relations, such as Saudi Arabia or China. And liberal policies actively tried to undermine democratic processes in cases where the outcome was seen to undermine their interests, such as in Gaza.

By the same token, policies designed to promote or enforce liberal norms and principles such as human rights were systematically tied to the constitution and reproduction of domestic liberalism itself. Hence, humanitarian interventions were undertaken where they coincided with 'national interests' (as in Kosovo); they were not undertaken where such interests were deemed lacking and the violation of human rights could be attributed to exogenous 'nonliberal' norms and practices (as in Rwanda); and human rights were prominently violated by liberal actors themselves where they were seen to directly threaten the constitution and survival of 'liberalism' itself (for example in the case of extraordinary rendition or in Guantanamo Bay).

The internal tensions of liberalism and the resultant 'inconsistent' policies moreover contribute to the constitution and reproduction of nonliberal actors, institutions, and practices. Both in the domestic and in the international sphere these policies, historically and today, entail the provision of material benefits and political rights to some actors through the denial of these benefits and rights to others. Indigenous economies were transformed and made dependent on liberal markets; boundaries were redrawn, old communities destroyed and new ones erected; populations were transplanted (for instance through the slave trade); traditional cultures were reformed (by missionary activities in Africa, for example) for purposes of colonial rule. The specifics of such policies, of course, varied from case to case and the relations between liberal and dependent actors had their twists and turns – culminating eventually in decolonization. Nevertheless, the results of these relations, which in some cases (going back to Locke's advocacy of colonialism) lasted for hundreds of years, are as varied as the local conditions combined with the entire range of liberal interests and policies allow. They have directly led to the establishment of the leading liberal power today, the United States of America; almost all contemporary African as well as many Middle Eastern states are in their boundaries as well as the composition of their populations a product of these developments; the newly independent states in Eastern Europe and the Balkans are a product not only of their previous 'alliance' with the Soviet Union (itself largely a product of liberal pressures) but also of the liberal political and economic pressures into which they emerged after the end of the Cold War. Hence, while these policies produced successful liberal states, they also produced states that can hardly be called liberal.

To be sure, there is controversy over the extent to which the economic weaknesses and political shortcomings of contemporary nonliberal states can be attributed to colonial era engagements with liberal powers (Russett et al. 2000). Yet, the very attempt to identify what can, or cannot, be attributed to different origins is based on the liberal assumption that politics, economics, culture, domestic and international, time and space constitute separate and separable spheres. For the purpose of the current argument, the point is best made by a brief counterfactual exercise: Is it possible to imagine the contemporary cultural, economic, and political entity of China without the experience of the opium wars, Japanese imperialism (itself a product of the international pressures exerted by liberal political and economic expansion), the introduction of Marxism (also a product of, and answer to, liberalism), and the adoption of liberal economic principles? Similarly, is it possible to imagine the ongoing conflict in Congo without Belgian imperialism, American intervention, a liberal world market seeking access to Congolese resources and providing the opportunity to buy arms? Is it possible to think of Saudi Arabia in separation from American oil companies and policies? Finally, is it possible to separate indigenous African cultures from the deep Christianity which infuses them since the colonial era? Surely, the answer to these questions is no. In all their variety, contemporary nonliberal actors, institutions, and practices are the result of, and fundamentally shaped by, a variety of more or less direct engagements with liberal political, economic and normative actors, policies, and practices which have combined over time with local traditions, institutions, and practices. In technical terms, they are products of uneven and combined development just as, indeed, liberal actors themselves are (Rosenberg 1996, 2007). To note this combination of forces, of course, neither entails a denial of genuine indigenous agency – either in the liberal or in the nonliberal world – nor does it place the responsibility for the outcome onto liberalism alone. Instead, it provides a consistent and dynamic account of nonliberal behavior.

As products of an engagement with liberalism, nonliberal actors are, first of all, familiar with, often attached to, and desirous of its positive achievements which accounts for a considerable openness to adopting policies that promise progress in that direction. As a result of this combined development, moreover, sections of nonliberal societies benefit from continued cooperation (Sørensen 2012: 126). At the same time, however, as 'deeply penetrated by, and in important ways dependent on, the industrial world and especially the world economy' (Russett et al. 2000: 416), nonliberal actors are uniquely aware of and indeed embody to varying degrees the 'dark side' of liberal policies – its production of unfreedom, poverty, and inequality. Hence, they frequently lack the domestic conditions for the establishment of liberalism, that is, the majority of their citizens are dependent for their survival on communal forms of production and distribution and hence also on the representation of such communal – as opposed to individual – interests through political institutions and practices. Moreover, they are 'constrained by the hierarchical nature of the international political and economic system' (Russett et al. 2000: 439). That is, in contrast to liberal actors for whom the international sphere offers opportunities for economic and political relief and expansion, the international sphere confronts many nonliberal actors with additional economic and political pressures (Sørensen 2012: 131–2; Ndi 2011; Brown 2009) – especially so since the end of the Cold War and the dominance of liberalism. Hence, many nonliberal actors had little choice but to adopt neoliberal economic policies and/or introduce democratic institutions. Yet, since these policies neither fitted the domestic conditions nor increased their economic or political independence nor provided tangible benefits to the majority of the population, they implemented structural adjustment policies half-heartedly or used democratic institutions to further communal interests and consolidate nonliberal regimes. The 'inconsistent' policies of nonliberal actors are thus perfectly consistent with a conception of liberalism that accounts for its fragmentary dynamics.

Above all, it is these fragmentary dynamics of liberalism which explain the rapidity with which the optimism of the early 1990s began to decline. This optimism, as we have seen, was based on the assumption that obstacles to the realization of liberal principles were external to liberalism, that such obstacles were the product of independent and exogenous developments. And with the major one of these obstacles, the Soviet Union, gone, nothing stood in the way of a general realization of liberal principles. These assumptions were widely reflected in the design of liberal policies in the early post-Cold War period. Successful democratization did not require any preconditions and could be kick-started through the introduction of elections (Carothers 2002). All that was needed to pacify civil conflicts was a replacement of nonliberal institutions with market democracies (Paris 2004). The problem of economic development required nothing but the removal of government intervention in the market (Williams 2012). The protection of human rights could simply be achieved by replacing nonliberal with liberal governments (Tesón 2003) which was also the solution to international insecurity generated by nonliberal or 'rogue' states like Afghanistan and Iraq. In all these cases, the solution was the removal of nonliberal institutions and practices that had been propped up by the power of the Soviet Union or eeked out a living in the spaces created by the superpower competition of the Cold War. With both the former and the latter gone, these nonliberal institutions and practices were thought to require nothing but a little push in order to collapse like a house of cards and make way for liberal institutions and practices that were, after all, deeply 'aligned with global developmental processes', 'congruent with the deeper forces of modernization, industrialization, and social mobilization', and provided a 'functional "fit"' between the underlying historical conditions and liberal institutions and practices (Ikenberry 2006: 146, 161). These assumptions explain the short-term design of liberal policies in the early 1990s and even, in the case of the Iraq war, into the 2000s. Democracy assistance was designed to terminate after the first successful election, peacebuilding operations adopted a 'quickly-in-and-out' approach, the implementation and results of structural adjustment programs were not monitored, humanitarian interventions were designed to stop the killing but not to rebuild institutions and the Iraq intervention (in)famously lacked any plans for the aftermath of the military phase (Carothers 2002; Paris 2004: 19; Williams 2012: 121; Packer 2006: 113, 147; Jahn 2007b: 220). And it was against these optimistic expectations that the liberal policies of the early 1990s quickly appeared to 'fail'. The analysis of these 'failures' led to an adjustment of liberal policies already from the mid-1990s onwards. Expectations, it was widely held, had been too optimistic; the economic, political, and cultural preconditions for functioning liberal market democracies were widely lacking and liberal actors themselves had to iron out their 'inconsistent' or half-hearted approach to the spread of liberal principles: in sum, more time was needed.

And yet, a conception of liberalism accounting for its fragmentary dynamics suggests that the heyday of liberalism in the early 1990s did not end so rapidly because liberals had overlooked the continued existence of substantial nonliberal forces but rather that these policies were themselves responsible for creating new nonliberal forces. It was the fact that the introduction of elections frequently contributed to the consolidation of *new* nonliberal regimes (after all, the current government in Russia differs radically from the previous Soviet ones), that the introduction of market democracies re*new*ed civil conflict (for example in Angola), that neoliberal economic policies generated *new* inequalities as well as *new* economic and financial crises, that interventions generated *new* insurgencies (like in Iraq) which led to what Ikenberry correctly calls a 'crisis of authority' (Ikenberry 2009). That is, it was the extensive, rapid, and high-handed nature of liberal policies themselves that intensified the liberal dynamic of fragmentation and generated a wide variety of nonliberal actors, forces, and practices – that is, to an internal 'crisis of authority' since serious external 'ideological challengers or geopolitical balancers are not to be found' (Ikenberry 2006: 143).

In sum, then, the mixed and paradoxical outcomes of liberal foreign policies during the post-Cold War period have their roots in the contradictory and fragmentary dynamics of liberalism. The impulse to spread liberal principles was as much rooted in an emancipatory interest as in the urgency to prove the validity of liberal principles and to maintain their achievements in core liberal states – leading to 'inconsistent' policies. These 'inconsistencies' were compounded by the internal fragmentation of liberalism into a variety of different actors and policy areas as well as by the equally contradictory interests of target societies. Yet, while these 'inconsistencies' stood in the way of an unequivocal realization of liberal principles, their outcomes are perfectly in line with the internal tensions and contradictions of liberalism. After all, these policies were in fact successful in spreading democratic institutions, liberal economic principles, and human rights to some sections of (international) society even while they produced 'illiberal democracies', engaged in protectionism, led to poverty, and violated the human rights of others. In light of this analysis, the liberal policies during the 1990s cannot be regarded as 'failures'. On the contrary, they produced exactly the results that a comprehensive conception of liberalism would expect. It was, in other words, not liberal practice which 'failed' liberal theory but liberal theory which 'failed' to grasp the dynamics of, and hence also misled, liberal practice.

If this analysis holds, the adoption of a comprehensive conception of liberalism which accounts for its core dynamics has two crucial implications for liberal policies. First, the internal tensions and resulting fragmentary dynamics at the core of liberalism suggest that the universal realization of liberal principles is logically impossible. Inasmuch as the attempt to realize the liberal political project is bound to produce and reproduce nonliberal actors, institutions, and practices, the realization of liberal principles remains limited to particular (if shifting) sections of (international) society. Yet, even while this particularity undermines the lofty promises of liberalism, it frees liberal policies from the need to pursue unrealistic or hubristic goals, and thus also from the unfortunate fate of being judged against goals it cannot possibly reach.

Secondly, a conception that theoretically accounts for 'the dilemmas and tensions in liberalism itself' (Sørensen 2012: 3) overcomes the separation of theory and practice that continues to haunt even the most insightful analyses that variously describe and discuss these tensions (Sørensen 2012; Ikenberry 2011) without, however, linking the results of these analyses back to the conception of liberalism itself. For it is this lacuna which accounts for 'the current difficulties of creating a liberal world order' consisting in the 'tensions in liberalism' itself as well as in confronting external challenges like 'a renewed balance of power competition between great powers, the existence of weak states, the phenomenon of international terrorism, or a confrontation between competing cultures' (Sørensen 2012: 3). Once the analysis of the tensions *within* liberalism is taken seriously and informs the conception *of* liberalism, we are not any longer confronted with a need to 'create a liberal world order': we already live in it. And the challenges for liberal policies then do not consist any longer in confronting external threats but in designing policies that avoid the production of internal fragmentation. Such a shift in focus may well provide liberalism's only chance to escape the tragic fate that the very policies designed to extend its reach simultaneously undermine it – that its moments of greatest triumph generate the causes of its most serious crises.

Bibliography

Acemoglu, D. and Robinson, J. A. (2006) *Economic Origins of Dictatorship and Democracy* (Cambridge: Cambridge University Press).

Adamson, F. (2005) 'Global Liberalism Versus Political Islam: Competing Ideological Frameworks in International Politics', *International Studies Review*, 7: 4, 547–69.

Ake, C. (1992) 'Devaluing Democracy', *Journal of Democracy*, 3: 3, 32–6.

Alvarez, J. E. (2001) 'Do Liberal States Behave Better? A Critique of Slaughter's Liberal Theory', *European Journal of International Law*, 12: 2, 183–246.

Angell, N. (1910) *The Great Illusion* (London: Heinemann).

Anghi, A. (2007) *Imperialism, Sovereignty and the Making of International Law* (Cambridge: Cambridge University Press).

Arblaster, A. (1984) *The Rise and Decline of Western Liberalism* (Oxford: Blackwell).

Archibugi, D. (2004) 'Cosmopolitan Democracy and its Critics', *European Journal of International Relations*, 10: 3, 437–73.

Archibugi, D. (2003) (ed.) *Debating Cosmopolitics* (London: Verso).

Archibugi, D. (1998) 'Principles of Cosmopolitan Democracy' in D. Archibugi, D. Held and M. Köhler (eds) *Re-Imagining Political Community: Studies in Cosmopolitan Democracy* (Cambridge: Polity) 198–228.

Archibugi, D. and Held, D. (eds) (1995) *Cosmopolitan Democracy: An Agenda for a New World Order* (Cambridge: Polity Press).

Armitage, D. (2004) 'John Locke, Carolina, and the "Two Treatise of Government"', *Political Theory*, 32: 5, 602–27.

Armitage, D. (2001) *The Ideological Origins of the British Empire* (Cambridge: Cambridge University Press).

Arneil, B. (1996) *John Locke and America. The Defence of English Colonialism* (Oxford: Clarendon).

Ashley, R. K. (1988) 'Untying the Sovereign State: A Double Reading of the Anarchy Problematique', *Millennium: Journal of International Studies*, 17: 2, 227–86.

Bacevich, A. J. (ed.) (2003) *The Imperial Tense: Prospects and Problems of American Empire* (Chicago: Ivan R. Dee) 93–101.

Bajoria, J. (2011) 'The Taliban in Afghanistan', http://www.cfr.org/afghanistan/taliban-afghanistan/p10551, 15 February 2013.

Baldwin, D. A. (ed.) (1993) *Neorealism and Neoliberalism: The Contemporary Debate* (New York: Columbia University Press).

Barbieri, K. (2002) *The Liberal Illusion. Does Trade Promote Peace?* (Ann Arbor: The University of Michigan Press).

Barkawi, T. and Laffey, M. (eds) (2001) *Democracy, Liberalism and War* (Boulder: Lynne Rienner).

Barry, B. (2005) *Why Social Justice Matters* (Cambridge: Polity Press).

Barry, B. (1995) *Justice as Impartiality* (Oxford: Clarendon Press).

Barton, F. D. and Crocker, B. (2003) 'Winning the Peace in Iraq', *The Washington Quarterly*, 26: 2, 7–22.

Bauer, P. T. (1981) *Equality, the Third World, and Economic Delusion* (London: Weidenfeld and Nicolson).

Behnke, A. (2012) 'Eternal Peace, Perpetual War? A Critical Investigation into Kant's Conceptualisation of War', *Journal of International Relations and Development*, 15: 2, 250–71.

Beitz, C. R. (1983) 'Cosmopolitan Ideals and National Sentiment', *The Journal of Philosophy*, 80: 10, 591–600.

Beitz, C. R. (1979) *Political Theory and International Relations* (Princeton: Princeton University Press).

Bell, D. (2006a) 'Empire in Nineteenth Century European Political Thought', in G. Claeys and G. Stedman Jones (eds) *Cambridge History of 19th Century Political Thought* (Cambridge: Cambridge University Press).

Bell, D. (2006b) 'Empire and International Relations in Victorian Political Thought', *Historical Journal*, 49: 1, 281–98.

Bellamy, A. J. (2005) 'Responsibility to Protect or Trojan Horse? The Crisis in Darfur and Human Rights After Iraq', *Ethics and International Affairs*, 19: 2, 31–54.

Berger, P. L. (1992) 'The Uncertain Triumph of Democratic Capitalism', *Journal of Democracy*, 3: 3, 7–16.

Berry, A. and Serieux, J. (2006) 'Riding the Elephants: The Evolution of World Economic Growth and Income Distribution at the End of the 20th Century (1980–2000)', DESA Working Paper No 27, http://www.un.org/esa/desa/papers/2006/wp27_2006.pdf, 16 February 2013.

Bhagwati, J. (2004) *In Defense of Globalization* (New York: Oxford University Press).

Bhagwati, J. (1992) 'Democracy and Development', *Journal of Democracy*, 3: 3, 37–44.

Bilefsky, D. (2012) 'Romania Strains to Build True Democracy', *International Herald Tribune*, 12 October.

Bishai, L. (2012) 'Liberal Internationalism and the Order vs Liberty Paradox', *Journal of International Relations and Development*, 15: 2, 201–23.

Bitterli, U. (1982) *Die 'Wilden' und die 'Zivilisierten': Die europäisch-überseeische Begegnung* (München: dtv).

Blair, T. (1999) 'Doctrine of the International Community', Speech to the Economic Club, Chicago Hilton 22 April, http://www.fco.gov.uk/news/speechtext.asp?2316, 16 February 2013.

Blaney, D. and Inayatullah, N. (2010) *Savage Economics: Wealth, Poverty and the Temporal Walls of Capitalism* (London: Routledge).

Blond, P. (2008) 'The Failure of Neo-Liberalism', *International Herald Tribune*, 23 January.

Boucher, D. (1994) 'British Idealism, the State, and International Relations', *Journal of the History of Ideas*, 55: 4, 671–94.

Boucher, D. (2006) 'Property and Propriety in International Relations: The Case of John Locke' in B. Jahn (ed.) *Classical Theory in International Relations* (Cambridge: Cambridge University Press) 156–77.

Boucoyannis, D. (2007) 'The International Wanderings of a Liberal Idea, or Why Liberals Can Learn to Stop Worrying and Love the Balance of Power', *Perspectives on Politics*, 5: 4, 703–27.

Bova, R. (1997) 'Democracy and Liberty: The Cultural Connection', *Journal of Democracy*, 8: 1, 112–26.

Brown, C. (2001) 'Cosmopolitanism, World Citizenship and Global Civil Society' in P. Jones and S. Caney (eds) *Human Rights and Global Diversity* (London: Frank Cass) 7–26.

Brown, C. (1997) 'Theories of Justice', *British Journal of Political Science*, 27: 2, 273–97.

Brown, C. and Ainley, K. (2005) *Understanding International Relations* (Basingstoke: Palgrave).

Brown, M. E., Lynn-Jones, S. M. and Miller, S. E. (1996) (eds) *Debating the Democratic Peace* (Cambridge: MIT Press).

Brown, W. (2009) 'Reconsidering the Aid Relationship: International Relations and Social Development', *Round Table*, 98: 402, 285–99.

Buchanan, A. (2003) 'Reforming the International Law of Humanitarian Intervention' in J. L. Holzgrefe and R. O. Keohane (eds) *Humanitarian Intervention. Ethical, Legal, and Political Dilemmas* (Cambridge: Cambridge University Press) 130–73.

Buchanan, A. and Keohane, R. O. (2004) 'The Preventive Use of Force: A Cosmopolitan Institutional Proposal', *Ethics and International Affairs*, 18: 1, 1–22.

Burchill, S. (2001) 'Liberalism' in S. Burchill et al. (eds) *Theories of International Relations* (Basingstoke: Palgrave) 55–83.

Bush, G. H. W. (1991) 'Address Before a Joint Session of Congress on the End of the Gulf War' (March 6) http://millercenter.org/president/speeches/detail/3430, 15 February 2013.

Cammack, P. (1997) *Capitalism and Democracy in the Third World: The Doctrine for Political Development* (London: Leicester University Press).

Campbell, D. (1992) *Writing Security: United States Foreign Policy and the Politics of Identity* (Minneapolis: University of Minnesota Press).

Carothers, T. (2004) *Critical Mission. Essays on Democracy Promotion* (Washington: Carnegie Endowment for International Peace).

Carothers, T. (2002) 'The End of the Transition Paradigm', *Journal of Democracy*, 13: 1, 5–21.

Carothers, T. (2000) 'Taking Stock of US Democracy Assistance', in M. Cox, G. J. Ikenberry and T. Inoguchi (eds) *American Democracy Promotion: Impulses, Strategies, and Impacts* (Oxford: Oxford University Press) 181–99.

Cass, D. Z. (2001) 'The "Constitutionalization" of International Trade Law: Judicial Norm-Generation as the Engine of Constitutional Development in International Trade', *European Journal of International Law*, 12: 1, 39–75.

Cassel, D. (2001) 'Does International Human Rights Law Make a Difference?' *Chicago Journal of International Law*, 2, 121–35.

Chandler, D. (2006) *Empire in Denial. The Politics of State-building* (London: Pluto Press).

Chappell, V. (1994) *The Cambridge Companion to Locke* (Cambridge: Cambridge University Press).

Charney, J. I. (1999) 'Anticipatory Humanitarian Intervention', *American Journal of International Law*, 93: 4, October, 834–41.

Chesterman, S. (2001) *Just War or Just Peace? Humanitarian Intervention and International Law* (Oxford: Oxford University Press).

Clark, I. (2009) 'Democracy in International Society: Promotion or Exclusion?' *Millennium: Journal of International Studies*, 37: 3, 563–81.

Clarke, P. (1978) *Liberals and Social Democrats* (Cambridge: Cambridge University Press).

Coady, C. A. J. (2002) *The Ethics of Armed Humanitarian Intervention*, Peaceworks No. 45. (Washington: United States Institute of Peace).

Cohen, B. J. (2008) *International Political Economy: An Intellectual History* (Princeton: Princeton University Press).

Cohen, J. L. (2004) 'Whose Sovereignty? Empire Versus International Law', *Ethics and International Affairs*, 18: 3, 1–24.

Cook, M. L. (2003) ' "Immaculate War": Constraints on Humanitarian Intervention' in A. F. Lang Jr (ed.) *Just Intervention* (Washington: Georgetown University Press) 145–154.

Cooper, R. (2002) 'The New Liberal Imperialism', http://www.guardian.co.uk/world/2002/apr/07/1/print, 16 February 2013.

Cox, M., Ikenberry, G. J. and Inoguchi, T. (2000) 'Introduction' in M. Cox, G. J. Ikenberry and T. Inoguchi (eds) *American Democracy Promotion: Impulses, Strategies, and Impacts* (Oxford: Oxford University Press) 1–17.

Cox, R. H. (1960) *Locke on War and Peace* (Oxford: Oxford University Press).

Cox, R. W. (1981) 'Social Forces, States, and World Orders: Beyond International Relations Theory', *Millennium: Journal of International Studies*, 10: 2, 126–55.

Cranston, M. (1985) *John Locke: A Biography* (Oxford: Oxford University Press).

Cutler, C. (2003) *Private Power and Global Authority: Transnational Merchant Law in the Global Political Economy* (Cambridge: Cambridge University Press).

David, S. R. (1992/93) 'Why the Third World Still Matters', *International Security*, 17: 3, 127–59.

de Tocqueville, A. (1994) *Democracy in America* (London: Everyman's Library).

De Waal, A. (2007) 'No Such Thing as Humanitarian Intervention. Why we Need to Rethink the "Responsibility to Protect" in Wartime', *Harvard International Review*, http://hir.harvard.edu/index.php?page= article&id= 1482&p= 1, 15 January 2010.

De Waal, A. (1997) 'Democratizing the Aid Encounter in Africa', *International Affairs*, 73: 4, 623–39.

De Waal, A. (1994) 'Dangerous Precedents? Famine Relief in Somalia, 1991–93' in J. Macrae and A. Zwi (eds) *War and Hunger: Rethinking International Responses to Complex Emergencies* (London: Zed Books).

De Zeeuw, J. and L. van de Goor (2006) 'Findings and Recommendations' in J. De Zeeuw and K. Kumar (eds) *Promoting Democracy in Postconflict Societies* (Boulder: Lynne Rienner) 275–90.

Desch, M. C. (2007) 'America's Liberal Illiberalism – The Ideological Origins of Overreaction in US Foreign Policy', *International Security*, 32: 3, 7–43.

Deudney, D. and Ikenberry, G. J. (1999) 'The Nature and Sources of Liberal International Order', *Review of International Studies*, 25: 2, 179–96.

Diamond, L. (1999) *Developing Democracy: Toward Consolidation* (Baltimore: Johns Hopkins University Press).

Diamond, L. (1996) 'Is the Third Wave Over?' *Journal of Democracy*, 7: 3, 20–37.

Di Muzio, T. (2012) 'The Liberal Renaissance and the End(s) of History', *Journal of International Relations and Development*, 15: 2, 158–76.

Dodge, T. (2012) 'The Resistable Rise of Nuri al-Maliki', http://www.opendemocracy.net/toby-dodge/resistible-rise-of-nuri-al-maliki, 15 February 2013.

Dodge, T. (2009) 'Coming Face to Face With Bloody Reality: Liberal Common Sense and the Ideological Failure of the Bush Doctrine in Iraq', *International Politics*, 46: 2/3, 253–75.

Dougherty, J. and Pfaltzgraff Jr, R. L. (1997) *Contending Theories of International Relations* (New York: Longman).

Doyle, M. W. (1997) *Ways of War and Peace* (New York: W. W. Norton).

Doyle, M. W. (1996) 'Kant, Liberal Legacies, and Foreign Affairs', in M. E. Brown, S. M. Lynn-Jones and S. E. Miller (eds) *Debating the Democratic Peace* (Cambridge: MIT Press) 3–57.

Doyle, M. W. (1986) 'Liberalism and World Politics', *American Political Science Review*, 80: 4, 1151–69.

Duffield, M. (2001) *Global Governance and the New Wars* (London: Zed Books).

Dunn, J. (1969) *The Political Thought of John Locke. A Historical Account of the Arguments of the 'Two Treatise of Government'* (Cambridge: Cambridge University Press).

Dunne, T. and Wheeler, N. J. (eds) (1999) *Human Rights in Global Politics* (Cambridge: Cambridge University Press).

Dunne, T. (1997) 'Liberalism' in J. Baylis and S. Smith (eds) *The Globalization of World Politics* (Oxford: Oxford University Press).

Elshtain, J. B. (2003) 'International Justice as Equal Regard and the Use of Force', *Ethics and International Affairs*, 17: 2, 63–75.

Evans, M. (2001) *The Edinburgh Companion to Contemporary Liberalism* (Edinburgh: Edinburgh University Press).

Falk, R. (1998) *Law in an Emerging Global Village: A Post-Westphalian Perspective* (Ardsley: Transnational Publishers).

Falk, R. (1995) *On Humane Governance: Towards a New Global Politics* (University Park PA: Pennsylvania State University).

Farer, T. J. (2003) 'Humanitarian Intervention Before and After 9/11: Legality and Legitimacy' in J. L. Holzgrefe and R. O. Keohane (eds) *Humanitarian Intervention. Ethical, Legal, and Political Dilemmas* (Cambridge: Cambridge University Press) 53–89.

Finkel, S. E., Perez-Linan, A., Seligson, M. and Azpuru, D. (2006) *Effects of US Foreign Assistance on Democracy Building: Results of a Cross-National Quantitative Study* (USAID, University of Pittsburgh, Vanderbilt University).

Franceschet, A. (2002) *Kant and Liberal Internationalism: Sovereignty, Justice and Global Reform* (Basingstoke: Palgrave Macmillan).

Franck, T. M. (1992) 'The Emerging Right to Democratic Governance', *American Journal of International Law*, 86: 1, 46–91.

Freeden, M. (2005) *Liberal Languages. Ideological Imaginations and Twentieth Century Progressive Thought* (Princeton: Princeton University Press).

Freedom House (2012) 'Freedom in the World 2013: Democratic Breakthroughs in the Balance', http://www.freedomhouse.org/sites/default/files/FIW%202013%20Charts%20and%20Graphs%20for%20Web.pdf, 16 February 2013.

Friedman, M. and Friedman R. D. (1962) *Capitalism and Freedom* (Chicago: University of Chicago Press).

Fritz, J.-S. (2005) 'Internationalism and the Promise of Science', in D. Long and B. C. Schmidt (eds) *Imperialism and Internationalism in the Discipline of International Relations* (Albany: State University of New York Press) 141–58.

Froning, D. (2001) 'Will Debt Relief Really Help?' *The Washington Quarterly*, 24: 3, 199–211.

Fukuyama, F. (1992b) *The End of History and the Last Man* (London: Penguin).

Fukuyama, F. (1992a) 'Capitalism and Democracy: The Missing Link', *Journal of Democracy*, 3: 3, 100–10.

Fukuyama, F. (1989) 'The End of History?' *National Interest*, Summer, 3–18.

Gardner, R. N. (1990) 'The Comeback of Liberal Internationalism', *The Washington Quarterly*, 13: 3, 23–39.

Gates, S., Knutsen, T. L. and Moses, J. W. (1996) 'Democracy and Peace: A More Sceptical View', *Journal of Peace Research*, 33: 1, 1–10.

Gills, B. (2000) 'American Power, Neoliberal Economic Globalization and "Low Intensity Democracy": An Unstable Trinity', in M. Cox, G. J. Ikenberry and T. Inoguchi (eds) *American Democracy Promotion: Impulses, Strategies, and Impacts* (Oxford: Oxford University Press) 326–44.

Gilpin, R. (1987) *The Political Economy of International Relations* (Princeton: Princeton University Press).

Gismondi, M. D. (2008) *Ethics, Liberalism and Realism in International Relations* (Abingdon: Routledge).

Glausser, W. (1990) 'Three Approaches to Locke and the Slave Trade', *Journal of the History of Ideas*, 51: 2, 199–216.

Gorman, D. (2005) 'Liberal Internationalism, the League of Nations Union, and the Mandates System', *Canadian Journal of International History*, 40: 3, 449–77.

Gradstein, M. and Milanovic, B (2004) 'Does Liberté = Egalité? A Survey of the Empirical Links Between Democracy and Inequality with Some Evidence on the Transition Economies', World Bank Policy Research Working Paper Series 2875, http://ideas.repec.org/p/wbk/wbrwps/2875.html, 16 February 2013.

Gray, J. (1986) *Liberalism* (Minneapolis: University of Minnesota Press).

Griffiths, M. (2011) *Rethinking International Relations Theory* (London: Palgrave Macmillan).

Gross, A. M. (2007) 'Human Proportions: Are Human Rights the Emperor's New Clothes of the International Law of Occupation?' *European Journal of International Law*, 18: 1, 1–35.

Grovogui, S. N. (2000) 'Legal Standing, Questionable Deeds: Western Mediation in Namibia', in C. Lynch and M. Loriaux (eds) *Law and Moral Action in World Politics* (Minneapolis: University of Minnesota Press) 175–202.

Guzzini, S. (1998) *Realism in International Relations and International Political Economy: The Continuing Story of a Death Foretold* (London: Routledge).

Haass, R. N. (2003) 'Toward Greater Democracy in the Muslim World', *The Washington Quarterly*, 26: 3, 137–48.

Hafner, G., Boon, K., Rübesame, A. and Huston, J. (1999) 'A Response to the American View as Presented by Ruth Wedgewood', *European Journal of International Law*, 10: 1.

Hagmann, T. (2012) 'Supporting Stability, Abetting Oppression', *New York Times*, 11 July 2012.

Hall, C. (2002) *Civilising Subjects: Metropole and Colony in the English Imagination 1830–1867* (Chicago: University of Chicago Press).

Hamre, J. J. and Sullivan, G. R. (2002) 'Toward Postconflict Reconstruction', *The Washington Quarterly*, 25: 4, 85–96.

Hasenclever, A., Mayer, P. and Rittberger, V. (1997) *Theories of International Regimes* (Cambridge: Cambridge University Press).

Haslam, J. (2002) *No Virtue Like Necessity: Realist Thought in International Relations since Machiavelli* (New Haven: Yale University Press).

Hayek, F. (2011) *The Constitution of Liberty* (Chicago: University of Chicago Press).

Hayek, F. (2001) *The Road to Serfdom* (London: Routledge).

Heathershaw, J. (2008) 'Unpacking the Liberal Peace: The Dividing and Merging of Peacebuilding Discourse', *Millennium: Journal of International Studies*, 36: 3, 597–621.

Hehir, A. (2010) *Humanitarian Intervention. An Introduction* (Basingstoke: Palgrave Macmillan).

Heinze, E. A. (2009) *Waging Humanitarian War. The Ethics, Law, and Politics of Humanitarian Intervention* (New York: State University of New York Press).

Held, D. (1997) *Models of Democracy* (Cambridge: Polity Press).

Held, D. (1996) *Democracy and the Global Order: From the Modern State to Cosmopolitan Governance* (Cambridge: Polity).

Hobson, C. and Kurki, M. (2012) (eds) *The Conceptual Politics of Democracy Promotion* (London: Routledge).

Hobson, C. (2009) 'Beyond the End of History: The Need for a Radical "Historicisation" of Democracy in International Relations', *Millennium: Journal of International Studies*, 37: 3, 631–57.

Hobson, J. A. (2006) *Imperialism: A Study* (New York: Cosimo).

Hoffmann, S. (1995) 'The Crisis of Liberal Internationalism', *Foreign Policy*, 98, 159–77.

Hoffmann, S. (1987) *Janus and Minerva. Essays in the Theory and Practice of International Politics* (Boulder: Westview).

Holden, B. (2000) (ed.) *Global Democracy: Key Debates* (London: Routledge).

Holzgrefe, J. L. and Robert O. Keohane (eds) (2003) *Humanitarian Intervention. Ethical, Legal, and Political Dilemmas* (Cambridge: Cambridge University Press).

Hont, I. (2005) *Jealousy of Trade. International Competition and the Nation-State in Historical Perspective* (Cambridge MA: Harvard University Press).

Hovden, E. and Keene, E. (2001) (eds) *The Globalization of Liberalism* (Basingstoke: Palgrave Macmillan).

Howard, M. (1978) *War and the Liberal Conscience* (Oxford: Oxford University Press).

Howe, A. (1997) *Free Trade and Liberal England, 1846–1946* (Oxford: Clarendon Press).

Huntington, S. P. (1993) 'The Clash of Civilizations?' *Foreign Affairs*, 72: 3, 22–49.

Huntington, S. P. (1991) *The Third Wave: Democratization in the Late Twentieth Century* (Oklahoma: University of Oklahoma Press).

Igarashi, M. (2013) *Genealogy of Trusteeship: From Colonial Administration to Peacebuilding*, University of Sussex, unpublished PhD thesis.

Ignatieff, M. (2003) 'State Failure and Nation-Building' in J. L. Holzgrefe and R. O. Keohane (eds) *Humanitarian Intervention. Ethical, Legal, and Political Dilemmas* (Cambridge: Cambridge University Press) 299–321.

Ignatieff, M. (1999) 'Counting Bodies in Kosovo', *New York Times*, 21 November.

Ikenberry, J. G. (2006) *Liberal Order and Imperial Ambition* (Cambridge: Polity).

Ikenberry, G. J. (2011) *Liberal Leviathan. The Origins, Crisis, and Transformation of the American World Order* (Princeton: Princeton University Press).

Ikenberry, G. J. (2009) 'Liberal Internationalism 3.0: America and the Dilemmas of Liberal World Order', *Perspectives on Politics*, 7: 1, 71–87.

Ikenberry, G. J. and Slaughter, A.-M. (2006) *The Princeton Project on National Security. Forging a World of Liberty Under Law, US National Security in the 21st Century* (Princeton: Woodrow Wilson School of Public and International Affairs, Princeton University).

Inayatullah, N. and Blaney, D. L. (2004) *International Relations and the Problem of Difference* (New York: Routledge).

Inayatullah, N. and Blaney, D. L. (2012) 'Liberal Fundamentals: Invisible, Invasive, Artful and Bloody Hands', *Journal of International Relations and Development*, 15: 2, 290–315.

Ivison, Duncan (2002) *Postcolonial Liberalism* (Cambridge: Cambridge University Press).

Ivison, D. (2003) 'Locke, Liberalism and Empire', in P. R. Anstey (ed.) *The Philosophy of John Locke: New Perspectives* (London: Routledge) 86–105.

Jackson, J. H. (1997) 'The WTO Dispute Settlement Understanding – Misunderstandings on the Nature of Legal Obligations', *American Journal of International Law*, 91: 1, 60–4.

Jackson, R. (2000) *The Global Covenant. Human Conduct in a World of States* (Oxford: Oxford University Press).

Jackson, R. and Sørensen, G. (2003) *Introduction to International Relations. Theories and Approaches* (Oxford: Oxford University Press).

Jahn, B. (2012b) 'Critique in a Time of Liberal World Order', *Journal of International Relations and Development*, 15, 145–57.

Jahn, B. (2012a) 'Humanitarian Intervention: What's in a Name?' *International Politics*, 49: 1, 36–58.

Jahn, B. (2009) 'Liberal Internationalism: From Ideology to Empirical Theory – and Back Again', *International Theory*, 1: 3, 409–38.

Jahn, B. (2007b) 'The Tragedy of Liberal Diplomacy: Democratization, Intervention, Statebuilding II', *Journal of Intervention and Statebuilding*, 1: 2, 211–29.

Jahn, B. (2007a) 'The Tragedy of Liberal Diplomacy: Democratization, Intervention, Statebuilding I', *Journal of Intervention and Statebuilding*, 1: 1, 88–106.

Jahn, B. (2005b) 'Barbarian Thoughts: Imperialism in the Philosophy of John Stuart Mill', *Review of International Studies*, 31, 599–618.

Jahn, B. (2005a) 'Kant, Mill, and Illiberal Legacies in International Affairs', *International Organization*, 59, 177–207.

Jahn, B. (2000) *The Cultural Construction of International Relations. The Invention of the State of Nature* (Basingstoke: Palgrave Macmillan).

Jahn, B. (1998) 'One Step Forward, Two Steps Back: Critical Theory as the Latest Edition of Liberal Internationalism', *Millennium: Journal of International Studies*, 27: 3, 613–41.

Jenkins, K. and Plowden, W. (2006) *Governance and Nationbuilding. The Failure of International Intervention* (Cheltenham: Edward Elgar).

Kagan, R. (2002) 'Power and Weakness', *Policy Review*, No 113, June.

Kant, I. (1957) *Perpetual Peace*, L. W. Beck (ed.) (London: Macmillan).

Keohane, R. O. (2003) 'Political Authority After Intervention: Gradations in Sovereignty' in J. L. Holzgrefe and R. O. Keohane (eds) *Humanitarian*

Intervention. Ethical, Legal, and Political Dilemmas (Cambridge: Cambridge University Press) 275–98.

Keohane, R. O. (2002) *Power and Governance in a Partially Globalized World* (London: Routledge).

Keohane, R. O. (1989) *International Institutions and State Power* (Boulder: Westview).

Keohane, R. O. (1986) (ed.) *Neo-Realism and Its Critics* (New York: Columbia University Press).

Keohane, R. O., Moravcsik, A. and Slaugher, A.-M. (2000) 'Legalized Dispute Resolution: Interstate and Transnational', *International Organization*, 54: 3, 457–88.

Keohane, R. O. and Nye, J. S. (1989) *Power and Interdependence* (New York: Harper Collins).

Keynes, J. M. (2006) *General Theory of Employment, Interest and Money* (New Delhi: Atlantic).

Kim, K. (1992) 'Marx, Schumpeter, and the East Asian Experience', *Journal of Democracy*, 3: 3, 17–31.

Kramer, D. J. (2012) 'Russia 2012: Increased Oppression, Rampant Corruption, Assisting Rogue Regimes', Testimony before the United States House Foreign Affairs Committee, http://www.freedomhouse.org/sites/default/files/inline_images/HFAC%20Kramer%20testimony%20on%20Russia%203-21-12.pdf, 15 February 2013.

Krugman, P. R. and Obstfeld, M. (2002) *International Economics: Theory and Policy* (Reading MA: Addison Wesley).

Kymlicka, W. (1995) *Multicultural Citizenship* (Oxford: Oxford University Press).

Kymlicka, W. (1989) *Liberalism, Community and Culture* (Oxford: Oxford University Press).

Lal, D. (1983) *The Poverty of Development Economics* (London: Institute of Economic Affairs).

Lang Jr., A. F. (2003) (ed.) *Just Intervention* (Washington: Georgetown University Press).

Lang Jr., A. F. (2001) *Agency and Ethics. The Politics of Military Intervention* (Albany: State University of New York Press).

Laslett, P. (1994) 'Introduction' in P. Laslett (ed.) *John Locke, Two Treatise of Government* (Cambridge: Cambridge University Press) 1–133.

Latham, M. E. (2000) *Modernization as Ideology: American Social Science and 'Nation Building' in the Kennedy Era* (Chapel Hill: The University of North Carolina Press).

Lebovics, H. (1986) 'The Uses of America in Locke's Second Treatise of Government', *Journal of the History of Ideas*, 47: 4, 567–81.

Linklater, A. (2000) 'The Good International Citizen and the Crisis in Kosovo' in A. Schnabel and R. Thakur (eds) *Kosovo and the Challenge of Humanitarian Intervention: Selective Indignation, Collective Action, and International Citizenship* (New York: UN University Press) 482–95.

Linklater, A. (1998) *The Transformation of Political Community* (Cambridge: Polity).

Linklater, A. (1990) *Beyond Realism and Marxism* (Basingstoke: Palgrave Macmillan).

List, F. (2013) *National System of Political Economy* (New York: Cosimo Publications).

Little, I. M. D. (1982) *Economic Development: Theory, Policy, and International Relations* (New York: Basic Books).

Locke, J. (1994) *Two Treatises of Government*, P. Laslett (ed.) (Cambridge: Cambridge University Press).

Locke, J. (1983) *A Letter Concerning Toleration*, J. H. Tully (ed.) (Indianapolis: Hackett Publishing Company).

Locke, J. (1959) *An Essay Concerning Human Understanding*, 2 Vols., collated and annotated by A. C. Fraser (New York: Dover).

Long, D. (1995) 'The Harvard School of Liberal International Theory: A Case for Closure', *Millennium: Journal of International Studies*, 24: 3, 489–505.

Long, D. and Schmidt, B. C.(eds) (2005) *Imperialism and Internationalism in the Discipline of International Relations* (Albany: State University of New York Press).

Long, D. and Wilson, P. (eds) (1995) *Thinkers of the Twenty Year's Crisis: Inter-war Idealism Reassessed* (Oxford: Clarendon Press).

MacGinty, R. and Richmond, O. (2007) (eds) 'The Liberal Peace and Post-War Reconstruction: Myth or Reality?' special issue of *Global Society*, 21: 4.

MacMillan, J. (1998) *On Liberal Peace. Democracy, War and the International Order* (London: I.B. Tauris).

MacMillan, J. (1995) 'A Kantian Protest Against the Peculiar Discourse of Inter-Liberal State Peace', *Millennium: Journal of International Studies*, 24: 3, 549–62.

MacPherson, C. B. (1962) *The Political Theory of Possessive Individualism* (Oxford: Oxford University Press).

McDonald, P. J. and Sweeney, K. (2007) 'The Achille's Heel of Liberal IR Theory? Globalization and Conflict in the Pre-World War I Era', *World Politics*, 59: 3, 370–403.

McFaul, M. (2005) 'Democracy Promotion as a World Value' *The Washington Quarterly*, 28: 1, 147–63.

McNally, D. (1988) *Political Economy and the Rise of Capitalism. A Reinterpretation* (Berkeley: University of California Press).

Manent, P. (1994) *An Intellectual History of Liberalism* (Princeton: Princeton University Press).

Marks, R. B. (2007) *The Origins of the Modern World. Fate and Fortune in the Rise of the West* (Lanham: Rowman and Littlefield).

Marten, K. Z. (2002/03) 'Defending Against Anarchy: From War to Peacekeeping in Afghanistan', *The Washington Quarterly*, 26: 1, 35–52.

May, C. (2000) *A Global Political Economy of Intellectual Property Rights* (London: Routledge).

Mazzini, G. (2009) *A Cosmopolitanism of Nations. Guiseppe Mazzini's Writings on Cosmopolitanism, Nationbuilding, and International Relations*, S. Recchia and N. Urbinati (eds) (Princeton: Princeton University Press).

Meek, R. L. (1976) *Social Science and the Ignoble Savage* (Cambridge: Cambridge University Press).

Megret, F. (2001) 'Epilogue to an Endless Debate: The International Criminal Court's Third Party Jurisdiction and the Looming Revolution of International Law', *European Journal of International Law*, 12: 2, 247–68.

Mehta, U. S. (1999) *Liberalism and Empire. A Study in Nineteenth-century British Liberal Thought* (Chicago, IL: The University of Chicago Press).

Melzer, A. M., Weinberger, J. and Zinman, M. R. (1995) (eds) *History and the Idea of Progress* (Ithaca: Cornell University Press).

Mill, J. S. (1998c) 'On the Subjection of Women' in J. Gray (ed.) *On Liberty and Other Essays* (Oxford: Oxford University Press) 471–582.

Mill, J. S. (1998b) 'Considerations on Representative Government' in J. Gray (ed.) *On Liberty and Other Essays* (Oxford: Oxford University Press) 203–467.

Mill, J. S. (1998a) 'On Liberty' in J. Gray (ed.) *On Liberty and Other Essays* (Oxford: Oxford University Press).

Mill, J. S. (1994) *Principles of Political Economy* (Oxford: Oxford University Press).

Mill, J. S. (1984) 'A Few Words on Non-Intervention' in J. M. Robson (ed.) *The Collected Works of John Stuart Mill*, Vol. XXI (Toronto: University of Toronto Press) 109–124.

Miller, B. (2010) 'Democracy Promotion: Offensive Liberalism versus the Rest (of IR Theory)', *Millennium: Journal of International Studies*, 38: 3, 561–91.

Miller, R. W. (2003) 'Respectable Oppressors, Hypocritical Liberators: Morality, Intervention, and Reality' in D. K. Chatterjee and D. E. Scheid (eds) *Ethics and Foreign Intervention* (Cambridge: Cambridge University Press) 215–250.

Møller, J. (2008) 'A Critical Note on "The Rise of Illiberal Democracy"', *Australian Journal of Political Science*, 43: 3, 555–61.

Moore, M. and Robinson, M. (1994) 'Can Foreign Aid Be Used to Promote Good Government in Developing Countries?' *Ethics and International Affairs*, 8: 1, 141–58.

Moravcsik, A. (1997) 'Taking Preferences Seriously: A Liberal Theory of International Politics', *International Organization*, 51: 4, 513–53.

Morrison, B. (2003) (ed.) *Transnational Democracy: A Critical Consideration of Sites and Sources* (Aldershot: Ashgate).

Morse, E. L. (1976) *Modernization and the Transformation of International Relations* (New York: The Free Press).

Moses, J. (2010) 'Liberal Internationalist Discourse and the Use of Force: Blair, Bush and Beyond', *International Politics*, 47: 1, 26–51.

Mousseau, M. (2000) 'Market Prosperity, Democratic Consolidation, and Democratic Peace', *Journal of Conflict Resolution,* 44: 4, 472–507.

Müllerson, R. (2009) *Democracy – A Destiny of Humankind?* (New York: Nova Science Publishers).

Nardin, T. (2003) 'The Moral Basis for Humanitarian Intervention' in A. F. Lang Jr. (ed.) *Just Intervention* (Washington: Georgetown University Press) 11–24.

Nardin, T. (1983) *Law, Morality and the Relations of States* (Princeton: Princeton University Press).

Nash, W. L. (2006) 'Iraq: Democracy or Civil War', Prepared Testimony Before the House Subcommittee on National Security, Emerging Threats, and International Relations, Council on Foreign Relations, 11 September, http://reform.house.gov/UploadedFiles/September%2011%20Nash%20Testimony.pdf

Ndi, A. (2011) 'Why Liberal Capitalism Has Failed to Stimulate a Democratic Culture in Africa: Rethinking Amarty Sen's Theory About Development as Freedom', *Journal of Developing Societies*, 27: 2, 177–200.

Nozick, R. (1974) *Anarchy, State, and Utopia* (New York: Basic Books).

O'Donnell, G. (1996a) 'Illusions About Consolidation', *Journal of Democracy*, 7: 2, 34–51.

O'Donnell, G. (1996b) 'Illusions and Conceptual Flaws', *Journal of Democracy*, 7: 4, 160–8.

Ollapally, D. (1995) 'Third World Nationalism and the US after the Cold War', *Political Science Quarterly*, 110: 3, 417–34.

O'Neill, O. (1986) *Faces of Hunger: An Essay on Poverty, Justice and Development* (London: Allen and Unwin).

Ong, G. G. (2003) 'Credibility Over Courage: NATO's Mis-Intervention in Kosovo', *The Journal of Strategic Studies*, 26: 3, 73–108.

Onuf, N. G. (1989) *World of Our Making* (Columbia: University of South Carolina Press).

Orr, R. (2002) 'Governing When Chaos Rules: Enhancing Governance and Participation', *The Washington Quarterly*, 25: 4, 139–52.

Owen, J. M. (1996) 'How Liberalism Produces Democratic Peace', in M. E. Brown, S. M. Lynn-Jones and S. E. Miller (eds) *Debating the Democratic Peace* (Cambridge: MIT Press) 116–54.

Packenham, R. A. (1973) *Liberal America and the Third World: Political Development Ideas in Foreign Aid and Social Science* (Princeton: Princeton University Press).

Packer, G. (2006) *The Assassins' Gate: America in Iraq* (London: Faber and Faber).

Pagden, A. (1995) *Lords of All the World. Ideologies of Empire in Spain, Britain and France c.1500–c.1800* (New Haven: Yale University Press).

Pagden, A. (1993) *European Encounters with the New World* (New Haven, CT: Yale University Press).

Paris, R. (2010) 'Saving Liberal Peacebuilding', *Review of International Studies*, 36: 2, 337–65.

Paris, R. (2004) *At War's End. Building Peace after Civil Conflict* (Cambridge: Cambridge University Press).

Paris, R. (1997) 'Peacebuilding and the Limits of Liberal Internationalism', *International Security*, 22: 2, 54–89.

Pasha, M. K. (2012) 'Islam, Nihilism and Liberal Secularity', *Journal of International Relations and Development*, 15: 2, 272–89.

Perelman, M. (2000) *The Invention of Capitalism. Classical Political Economy and the Secret History of Primitive Accumulation* (Durham: Duke University Press).

Peterson, V. S. (1992) *Gendered States: Feminist (Re) Visions of International Relations Theory* (Boulder: Lynne Rienner).

Pitts, J. (2005) *A Turn to Empire. The Rise of Imperial Liberalism in Britain and France* (Princeton, NJ: Princeton University Press).

Plattner, M. F. (2008) *Democracy Without Borders? Global Challenges to Liberal Democracy* (Lanham: Rowman and Littlefield).

Pogge, T. W. (2004) 'The First United Nations Millennium Development Goal: A Cause for Celebration?' *Journal of Human Development*, 5: 3, 377–97.

Pogge, T. W. (2002) *World Poverty and Human Rights: Cosmopolitan Responsibilities and Reforms* (Cambridge: Polity Press).

Pogge, T. W. (1989) *Realizing Rawls* (Ithaca: Cornell University Press).

Pomeranz, K. and Topik S. (1999) *The World that Trade Created* (Armonk NY: M. E. Sharpe).

Porter, A. (1999) 'Trusteeship, Anti-Slavery, and Humanitarianism' in *The Oxford History of the British Empire*, Vol. III (Oxford: Oxford University Press) 198–99.

Przeworski, A. (1992) 'The Neoliberal Fallacy', *Journal of Democracy*, 3: 3, 45–58.

Przeworski, A., Alvarez, H. E., Cheibub, J. A. and Limongi, F. (2000) *Democracy and Development. Political Institutions and Well-Being in the World, 1950–1990* (Cambridge: Cambridge University Press).

Pugh, M. (2012) *Liberal Internationalism. The Interwar Movement for Peace in Britain* (Basingstoke: Palgrave Macmillan).

Pye, L. W. and Verba, S. (eds) (1965) *Political Culture and Political Development* (Princeton: Princeton University Press).

Rapaczynski, A. (1987) *Nature and Politics: Liberalism in the Philosophies of Hobbes, Locke, and Rousseau* (Ithaca: Cornell University Press).

Rawls, J. (2001) *The Law of Peoples* (Cambridge: Harvard University Press).

Rawls, J. (1971) *A Theory of Justice* (Cambridge: Harvard University Press).

Reus-Smit, C. (2001) 'The Strange Death of Liberal International Theory', *European Journal of International Law*, 12: 3, 573–93.

Reus-Smit, C. (ed.) (2004) *The Politics of International Law* (Cambridge: Cambridge University Press).

Richardson, J. L. (2001) *Contending Liberalisms in World Politics. Ideology and Power* (Boulder: Lynne Rienner).

Richardson, J. L. (1997) 'Contending Liberalisms: Past and Present', *European Journal of International Relations*, 3: 1, 5–33.

Roberts, A. (2004) 'Righting Wrongs or Wronging Rights? The United States and Human Rights Post-September 11', *European Journal of International Law*, 15: 4, 721–49.

Rorty, R. (1989) *Contingency, Irony and Solidarity* (Cambridge: Cambridge University Press).

Rose, G. (2000/1) 'Democracy Promotion and American Foreign Policy: A Review Essay', *International Security*, 25: 3, 186–203.

Rosenau, J. N. and Czempiel, E.-O. (eds) (1992) *Governance Without Government: Order and Change in World Politics* (Cambridge: Cambridge University Press).

Rosenberg, J. (2007) 'International Relations – The "Higher Bullshit": A Reply to the Globalization Theory Debate', *International Politics*, 44: 4, 450–82.

Rosenberg, J. (2005) 'Globalisation Theory: A Post Mortem', *International Politics*, 42: 1, 2–74.

Rosenberg, J. (1996) 'Why is There No International Historical Sociology?' *European Journal of International Relations*, 12: 3, 307–40.

Rosenberg, J. (1994) *The Empire of Civil Society* (London: Verso).

Rostow, W. W. (1971) *The Stages of Economic Growth: A Non-Communist Manifesto* (Cambridge: Cambridge University Press).

Rotberg, R. I. (2002) 'The New Nature of Nation-State Failure', *The Washington Quarterly*, 25: 3, 85–96.

Rubin, B. R. (2006b) 'Still Ours to Lose: Afghanistan on the Brink', Testimony for the House Committee on International Relations and the Senate Committee on Foreign Relations, Council on Foreign Relations, http://www.cfr.org/publication/11486/still_ours_to_lose.html

Rubin, B. R. (2006a) 'Afghanistan's Uncertain Transition from Turmoil to Normalcy', Council on Foreign Relations, CSR No.12, March, http://www.cfr.org/content/publications/attachments/Afghanistan_CSR.pdf

Ruggie, J. G. (1982) 'International Regimes, Transactions, and Change: Embedded Liberalism in the Postwar Economic Order', *International Organization*, 36: 2, 379–415.

Runyan, A. S. and Peterson, V. S. (1991) 'The Radical Future of Realism: Feminist Subversions of IR Theory', *Alternatives*, 16: 1, 67–106.

Russell, A. (2001) 'Trade, Money and Markets' in B. White et al. (eds) *Issues in World Politics* (Basingstoke: Palgrave Macmillan) 35–54.

Russett, B. (1996b) 'Why Democratic Peace?' in M. E. Brown et al. (eds) *Debating the Democratic Peace* (Cambridge: MIT Press) 58–81.

Russett, B. (1996a) 'The Fact of Democratic Peace' in M. E. Brown et al. (eds) *Debating the Democratic Peace* (Cambridge: MIT Press) 82–115.

Russett, B., Harvey, S. and Kinsella, D. (2000) *World Politics. The Menu for Choice* (Boston: Bedford/St Martin's).

Rutland, P. (2000) 'Russia: Limping Along Towards American Democracy?' in M. Cox, G. J. Ikenberry and T. Inoguchi (eds) *American Democracy Promotion: Impulses, Strategies, and Impacts* (Oxford: Oxford University Press) 243–66.

Sachs, J. D. (2001) 'The Strategic Significance of Global Inequality', *The Washington Quarterly*, 24: 3, 187–98.

Saint-Simon, H. (1975) *Selected Writings on Science, Industry and Social Organisation*, K. Taylor (ed.) (London: Taylor and Francis).

Sandel, M. J. (1984) *Liberalism and its Critics* (New York: New York University Press).

Sartori, G. (1995) 'How Far Can Free Government Travel?' *Journal of Democracy*, 6: 3, 101–11.

Schabas, W. (2004) 'United States Hostility to the International Criminal Court: It's All About the Security Council', *European Journal of International Law*, 15: 4, 701–20.

Schmidt, B. C. (2005) 'Paul S. Reinsch and the Study of Imperialism and Internationalism', in D. Long and B. C. Schmidt (eds) *Imperialism and Internationalism in the Discipline of International Relations* (Albany: State University of New York Press) 43–69.

Schmitter, P. (1994) 'Dangers and Dilemmas of Democracy', *Journal of Democracy*, 5: 2, 57–74.

Seligman, A. B. (2009) 'Democracy, Civil Society, and the Problem of Toleration' in Z. Barany and R. G. Moser (eds) *Is Democracy Exportable?* (Cambridge: Cambridge University Press) 110–28.

Sell, S. (2003) *Private Power, Public Law: The Globalization of Intellectual Property Rights* (Cambridge: Cambridge University Press).

Shafer, D. M. (1988) *Deadly Paradigms: The Failure of US Counterinsurgency Policy* (Princeton: Princeton University Press).

Shaw, M. (2002) 'Risk-Transfer Militarism, Small Massacres, and the Historic Legitimacy of War', *International Relations*, 16: 2, 343–60.

Shearmur, J. (1992) 'In Defense of Neoliberalism', *Journal of Democracy*, 3: 3, 75–81.

Sheehan, M. (1995) *The Balance of Power. History and Theory* (London: Routledge).

Shilliam, R. (2009) *German Thought and International Relations: The Rise and Fall of a Liberal Project* (Basingstoke: Palgrave Macmillan).

Shilliam, R. (2007) 'Morgenthau in Context: German Backwardness, German Intellectuals and the Rise and Fall of a Liberal Project', *European Journal of International Relations*, 13: 3, 299–327.

Shimko, K. L. (2005) *International Relations. Perspectives and Controversies* (Boston: Houghton Mifflin).

Shue, H. (1996) *Basic Rights: Subsistence, Affluence, and US Foreign Policy* (Princeton: Princeton University Press).

Skinner, Q. (1998) *Liberty Before Liberalism* (Cambridge: Cambridge University Press).

Simpson, G. (2004) *Great Powers and Outlaw States. Unequal Sovereigns in the International Legal Order* (Cambridge: Cambridge University Press).

Simpson, G. (2001) 'Two Liberalisms', *European Journal of International Law*, 12: 3, 537–71.

Singer, P. (1993) *Practical Ethics* (Cambridge: Cambridge University Press).

Singer, P. (1972) 'Famine, Affluence, and Morality', *Philosophy and Public Affairs*, 1: 1, 229–43.

Slaughter, A.-M. (2000) 'Governing the Global Economy through Government Networks' in M. Beyers (ed.) *The Role of Law in International Politics* (Oxford: Oxford University Press) 177–206.

Slaughter, A.-M. (1995) 'International Law in a World of Liberal States', *European Journal of International Law*, 6, 1–39.

Smith, A. (1952) *An Inquiry into the Nature and Causes of the Wealth of Nations* (Chicago: William Benton).

Smith, M. J. (1992) 'Liberalism and International Reform' in T. Nardin and D. Mapel (eds) *Traditions of International Ethics* (Cambridge: Cambridge University Press) 201–24.

Smith, M. J. (1986) *Realist Thought from Weber to Kissinger* (Baton Rouge: Louisiana State University Press).

Smith, T. (2007) *A Pact With the Devil. Washington's Bid for World Supremacy and the Betrayal of the American Promise* (New York: Routledge).

Sørensen, G. (2012) *A Liberal World Order in Crisis. Choosing between Imposition and Restraint* (Ithaca: Cornell University Press).

Sørensen, G. (2000) 'The Impasse of Third World Democratization: Africa Revisited', in M. Cox, G. J. Ikenberry and T. Inoguchi (eds) *American Democracy Promotion. Impulses, Strategies, and Impacts* (Oxford: Oxford University Press) 287–307.

Sørensen, G. (1993) *Democracy and Democratization* (Boulder: Westview).

Spegele, R. D. (1996) *Political Realism in International Theory* (Cambridge: Cambridge University Press).

Stanley, B. (1990) *The Bible and the Flag: Protestant Missions and British Imperialism in the Nineteenth and Twentieth Centuries* (Leicerster: Apollos).

Stavrianakis, A. (2012) 'Missing the Target: NGOs, Global Civil Society and the Arms Trade', *Journal of International Relations and Development*, 15: 2, 224–49.

Strange, S. (1988) *States and Markets* (London: Continuum).

Sylvest, C. (2009) *British Liberal Internationalism, 1880–1930: Making Progress?* (Manchester: Manchester University Press).

Sylvest, C. (2005) 'Continuity and Change in British Liberal Internationalism, c. 1900–1930', *Review of International Studies*, 31: 2, 263–83.

Talavera, A. F. (1992) 'The Future of an Illusion', *Journal of Democracy*, 3: 3, 111–7.

Tan, K.-C. (2010) 'Poverty and Global Distributive Justice' in D. Bell (ed.) *Ethics and World Politics* (Oxford: Oxford University Press) 256–73.

Tansey, O. (2008) 'The Complexity of Western Diplomacy: A Reply to Beate Jahn', *Journal of Intervention and Statebuilding*, 2: 1, 87–94.

Teschke, B. (2003) *The Myth of 1648: Class, Geopolitics and the Making of Modern International Relations* (London: Verso).

Tesón, F. R. (2005) *Humanitarian Intervention: An Enquiry Into Law and Morality* (Ardsley NY: Transnational Publishers).

Tesón, F. R. (2003) 'The Liberal Case for Humanitarian Intervention' in J. L. Holzgrefe and R. O. Keohane (eds) *Humanitarian Intervention: Ethical, Legal, and Political Dilemmas* (Cambridge: Cambridge University Press) 93–129.

Thomas, C. and Reader, M. (2001) 'Development and Inequality' in B. White et al. (eds) *Issues in World Politics* (Basingstoke: Palgrave Macmillan) 74–92.

Tickner, J. A. (1988) 'Hans Morgenthau's Political Principles of Political Realism: A Feminist Reformulation', *Millennium: Journal of International Studies*, 17: 3, 429–440.

Tilly, C. (2004) *Contention and Democracy in Europe, 1650–2000* (New York: Cambridge University Press).

Todorov, T. (1999) *The Conquest of America. The Question of the Other* (Norman: University of Oklahoma Press).

Tuck, R. (1999) *The Rights of War and Peace. Political Thought and the International Order from Grotius to Kant* (Oxford: Oxford University Press).

Tully, J. (1993) *An Approach to Political Philosophy: Locke in Contexts* (Cambridge: Cambridge University Press).

Tully, J. (1988) *Meaning and Context: Quentin Skinner and his Critics* (Princeton: Princeton University Press).

Tully, J. (1982) *A Discourse on Property. John Locke and his Adversaries* (Cambridge: Cambridge University Press).

Van de Haar, E. (2009) *Classical Liberalism and International Relations Theory. Hume, Smith, Mises, and Hayek* (Basingstoke: Palgrave Macmillan).

Vanberg, V. J. (2008) 'On the Complementarity of Liberalism and Democracy – A Reading of F. A. Hayek and J. M. Buchanan', *Journal of Institutional Economics*, 4: 2, 139–61.

Vasquez, J. A. (1998) *The Power of Power Politics. From Classical Realism to Neotraditionalism* (Cambridge: Cambridge University Press).

Vitalis, R. (2005) 'Birth of a Discipline' in D. Long and B. C. Schmidt (eds) *Imperialism and Internationalism in the Discipline of International Relations* (Albany: State University of New York Press) 159–81.

von Hippel, K. (1999) 'Democracy by Force: A Renewed Commitment to Nation Building', *The Washington Quarterly*, 23: 1, 95–112.

Walker, R. B. J. (2010) *After the Globe, Before the World* (London: Routledge).

Walker, R. B. J. (1993) *Inside/Outside: International Relations as Political Theory* (Cambridge: Cambridge University Press).

Walker, R. B. J. (1987) 'Realism, Change, and International Political Theory', *International Studies Quarterly*, 31: 1, 65–86.

Walker, T. C. (2008) 'Two Faces of Liberalism: Kant, Paine, and the Question of Intervention', *International Studies Quarterly*, 52: 3, 449–68.

Waltz, K. (1979) *Theory of International Politics* (New York: McGraw-Hill).

Walzer, M. (1997) (ed.) *Toward a Global Civil Society* (New York: Berghahn Books).

Washbrook, D. (1997) 'From Comparative Sociology to Global History: Britain and India in the Pre-History of Modernity', *Journal of the Economic and Social History of the Orient*, 40: 4, 410–443.

Weber, C. (2010) 'After Liberalism', *Millennium: Journal of International Studies*, 38: 3, 553–60.

Weber, M. (1984) *The Protestant Ethic and the Spirit of Capitalism* (London: Unwin).

Wedgwood, R. (1999) 'The ICC – An American View', *European Journal of International Law*, 10: 1, 93–107.

Weiler, P. (1982) *The New Liberalism. Liberal Social Theory in Great Britain 1889–1914* (New York: Garland).

Weiss, L. (2005) 'Global Governance, National Strategies: How Industrialized States Make Room to Move Under the WTO', *Review of International Political Economy*, 12: 5, 723–49.

Wendt, A. (1999) *Social Theory of International Politics* (Cambridge: Cambridge University Press).

Westad, O. A. (2005) *The Global Cold War* (Cambridge: Cambridge University Press).

Wheeler, N. J. (2004) 'The Humanitarian Responsibilities of Sovereignty' in J. Welsh (ed.) *Humanitarian Intervention in International Relations* (Oxford: Oxford University Press) 29–52.

Wheeler, N. J. (2000) *Saving Strangers. Humanitarian Intervention in International Society* (Oxford: Oxford University Press).

Whitehead, L. (2009) 'Losing "the Force"? The "Dark Side" of Democratization After Iraq', *Democratization*, 16: 2, 215–42.

Wight, M. (1966) 'Why is there no International Theory?' in M. Wight and H. Butterfield (eds) *Diplomatic Investigations: Essays in the Theory of International Politics* (London: Allen and Unwin) 17–33.

Williams, D. (2012) *International Development and Global Politics. History, Theory and Practice* (London: Routledge).

Williams, D. (2008) *The World Bank and Social Transformation in International Politics* (London: Routledge).

Williams, D. and Young, T. (1994) 'Governance, the World Bank, and Liberal Theory', *Political Studies*, 42: 1, 84–100.

Williams, H. L. (1996) *International Relations and the Limits of Political Theory* (Basingstoke: Palgrave Macmillan).

Williams, M. C. (2005) *The Realist Tradition and the Limits of International Relations* (Cambridge: Cambridge University Press).

Windsor, J. L. (2003) 'Promoting Democratization Can Combat Terrorism', *The Washington Quarterly*, 26: 3, 43–58.

Wolf, M. (2004) *Why Globalization Works* (New Haven: Yale University Press).

Woolhouse, R. (2007) *Locke: A Biography* (Cambridge: Cambridge University Press).

WTO Preamble (1994) http://www.wto.org/english/res_e/booksp_e/analytic_index_e/wto_agree_01_e.htm#p, 26 October 2012

Wyatt-Walter, A. (1996) 'Adam Smith and the Liberal Tradition in International Relations', *Review of International Studies*, 22, 5–28.

Young, T. (1995) 'A Project to be Realised: Global Liberalism and Contemporary Africa', *Millennium: Journal of International Studies*, 24: 3, 527–46.

Zacher, M. W. and Matthew, R. A. (1995) 'Liberal International Theory: Common Threads, Divergent Strands' in C. W. Kegley Jr. (ed.) *Controversies in International Relations Theory. Realism and the Neoliberal Challenge* (New York: St. Martin's Press) 107–50.

Zakaria, F. (1997) 'The Rise of Illiberal Democracy', *Foreign Affairs*, 76, 22–43.

Index

Note: Locators with letter 'n' refer to notes.

Runyan, A. S., 15
Russell, A., 116
Russett, B., 22, 23, 74, 75, 123, 130,
    156, 157, 158, 191, 192
Russia, 3, 24, 66, 83–4, 116–17
Rutland, P., 83
Rwanda, 85, 149, 159

Sachs, J. D., 76
sanctions, 79, 82, 165
Sandel, M. J., 28
Sartori, G., 26, 61, 78, 79, 92, 183, 184
Schabas, W., 167
Schlesinger, A., 20
Schmidt, B. C., 16, 17, 18, 174
Schmitter, P., 61, 108n3
Seattle protests, 4
secessionist movements, 129
self-determination, 25, 70, 155
self-preservation, 43
Seligman, A. B., 62n11
Sell, S., 112
Serbia, 86, 164
Shafer, D. M., 16, 20
Shaftesbury, Earl of, 42, 49–50, 52,
    56, 62–3
Shaw, M., 159
Shearmur, J., 26
Sheehan, M., 16n2
Shilliam, R., 174, 176
Shimko, K. L., 15n1, 102–3, 105, 111,
    114, 115, 119
Shue, H., 138n2
Sierra Leone, 150
Simpson, G., 166
Singapore, 116
Singer, P., 138n2
Skinner, Q., 54, 54n7
Slaughter, A.-M., 3, 30, 31, 80, 140,
    148, 162, 178, 189
slavery/the slave trade, 25, 29, 32, 42
Smith, A., 103, 104, 120, 122, 127,
    176, 178
Smith, M. J., 20
Smith, T., 89
Somalia, 150
Sørensen, G., 1, 5, 16, 20, 22, 84, 145,
    179, 180, 188, 192, 195
South Africa, 78, 86

South Korea, 115–16
sovereignty, 3, 46, 56–7, 67, 123,
    141–2, 148, 151
Soviet Union, 19–20, 111, 130, 167
Spanish colonialism, cruelty of, 50
Spegele, R. D., 16n2
Staley, E. A., 18
Stanley, B., 182
state centrism, 19
state of nature, 43–8, 51–4, 58–60,
    103, 155
statebuilding, 84, 159
Stavrianakis, A., 32
Strange, S., 103n1
strategic aid, 116, 157
structural adjustment, 85, 107, 111,
    114–15, 118, 128–9
structural liberalism, 30–1, 33
A Study of History, Civilization on Trial
    (Toynbee), 17
subsistence rights, 138
Sullivan, G. R., 76, 90
Sweeney, K., 185
Sylvest, C., 17
Syria, 149
systemic aid, 157

Taiwan, 116
Talavera, A. F., 61, 63
Taliban, 87
taming of politics, 61
Tan, K.-C., 138n2
Tansey, O., 36
Tanzania, 84, 149
Taylor, C., 85
Teschke, B., 15
Tesón, F. R., 25, 141n5, 142, 149, 150,
    158, 160, 161, 162, 193
Thailand, 115
Thatcher, M., 110
Theory of Justice (Rawls), 19, 31, 138
Third Wave, of democratization, 78,
    88
Third World, 2, 20, 69, 76–7, 103,
    107–12, 115, 118, 128
Thomas, C., 146, 157
Tickner, J. A., 15
Tilly, C., 64
Todorov, T., 44n3

Printed and bound by CPI Group (UK) Ltd, Croydon, CR0 4YY

·